CASS
FORUM
中国社会科学论坛

中国社会科学论坛文集

现代社会生活方式的文化根源

The Cultural Origin of Lifestyle in Modern Society

萧俊明 / 主编

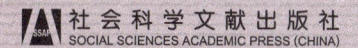

目 录

在"现代社会生活方式的文化根源"国际研讨会上的致辞 …… 武　寅 / 001

在"现代社会生活方式的文化根源"国际研讨会上的基调发言
……………………………………………………… 朝戈金 / 006

现代化进程与民族地区的传统文化 ……………… 朝　克 / 013

当代希腊社会中的文化自我觉识 ……… 斯特利奥斯·维尔维扎基斯 / 036

儒家政治及其矫正：从激进主义到渐进主义 …………… 陆建德 / 062

韩非子与现代性 ……………………………………… 白彤东 / 089

关于佛教与文化的反思 ……………… 素旺那·沙他－阿南德 / 118

私人与公共生活之间：来自中国处境的宗教多样性的挑战
……………………………………………………… 谢志斌 / 132

狂野的东方
　　——抑或体制变革后的生活 ……………… 霍尔腾西娅·霍苏 / 145

韩流的文化启示
　　——兼论韩流对现代社会生活方式的影响及其文化根源探析
………………………………………………………… 朴光海 / 161

现代韩国人的生活方式与巫俗文化的关系 ………… 黄棕源 / 183

文化多样性的假想与宗教的永恒性 ………… 西尔维娅·曼奇尼 / 208

编后记 ……………………………………………………………… / 246

Contents

Opening Address at the 2010 CASS Forum on the Cultural Origin
of Lifestyle in Modern Society *Wu Yin* / 003

Keynote Speech at the CASS Forum on the Cultural Origin of Lifestyle
in Modern Society *B. Chogjin* / 009

Modernization and the Traditional Cultures of Chinese
Ethnic Regions *Chao Ke* / 024

Cultural Self-awareness in Contemporary Greek Society
Stelios Virvidakis / 047

Confucian Politics and Its Redress: From Radicalism to
Gradualism *Lu Jiande* / 074

Han Fei Zi and Modernity *Bai Tongdong* / 101

Reflections on Buddhism and Culture *Suwanna Satha-Anand* / 124

Between Private and Public Life: The Challenge of Religious
Diversity in the Chinese Context *Xie Zhibin* / 137

现代社会生活方式的文化根源

Wild East-Or the Life after System-change　　　　　*Hortenzia Hosszú* / 152

The Cultural Implications of the Korean Wave: Its Cultural Origin and

Impacts on Chinese Lifestyle in Modern Society　　*Piao Guanghai* / 171

The Lifestyle of Contemporary Koreans and Its Relationship to

Shamanist Culture　　　　　　　　　　　　　*Hwang Jongwon* / 195

Imaginaries of Cultural Diversity and the Permanence of the Religious

　　　　　　　　　　　　　　　　　　　　　　Silvia Mancini / 225

Editor's Afterword　　　　　　　　　　　　　　　　　　　/ 246

在"现代社会生活方式的文化根源"国际研讨会上的致辞

武 寅[*]

尊敬的各位来宾,上午好。

首先,我代表中国社会科学院对这次论坛的召开表示衷心的祝贺,对前来参加此次论坛的中外客人表示热烈的欢迎。

举办中国社会科学论坛(CASS FORUM)是(中国社会科学院)2010年推出的一项重大举措,目的是要充分发挥中国社会科学院科研实力和人才资源优势,围绕中国经济社会发展以及全球关注的重大问题,围绕中华文化的传承与弘扬、中外文明的交流与互动,展开高层次、高水平的对话和研讨,增进世界对中国的了解,促进中外优秀文明成果的交流,为中国的和谐发展、世界的和谐发展贡献智慧和力量。按照计划,2010年中国社会科学论坛将举办18场国际学术研讨会。今天这个研讨会就是其中之一。

选择"生活方式"和"文化"作为本次论坛的主题主要是基于对文化的理解。

第一,文化不应是一个抽象的普遍概念,而应该是活生生的生活经验。这些生活经验的意义和价值总是通过特定的生活方式体现出来。后者作为文化的表现方式,既可以使我们看到不同文化元素在现代化进程中的整合与进化,又可以使我们切身感受到民族认同和文化认同的形成。只有在这样生动和具体的文化中,我们才可能触摸到文化传统的源流与脉络,才可能在现代

---

[*] 武寅,中国社会科学院副院长。

中找到传统,在传统中审视现代。

第二,具体的和特殊的文化也是多样的。强调文化多样性的意义在于促进不同文化之间的相互理解、相互对话、相互尊重。不同民族、不同宗教、不同文化之间虽然存在差异,但并不存在必然的或与生俱来的隔阂与冲突。从这个意义上讲,不同文化乃至不同领域之间的相互了解和相互交流正是消除屏障避免冲突的最好途径。本届论坛特意邀请了来自多个国家、多个民族、多个学科的学者到会发言(其中中国的四位代表来自三个民族四个领域),正是为了实现这样的了解和交流。跨文化、跨学科的交流可以为我们理解不同的文化提供多样的视角,带来不无裨益的见识。因此,它的价值和意义不仅是学术的和理论的,更是实践的和现实的。

第三,强调文化的特殊性和多样性也是拒绝文化上的普遍主义。换句话说,拒绝文化上的普遍主义或普遍价值也正是为了尊重差异、包容多样。从理论根源上讲,所谓普遍主义或普遍价值是一种形而上学的绝对化,是本质主义的登峰造极,这是我们所不能认同的。当然,我们也不会因此而走向另一个极端,过于强调每个文化的个性而否认文化融合的可能性。尊重差异、包容多样并不是以一种文化相对主义来对抗文化普遍主义,而是要倡导和谐,寻求共识。和谐,至少就中国文化而言,是其精髓所在,也是其追求的最高境界。和谐社会,无论从国家范围来讲,还是从全球范围来讲,都是人类生活的理想境界。今天,我们大家也正是为了这一共同理想聚在这里。

希望大家围绕会议主题各抒己见,畅所欲言。通过本次论坛为实现我们的追求,为中国的和谐发展、世界的和谐发展贡献智慧和力量。

最后,预祝本次论坛取得圆满成功。谢谢!

Opening Address at the 2010 CASS Forum on the Cultural Origin of Lifestyle in Modern Society

Wu Yin[*]

Good morning, ladies and gentlemen,

First, please allow me, on behalf of the Chinese Academy of Social Sciences, to extend my warm congratulations on the opening of CASS Forum. It is a great pleasure to welcome all the participants to CASS Forum in Beijing.

CASS Forum is an important strategy newly adopted by CASS in 2010 to take advantage of the research capacity of CASS, to increase CASS' engagement in high-level dialogues with the international community, to enhance people's understanding of China, and to encourage greater interaction and exchanges between China and other countries. The forum focuses on issues of China's social and economic development and those issues of global importance, with a particular stress on the inheritance and development of traditional Chinese cultures and the exchanges between Chinese and foreign civilizations, so as to contribute its bit to the harmonious development of China and the world. As scheduled, CASS Forum 2010 is going to include a total of 18 international symposia or conferences. This symposium is one of them.

The theme of the forum is 'The Cultural Origin of Lifestyle in Modern Society.' 'Lifestyle' and 'culture' are chosen here based upon our

---

[*] Wu Yin is Vice President of CASS.

understanding of culture.

First of all, culture is not an abstract universal concept, but the lived experiences of people. The significance and values of these lived experiences are always manifest in the form of a particular lifestyle. Through lifestyle, we can gain a view of how different cultural elements are integrated and evolve in the course of modernization, and how national identity and cultural identity have emerged and taken shape. Only in these living and specific cultures can we trace the origin and development of cultural traditions, discover traditions from the perspective of modernity, and examine modernity from the perspective of traditions.

Second, cultures, with their specificity and uniqueness, are also diverse. Cultural diversity is emphasized here to facilitate mutual understanding, dialogue and respect across different cultures. There is no inherent or necessary conflict between nations, religions or cultures, despite the differences between them. In this sense, mutual understanding and exchanges across cultures and even across areas of discipline are the best way of removing misunderstanding and avoiding conflicts. With these in view, CASS Forum has invited scholars from various countries, nations or discipline's (of whom are 4 Chinese scholars from 3 ethnic groups and 4 discipline's). Intercultural and inter-disciplinary exchanges as such can provide us with new perspectives and insights. Therefore, they are important both in theory and practice, and in academics and reality.

Third, by emphasizing the particularity and diversity of cultures, we reject the so-called cultural universalism. In other words, we reject cultural universalism or universal values so as to show respect for cultural variety and diversity. By origin, the so-called universalism (or universal values) is a metaphysical absolution, and an extreme form of essentialism. This is what we can hardly agree with. But, of course, we will not go to the other extreme of overemphasizing cultural particularity and denying the possibility of cultural convergence. By recognizing variety and diversity, we do not mean to confront cultural universalism with cultural relativism. Rather, we mean to advocate the idea of harmony and seek consensus among different cultures. In China at least, harmony constitutes the essence and ultimate goal of the Chinese culture. A harmonious society represents an ideal living state of human beings whether in a particular country or throughout the world. And it is precisely out of this common goal that we are gathering here today.

I hope that all participants will engage actively in the forum and express freely their views, so as to contribute to the achievement of our goal, and to the harmonious development of China and the world.

Finally, let me wish the forum full success! Thank you.

在"现代社会生活方式的文化根源"
国际研讨会上的基调发言

朝戈金[*]

尊敬的主席先生、女士们、先生们:

我很荣幸能够利用这次简短发言的机会,对国内外的代表表示欢迎,并预祝这次论坛取得圆满成功。

"海纳百川,有容乃大",这是我最喜欢的一句中国谚语。它的意思是一个人应当像大海接纳一切大江小河那样,具有宽广的胸襟,吸取别人的长处。今天,我们能够齐聚一堂,探讨大家感兴趣的诸多话题,并分享我们的学科知识,这是一个美好的经历。这次论坛的主题是:现代社会生活方式的文化根源。应当说,探讨这个话题恰逢其时,也正当其地,为什么这样说呢?

首先,我们要讨论的是文化根源。中国是一个拥有悠久历史和优秀文化传统的国家。其文化的丰富性从浩瀚的历史文献、无以计数的考古遗址和数不清的"文化遗存"(爱德华·泰勒)中可见一斑。因此,从"全球思考"的角度看,中国文化的多样性将带给我们富有意义的理念和实践。

其次,如果我们把整个中国看成一个现代社会,那么我们就会看到多种多样的生活方式。东西之间、城乡之间都存在巨大的差异。在中国的中部和东部,人们享受着现代设施的便利,如电子商务、第三代手机通信等。而在中国的西部地区,特别是在西部的农村,套牛拉犁仍然是种植庄稼的手段。

---

[*] 朝戈金,中国社会科学院学部委员、国际哲学与人文科学理事会副主席。

而在一些畜牧地区，游牧人民仍然过着住毡房、逐畜而居的生活。他们的生活方式与生活在都市中的人们的生活方式是迥然不同的。

再次，中国拥有56个民族，近130种语言。每个民族都有自己独特的文化传统，从而使中国文化呈现出丰富多样的特点。我坚信，文化只有在比较中才能得以解释。我们都知道，中国是进行这种比较研究的最佳场所之一。

最后，21世纪的第一个十年行将结束，传统文化正在迅速消失。诸多文化形式，如史诗说唱、民间手艺、农村表演艺术、祭祖敬神仪式以及传统节日庆典等，都在逐渐淡出人们的日常生活。我们有责任保护这些文化遗产，留存我们曾经走过的历史足迹，并展望我们的未来。

基于以上几点，我想再次强调，文化根源这一主题急需得到国际社会的关注和学术界的深度参与。

如果要选择一个能够连接古今的有代表性的东西来彰显文化的力量和动力，那么作为一个民俗学者，我会选择"口头传统"。

如果要问口头传统是什么，有些人会回答说，口头传统与一些日常的、老式的、古旧的、农村的、腐朽的、草根的、落后的，甚至是原始的东西有关。但是口头传统所涵盖的意义远远不止这些。姑且不论那些没有文字的社会，单说我们所有关于宇宙和自然的知识、所有关于鬼神的思想、所有的口头表达艺术（如神化、史诗、传说、故事、萨迦、民谣、歌词等）、所有的历史记忆、所有流传下来并不断发展的智慧，以及道德准则等，统统都保存在口头传统中。

这就是说，口头传统是一门古老而永恒的技能，我们人类持有这门技能已经有10万至20万年的历史了。虽然不同的文明创造了不同的文字，但是口头交流仍然是当今世界信息交流的一个重要方式。我想，这也正是联合国教科文组织把口头传统列为五大无形文化遗产之首的原因所在。

现在的学者们倾向于认为，纯口头性和纯文字性是位于我们交际频谱上的两个端点。在这两个端点中间存在大量的过渡形式。简言之，口头性和文字性是相互重叠的。口头传统作为一种历史悠久的技能，将永远存在。

由于时间的关系，我们无法细述口头传统在日常生活中的普及性，以及它在当代情境（文学、电影、电视、卡通、大众媒体、路牌、装潢和广告）中被体验、共享和实践的种种方式。我们仅从中国的不同口头文化流派中择取一个例子，例如，《格萨尔王》史诗就凸显了这种强烈的联系：从传统功能到现代艺术、从"局内人"到"局外人",以及从遥远的青藏高原和蒙古高原到2010年的上海世博会。

藏族有句谚语:"每个人嘴里都有一部《格萨尔王》。"在地方群体中,史诗表演不仅是宗教信仰、本土知识、地方智慧、民间记忆和母语表达的一个主要载体,还是其他传统艺术形式(如唐卡绘画、石雕、藏剧、壁画、雕刻和建筑)和当代民族文学艺术(如小说、诗歌、电视剧、广播剧和美术)的一个恒久的灵感来源。此外,格萨尔史诗还作为广告创意、创新行业、数字媒体、网络游戏和教科书的一个丰富的文化和艺术源泉,为听众(无论老幼、也无论内行外行)提供了一种文化多样性和历史持续性的感觉,为中国文化和世界文明宝库提供了一个不竭的创造性源泉。

作为世界上最长的史诗,《格萨尔王》是本土文化多样性的一个独特源泉,是持久而又充满活力的人类创造性的证据。这个为多个民族所共有的口头史诗传统,代表着博大精深的文化根源,昭示了口头传统和口头艺术的活力,体现了传统民俗和口头文化所取得的成就。

根据美国人类学家戴尔·海姆斯的传统化观点,过去是积极建构和生产的。经过长年的传播,格萨尔史诗的文化特质已经超越了口头和书面、城市与乡村、语言与群体,流派与类别,以及时空之间的界限。因此,这一历史悠久的口头传统将成为人类的真正的"共同遗产"。

在这里,我想说,这个多学科话语论坛的召开恰逢其时。它能够让我们退一步,审视我们所采取的立场,以及我们看待整个人类的过去、现在和未来等重要问题的方式。我确信,接下来的发言和讨论将对我们所有人都是不无裨益的。

中国的孔子曾经说过,"有朋自远方来,不亦乐乎?"我今天也感同身受。亲爱的朋友们,我希望你们能够尽情参与到讨论中来,并祝你们在北京生活愉快!谢谢!

Keynote Speech at the CASS Forum on the Cultural Origin of Lifestyle in Modern Society

B. Chogjin[*]

Distinguished chairman, ladies and gentlemen,

It is a great honor for me to make a very brief speech to welcome domestic and foreign participants, and deliver my good wishes to a successful forum in advance.

'The ocean admits hundreds of rivers for its capacity to hold (海纳百川，有容乃大).' This is one of my favorite Chinese aphorisms, it means one should be as encompassing as the vast ocean which admits hundreds of rivers and should draw upon other's strengths. It would be a wonderful experience to meet you all here to discuss topics we all concern and to share our expertise.

The topic of this forum is 'The Cultural Origin of Lifestyle in Modern Society'. I must say that it is a right time and right place to discuss such a topic. My point is supported by the following four factors:

Firstly, we are going to talk about cultural origin, and China is a country with a long history and splendid cultural traditions. Its rich culture can be observed via voluminous historical documents and numerous archeological sites, as well as countless 'survival in culture, in the words of Edward Taylor.' Thus, if we

---

[*] B. Chogjin is Academy Member of Chinese Academy of Social Sciences and Vice President of International Council of Social Sciences.

'think globally', China's diversified culture may bring us very interesting ideas and practice.

Secondly, if we take China as a whole a Modern Society, we can get a wide spectrum of lifestyles. Huge gaps lie between different regions from east to west, between rural and urban areas. In the middle and east part of China, people enjoy modern facilities like e-commerce, third-generation mobile telecommunication, and so on, while in the west part, especially in rural areas, cattle and plow are still used to raise crops. And in some animal husbandry regions, nomadic peoples are still living in traditional yurts, moving about with their domestic animals. Their lifestyle, by any means, is quite different from that of people living in metropolitan areas.

Thirdly, China is such a country that there are about one hundred and thirty languages spoken! Fifty six ethnic groups with their unique cultural traditions make this country's cultural profile a rich and plural one. I strongly believe that culture can only be explained by comparison. And we all know that China is one of the most suitable places to make such comparative studies.

Fourthly, it is now the end of the first decade of the twenty-first century. Traditional cultures are declining swiftly. A large amount of cultural forms, like epic singing, folk handicraft, rural performing arts, rituals of ancestor cult or rites of evoking deities, traditional festivals and ceremonies, and the like, are all gradually fading out of people's daily life. It is our duty to safeguard the cultural heritage, so as to keep our past footprint and foresee our future.

With the four above-mentioned factors, I'd like to stress again that the topic of cultural origin calls for ungent attention from the international society, as well as academia's in-depth participation.

If we choose one representative item to link the past with the present and to show cultural power and dynamics, as a folklorist, I would prefer 'oral tradition.'

When you ask people what oral tradition is, some people will tell you that oral tradition has to do with something common, old fashioned, quaint, rural, rustic, grass-roots, backward or even primitive. But oral tradition means much more than that. No need to mention in those non-literacy societies, all the knowledge about the universe and nature, all the ideas about deities and ghosts, all the oral expressive arts, like myth, epic, legend, tale, saga, ballad, lyric and so on, all the historical memories, all the surviving and developing wisdoms, and moral principles, are totally kept in oral tradition.

That's to say, oral tradition is age-old but an everlasting skill that we mankind have been using for approximately for 100,000—200,000 years. And though different civilizations invented a lot of different scripts, exchanging information orally is still a major way for us today in every corner on this planet. I think that is the reason why in the UNESCO's relevant documents, oral tradition comes first on the list of five principal domains of the Intangible Cultural Heritage.

Nowadays, scholars tend to agree that pure form of orality and literacy are two ends of our communication spectrum, in between there are a lot of intermediate forms. In a word, orality and literacy are overlapping with each other. And oral tradition, as a time-honored ability, will last forever.

Due to the limit of time, we can hardly describe the pervasiveness of oral tradition in everyday life as it is lived, shared and practiced in contemporary settings, including its modern uses in literature, film, television, cartoon, comic strip, mass media, street sign, decoration, and advertising. Picking up one example from diverse oral genres in China, epic King Gesar gives us a strong connection— from traditional functions to modern arts, from 'the insider' to 'the outsider,' and from the remote Qinghai-Tibet Plateau and Mongolian Plateau to the coastal Shanghai EXPO 2010.

As a Tibetan proverb goes, 'On every person's lips there is a canto of King Gesar.' Epic performances in local communities have been not only the primary vehicle for religious belief, indigenous knowledge, local wisdom, folk memory, and mother-tongue expression; but also a constant source of inspiration for other traditional art forms, including Thangka painting, stone-carving, Tibetan opera, mural, sculpture, architecture, as well as contemporary ethnic literature and arts, such as novel, poetry, TV play, radio drama, fine arts, and so on; in addition, as a wealth of cultural and artistic resources for advertising design, creative industry, digital media, network game, school textbook, and so forth, the Gesar epic imbues the audience with a sense of cultural diversity and historical continuity, and, in turn, contributes unceasingly with their creative inspiration to the treasure-house of Chinese culture and global civilization.

As the longest epic in the world, King Gesar is unique as a wellspring of indigenous cultural diversity and evidence of sustainable, yet dynamic, human creativity. This oral epic tradition, shared by multiple ethnic groups, represents the broad and deep spectrum of cultural origins, demonstrates the vitality of oral tradition and verbal arts, and epitomizes the achievements of traditional folklore and oral culture.

According to American anthropologist Dell Hymes and his idea of traditionalization, the past is actively constructed and produced. Through long years of its dissemination, the cultural traits of epic Gesar move beyond the boundaries between orality and literacy, between the rural and the urban, between language and community, between genre and type, and between space and time. Consequently, this time-honored oral tradition will become a real 'common heritage' of human beings.

Here I'd like to say, this forum of a multi-disciplinary discourse comes at a welcome time, it permits us to take a step back and see where the position we take, and how we deal with the crucial issues concerning the past, the present and the future of human beings as a whole. I'm sure the forthcoming presentations and discussions will be beneficial to all of us.

Last but not least, Chinese ancient sage Confucius once said, 'What a joy it is to have friends coming from afar!' I really have the same feeling today. Dear friends, I hope you enjoy our getting together here, and have a nice stay in Beijing.

Thank you for your attention.

现代化进程与民族地区的传统文化

朝 克[*]

一

众所周知,中国是一个由多民族相互交融、多种民族文化相互辉映,拥有世人所感叹而倾慕的极其丰富的民族语言文字、民族文化的国家。人类已经走入 21 世纪,我国少数民族在不断加强本民族语言文字的使用和保护的基础上,用新的发展的思想理念和全新的科学技术手段建设着他们的现代社会生活。同时,边疆民族地区和内陆发达地区间的交流和沟通的日益频繁和不断加深,为我国少数民族生活的广大农村牧区的现代化进程不断注入新的活力。而且,少数民族同胞为了进一步改善他们传统的生活方式,为了更快地融入现代社会生活,为了建设更加理想、更加美好而充满生机和现代化气息的文明、进步、繁荣发展的新型农村牧区,正在有计划、有步骤地实施着一场以科学发展观为主导的农村牧区的现代化建设。我们认为,我国少数民族生活的广大农村牧区要实施现代化建设,就是不断改变他们过去的那些不适合于现代社会发展的生活方式,同时不断强化现代化的社会生活意识、完

---

[*] 朝克(Chao Ke),男,1957 年出生。2004 年在日本获得语言文化学博士学位。中国社会科学院科研局副局长、研究生院博士生导师。主要研究领域:满通古斯语言文化研究。主要著述有《鄂温克语形态语音论与名词形态论》(日文版,2003)、《满通古斯语及其文化》(日文版,2002)、《满通古斯诸语比较研究》(汉文版,1997)等。第九、十、十一届全国人大代表,中宣部"四个一批"人才。

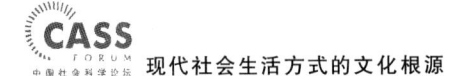

善现代社会生活内容。不过，我们提倡的科学发展观，我们所追求的现代化建设和现代社会生活，必须要尊重少数民族的意愿，尊重他们用生命和信仰传承的民族语言文化，要从少数民族对于现代社会生活的具体需求的实际出发，要实事求是，要因地制宜，要扎实而牢固地融入长期而可持续稳步发展的科学发展思想理念。这样才能把少数民族生活的广大农村牧区建设成为不远离他们传统文化、不丢掉他们历史记忆而使他们能够安居乐业，尽情享受物质文明和精神文明的现代社会生活的理想家园。

伴随少数民族生活的广大农村牧区经济状况的不断改变，生活环境和质量的不断改善，以及政治地位的不断提高，作为他们精神生活的重要组成部分的民族文化，尤其是那些属于边远地区而还未完全受到当今主流文化的冲击和影响的独具特色的民族文化，越来越多地引起世人的兴趣和关注。无论是生活在南国海滨或山区的南方少数民族，还是生活在辽阔戈壁或草原的北方少数民族，不管有多少人口，他们都有用一代又一代的生命传承下来的并成为他们精神生活的主要依靠，成为他们传承真善美的道德素养，乃至成为他们同历史和未来进行沟通与交流的精神桥梁的语言文化。因为，在这些民族的语言文化里，包含着他们走过的每一段历史，承载着他们不同时期的不同思考和不同的生活，甚至包含着他们从远古至今传承的思想、信仰和追求。当人们融入他们生存的特定社会环境和生活氛围，进入属于他们独具风格的民族文化和文明世界深处，用心灵去和他们进行深层次的交流时，就会发现许多被现代人遗忘的弥足珍贵的远古文化和文明。我们感到万分庆幸的是，他们竟然在铺天盖地的现代文化和文明的思潮的冲击下，用活生生的生命和坚定不移的信念把他们本民族的这些文化和文明保存下来。假设没有他们或他们的这种执着，也许我们早已失去许多历史的记忆，以及与我们血脉相承的早期的文明与文化。特别是，人口较少民族的濒危语言文化，在当今人类文化与文明走向一体化的世界大背景下，显得更加珍贵。毫无疑问，少数民族的这些优秀的传统文化和文明，为民族地区的现代化进程以及现代社会生活方式的形成发挥着不容忽视的重要作用。例如，少数民族现代化及其现代社会生活方式草原文化、雪原文化、高山文化、戈壁文化、森林文化以及独特的农耕文化等。

二

我们必须理性地看到，在我国少数民族地区的现代化进程和现代社会生活方式转变过程中，发达地区和少数民族地区逐渐缩小差异，从而在诸多方面逐步走向一体化。特别是，一些经济发达地区同经济欠发达的少数民族地区进行着多层面、多角度、多种形式和内容的经济合作的同时，把发达地区的文化和生活方式逐渐传播到少数民族生活的广大农村，结果少数民族的那些十分珍贵而优秀的文化和文明，却在以经济发展为核心的强大的现代化建设以及现代社会生活面前显得十分脆弱，进而面临着不同程度的危机，甚至人口较少民族的语言文化已经进入濒危状态。在这一现实面前，国家和各级政府颁布了一系列行之有效的民族语言文化保护和抢救的政策，这使少数民族从自身的角度自觉而强烈地感受到，对逐渐消亡的本民族语言文化进行保护和抢救的紧迫性和重要性。同时，采取行之有效的方法和手段，使少数民族的语言文化科学地融入现代文明和现代社会生活中，从而让它们为民族地区的社会经济的发展发挥作用。而且，人类文明的进程也不断证实，一切现代文化和文明只有同传统文化和文明密切而科学地相结合才能有生命力。反过来说，一切现代文化或文明，都和传统的文化和文明有着必然的和不可分割的内在联系，人类的一切现代文化和文明都来源于远古和历史，并不断走向未来。再说，正因为有了多样性的民族文化和文明，我们才拥有了今天丰富多彩的世界和丰富多彩的思维空间。我们知道，在我国东北风景秀丽、自然环境优美的广大农村牧区生活着蒙、满、朝、回、锡伯、达斡尔、鄂温克、鄂伦春、赫哲、柯尔克孜、俄罗斯等20多个少数民族。他们千百年来，一直生活在广阔的黑土地上、富饶的大兴安岭和小兴安岭里、巍巍的长白山脚下、美丽的大赉湖和呼伦湖畔、辽阔的呼伦贝尔草原上、奔腾的三江流域、地下森林奇观旁、樟子松林白桦林里、松花江柳树岛上、镜泊湖景区和北极漠河不夜景区、风光秀丽的尼尔基水库边。他们生活的土地上，有世界著名的倭肯哈达新石器时期洞穴、十八站旧石器文化遗址、早期村屯土墙遗址、辽金泰州塔子城、金代蒲峪路古城遗址、契丹遗址、亚沟女真人摩崖石刻、清代宁古塔城址、阿城旧址、瓦里霍吞古城遗址、完颜阿骨打墓、墨日根古城遗址等名胜古迹。在漫长的历史进程中，他们用共同的劳动和智慧创造并奉献给人类温寒带地区的东北农业文明、朝鲜族长白山水稻文化、布里亚特蒙古族人的牧骆驼文化、巴尔虎蒙古人的牧羊文化、厄鲁特蒙古人的牧牛文化、呼伦贝尔草原的牧马文化、赫哲族的三江渔猎鱼皮文化、鄂伦春人的森林文化和兴安岭文化、敖鲁古雅鄂温克人的驯鹿文化、鄂温克人的草原文化、满族海猎文化、满族家子屯村文化等。另外，他们在衣食住行等方面独具风格，服饰方面有满族旗袍与骨饰、蒙古族风格各异的长袍长靴子、锡伯族刺绣、朝鲜族船形鞋和五彩上衣及则高利长裙、鄂伦春族兽皮衣饰、达斡尔族蓝衣袍和狍腿靴、鄂温克族四季分明的皮衣类、赫哲族鱼皮衣等；饮食方面有满族酸茶与渍菜白肉火锅、朝鲜族狗肉汤与辣白菜、蒙古族乳食宴和手抓肉、布里亚特蒙古人酸面包、厄鲁特蒙古人烤牛排、巴尔虎蒙古人全羊席、锡伯族烤大饼和油茶饮食、达斡尔族柳蒿菜芽炖猪排、鄂温克族奶面片和鹿肉宴、鄂伦春族猴头炖野鸡、赫哲族拌菜生鱼片与"苏日卡"；住房方面有满族章茅屋顶炕粮烟筒独竖屋外的土房、朝鲜族高丽营子和大炕屋、蒙古族蒙古包、锡伯族草木房、达斡尔族的草房、鄂温克族和鄂伦春族桦树皮仙人住和游牧包、通古斯鄂温克的木克楞木屋、鄂伦春雪原林海的雪屋、赫哲族"撮兰库"房等；婚礼方面有蒙古族草原马背婚礼、满族乡土婚俗、赫哲族渔乡"萨日力尼"婚俗、朝鲜族娶亲奠雁礼、锡伯族换酒盅和抢猪肘子婚俗、达斡尔族烟荷包装钱认婿习俗、鄂伦春族赛马婚俗、鄂温克族篝火婚俗；礼仪习俗方面还有蒙古族鼻烟壶文化、满族占卦文化、满族擦肩礼与社交礼俗、锡伯族莫昆文化、鄂温克和鄂伦春的乌力楞文化、达斡尔族装烟礼与大叶烟文化等。

　　北方民族在节庆方面表现得更加丰富和独特，例如有蒙古族四月敖包节接羊羔节、蒙古族八月那达慕节、蒙古族十月伊德喜节；朝鲜族月亮屋节、朝鲜族流头节、朝鲜族嘉俳节、朝鲜族四月初八灯夕节；满族赶庙会节；锡伯族正月十五抹黑节、锡伯族正月二十五填仓节、锡伯族二月二喜利妈妈节、锡伯族四月十八西迁节、锡伯族七月十五鬼节；柯尔克孜族开斋节、柯尔克孜族古尔邦节、柯尔克孜族诺劳孜节；鄂温克族六月十八瑟宾节、鄂温克族十二月雪原节；鄂伦春篝火节；赫哲族四月渔业节、赫哲族秋季大马哈鱼丰收节、赫哲族三月三路神节、赫哲族九月九鹿神节、赫哲族八月乌日贡节等。在游戏方面很有代表性的有朝鲜族板舞戏跳板游戏、朝鲜族半仙之戏秋千游戏、锡伯族抓嘎拉哈游戏和皮影戏、赫哲族狗爬犁比赛叉草球游戏、达斡尔族曲棍球、鄂温克族抢苏游戏、鄂伦春族驯鹿棋等。在精神生活方面，北方民族同样创造了极其丰厚而灿烂的文化和文明，其中歌舞方面有蒙古族好来宝说唱、蒙古族长调、蒙古族马头琴拉唱、朝鲜族伽倻琴弹唱、朝鲜族长白山民歌、达斡尔族长唱"乌钦"、鄂伦春族摩苏昆长篇讲唱、鄂温克族萨满歌、赫哲族渔歌与伊玛堪长篇讲唱、满族阿那忽乐曲和奏墨克纳曲及吹锣板曲、锡伯族送粮曲、满族悠悠调、锡伯族秧歌调、蒙古族挤奶舞和鹰舞、满族笊篱姑娘舞和秧歌舞、满族猎舞和萨满舞、满族莽式舞及庆隆舞、锡伯族打谷舞、朝鲜族长鼓舞与帽带舞、鄂温克和鄂伦春族斗熊舞和哲辉楞舞、鄂温克和鄂伦春及达斡尔族阿罕拜舞。与此相关，还有蒙古族马头琴传说、满族两世罕王传、满族说部、满族神话、赫哲族伊玛堪长篇故事、锡伯族傻姑爷儿传说、锡伯族说"古艺儿"等。而且，北方绝大多数民族早期有万物有灵的萨满信仰，他们有熊图腾、山神崇拜、多神信仰、供奉蛇神、喜利妈妈崇拜、檀君教信仰、柳祭、渔祭、东正教等。北方民族使用的语言文字主要有蒙古语蒙古文、朝鲜语朝鲜文、满语、达斡尔语、鄂温克语、鄂伦春语、赫哲语、柯尔克孜语和俄罗斯语等。

所有这些风光如画的山河、森林、草原，名扬四海的远古洞穴、早期土墙、古城遗址，还有独具风格而色彩斑斓的民族语言文字、宅院、房屋、崖壁画、木雕器具、骨雕制品、皮毛衣食、刺绣、节庆、歌舞、神话故事、娱乐、兽皮艺术、桦树皮艺术品、族谱、婚俗、礼仪、宗教信仰等，均有浓郁而各具特色的民族风情和韵味。对于北方少数民族的这些古老文明和传统文化，我们必须要理性而科学地认识并好好保护，保护好我们人类自己的文化生态的多样性和丰富性。特别是，在现代化建设和构建现代社会生活方式的时候，一定要保护好少数民族独特而弥足珍贵的文化和文明，包括他们的物质生活和精神生活的一切精髓。然而，我们也不得不冷静地审视和思考，当今少数民族地区的现代化建设和现代社会生活方式的构建，对于少数民族传统文化和古老文明的传承和保护也造成一定负面影响。特别是，那些人口少、经济又不太发达且处于强势文化的背景之下、自身正经历着跨越式发展阶段的少数民族农村牧区，他们的民族语言文化逐渐走向濒危或已经进入濒危阶段。对于这些现象，国家各有关方面已给予高度重视，进而明确提出"在现代化的新农村建设中一定要保护好民族特色"，并将民族民间传统文化的保护和抢救列入全国人大常委会的立法计划《中华人民共和国民族民间传统文化保护法（草案）》，从而为做好民族民间传统文化保护工作奠定了法律、政策和理论方面的坚实基础。

文化部门的领导及专家学者更加清楚地认识到，少数民族濒危的语言文化的抢救与保护工作的紧迫性和重要性。严格地说，如果我们在少数民族地区的现代化建设和现代社会生活方式的构建中，不主动自觉地保护民族语言文化，那么我们就会不断地失去更多、更珍贵、更优秀、更加丰富多彩而独具风格的少数民族语言文化遗产，同时，也为民族地区的社会经济的繁荣发展带来一定负面影响。因为，民族语言文化是一个民族生存和发展的重要因素和条件，也是一个民族的灵魂。

三

我国历来重视保护、弘扬少数民族语言和他们的传统文化及古老文明，并把它们作为现代社会生活不可忽视的重要组成部分。例如，20世纪50年代至60年代期间，我国政府就向民族地区派遣民族语言文化方面的专家学者，对民族语言文化做过全面的田野调查，收集整理了数量可观的民族语言文化资料，当时还提出了民族语言文化保护工作的基本方案。另外，于20世纪70年代末至80年代末的10年时间里，对少数民族乡村的语言文化保存现状再次进行了大调查。在此基础上，关于中国民族语言、民族古老文明、民族传承文化等方面的大量书籍相继出版，这使我国广大农村牧区的民族语言文化的保护、整理、研究工作，无论在实际调查，还是在理论研究方面都上了一个新台阶，并取得了十分辉煌的成绩。同时，也培养了一批理论性强、有丰富的田野调查实践经验和实际问题分析能力的民族语言和传统文化研究专家学者。20世纪90年代以后，国家又拨专项资金，组织一批民族语言和民族传统文化等方面的专家学者，对偏远山村和边疆农村牧区的少数民族语言文化开展了全面、系统的调查、整理和抢救，撰写出版了一整套资料性和研究性相结合的民族语言、文化、宗教等方面的书籍。该项工程一直延续到现在，已取得了鼓舞人心的学术成果，还为民族地区的现代化建设和现代社会生活方式的构建起到了积极的推动作用。例如，近些年，东北地区成功举办民族冬运会、民族冰雪节、民族篝火节、草原民族国际那达慕、草原民族敖包盛会，兴建了各具特色的蒙古族草原风情园、满族乡村风情园、朝鲜族民族风情园、达斡尔族民俗风情园、鄂温克族民俗风情园、鄂伦春族民俗风情园、赫哲族民俗风情园、俄罗斯族民俗风情园、萨满文化民俗博物馆、鄂温克族民俗博物馆、鄂温克族驯鹿文化博物馆、达斡尔族民俗博物馆、鄂伦春族民俗风情园、赫哲族民俗博物馆、北极漠河不夜城旅游景区、兴安岭森林旅游景区、红花尔基樟子松旅游景区、赫哲族三江旅游风景区、俄罗斯族风情旅游村等。东北民族地区每年还举行以民族文化为中心的各种规模和形式的文化复兴活动，从而不断提高东北地区少数民族古老文明和优秀传统文化的知名度以及历史的、现实的社会地位。东北地区诸多民族居住地甚至是一些乡村还有具有浓厚民族特色文化广场、民族特色文化公园、民族特色文化体育馆、民族文化成果陈列馆、民族文艺队、民族特色文化夜校、民族乡村陈列馆、民族特色五好家庭、民族特色文明户等。所有这些，为东北地区面临危机甚至逐渐进入濒危的民族语言文字、古老文明、优秀传统文化的保护和抢救发挥着极其重要的作用。

然而，将民族语言文化融入现代社会生活也不是一件简单的事情。对此，首先要强化对于这些民族语言文化的保护和抢救工作。由于民族语言文化的保护和抢救工作涉及面非常广，许多民族又居住于偏远山林地带和农村牧区，因此需要不断强化工作力度，需要一定时间和相当数量的人力、相当数额的财力投入，才能逐步完成民族语言文化保护和抢救这一伟大工程。经过半个多世纪的努力，我国广大农村牧区的民族语言文化的保护、抢救和整理、分析研究工作已取得了巨大成就。同时，也给正在具体实施的农村现代化建设和现代社会生活方式的构建如何更好地保护民族语言文化积累了丰厚的实践经验和理论基础。在过去的岁月里，一些条件较好的少数民族集聚的农村具体实施的经济建设及现代化建设和现代社会生活方式的构建中，在民族语言文化的保护和抢救方面所获得的成绩，也为东北广大农村牧区更好地保护民族语言文化起到了表率作用，从而给农村牧区的现代化进程和现代社会生活方式的构建注入了新的活力和生命力。

少数民族集中生活的广大农村牧区是我国民族语言文化保护最好的地区，尤其是生活在偏远山林、农村、牧区的少数民族把他们的语言文化保存得较完整。所以，在农村牧区的现代化建设和现代社会生活方式的构建中，一定要把他们的民族语言文化保护放在重要位置，因为这是民族地区繁荣发展的重要因素。党的十六大指出："要立足于改革开放和现代化实践，着眼于世界文化发展前沿，发扬民族文化的优越传统。"我国少数民族生活的广大农村牧区面对今天、面对未来、面对世界，追求现代化发展和先进文化的同时，还必须理性地面对自己的历史，面对本民族语言文字、优秀古老的文明、优秀传统的文化，使一切古老文明和当今文明科学结合、和谐共存，使我们祖先创造的远古声音、古老文明、传统文化与当今世界的科学技术融为一体，相互映照，共同繁荣发展，共创灿烂辉煌。

四

我们应该科学地认识到，不同民族语言文化在不同民族的不同历史进程中，发挥过或继续发挥着凝聚民族整体、振奋民族精神、鼓舞民族进步和发展的巨大推动作用。我国不同民族的不同语言文字、口头传承文学以及所有精神文化和物质文化等共同构筑了博大而辉煌的中华文明和文化世界。在这一灿烂辉煌的文明与文化世界里，你中有我，我中有你，你离不开我，我也离不开你，共同繁荣发展。每一个民族的语言文字、宗教信仰、文学艺术等精神文化以及衣食住行等方面展示的物质文化，都是中华万古文明的重要组成部分，是维系中华整体民族精神与情感的纽带，是传承中华悠久历史文明的重要载体。正因为如此，我们在少数民族地区的现代化建设和构建现代社会生活方式中一定要想出一切行之有效的具体措施和方法，保护和抢救少数民族地区的语言文化，进而，将这些文明和文化科学、合理、理想、艺术地融入民族地区的现代化建设和构建现代社会生活方式的基本思路之中，作为构建现代社会生活方式的重要组成内容，使它们为现代文明和文化增添新的内容和活力，从而建立健全既有民族语言文化特色又有现代化色彩的农村牧区。

我们深深地懂得，我国不同民族的古老文明和传统文化间有着错综复杂的深层次内在联系，包括那些人口较少民族的精神文化和物质文化也是如此。当我们从历史唯物主义的理论视角透过现代文明进行理性思考时，就会清醒地认识到它们之间存在的诸多历史渊源，甚至是血脉相承、骨肉相连的亲缘关系。由此，我们有责任、有义务去珍惜、保护和抢救我们这个多民族家庭的每一个成员的古老文明和优秀传统文化，就像爱护我们生存的星球、爱护我们人类自己一样，爱护历史和祖先留给我们的一切往日的劳动、智慧、创造、文明和记忆，让它们为我国农村牧区的科学发展更好地服务。这需要我们不断弘扬贴近民族发展实际需求、贴近民族进步思想和精神需求的优秀传统文化，从而为我国构建全新意义的、包容一切优秀而先进文明和文化的、和谐而科学发展的现代社会生活做出积极贡献。我国民族语言文化与当今发达社会的主流语言文化科学紧密相结合，才能够获得新的生命力，发挥其独有的文化价值和无可忽视的重要经济价值，进而给我国民族地区日新月异的生活带来强健的生命基因，增强优秀而先进的文化的生命力与感召力。在这一点上，民族地区的民族语言文化，包括那些人口较少民族的语言文化均有其特殊而重要的使用价值和现实意义。

不论民族大小，任何一个民族的精神文化和物质文化都有其特定内涵和特殊价值。例如，从不同民族的语言表现形式以及语言结构、语言文化和口头传承文学中，往往能够了解到不同民族的历史背景、生存环境和不同社会结构、发展过程、思维模式。这对于农村牧区的科学发展理念，对于在农村牧区构建和谐社会，有其不可替代的重要意义。我们知道，在广大农村牧区保存的民族古老文明和传统文化，往往代表着他们同自然界的接触、交流中产生的思维规则和表述方式，其中包含着他们勤劳勇敢、团结友爱、热爱生活、热爱大自然、与自然界万物和谐共存的美好品德和情操，代表着他们对于真善美的追求和钟爱。也就是说，这些民族的古老文明和优秀传统文化，来源于自然回归于自然，来自于生活服务于生活，是代表着广大人民群众的高尚的思想品德和不断追求美好生活的坚定信念；是净化广大人民群众的精神世界和物质世界，给他们带来精神享受和物质享受、精神教育和物质教育、精神力量和物质力量的精神生活内涵以及物质生活产物；是教育现代人提高民族自信、自尊、自爱、自强、自觉，促进各民族间的文化交流，增强民族团结的重要内容，在对外宣传我国优秀传统文化等诸多方面将发挥重要作用。尤其是那些没有文字而人口较少民族的古老文明和优秀传统文化，在该民族的历史进程中，一直支撑着他们的生命和精神，凝聚着他们的力量和信仰，使他们从远古平静而自然地走入了现代文明社会。

然而，就像上面所提到的，在科学技术和现代文明飞速发展的今天，尤其是在具体实施和加快农村牧区现代化建设的关键时刻，我国广大农村牧区保存完好的民族语言文化，尤其是那些人口较少民族的精神文明和物质文化，是否能继续保存下去是摆在我们面前的严肃命题。我们真不愿意就这样让它们消失得无影无踪。所以，我们深切地感受到，不惜代价地保护和抢救农村牧区弥足珍贵的民族语言文化的紧迫性和重要性。

如上所说，无论民族大小、人口多少，他们的语言文化都承载着他们的历史，同他们生存的特定自然条件和社会环境以及政治经济制度有着不可分割的必然联系，是经过千百代的不断努力共同创造的产物。其中，包含他们的祖先走过的每一段历史、每一次变革、每一个进步和发展。我们都是从历史走来，都有着悠久而文明的历史，而历史的一切和一切的历史都活在我们的精神世界和物质世界之中。这也是我们力求要保护和抢救当今在广大农村牧区保存的民族语言文化的重要原因。因此，我们说，保护和抢救少数民族生活的广大农村牧区的语言文字、古老文明以及优秀文化，是我们今天语言文化保护和抢救工程中不可缺少的组成部分。

五

我国少数民族生活的广大农村牧区保存的语言文化，包括那些严重濒危的人口较少民族的语言文化，是我们建设现代化强国和现代社会生活方式的重要组成部分，是体现民族团结、民族语言文化繁荣发展的内在合力。我们这一由多民族组成的文明古国，之所以能耀眼夺目地屹立于世界东方，同各民族的共同努力和拼搏、共同的劳动和智慧是分不开的，也和各民族古老文明和优秀传统文化所发挥的特殊精神作用无法分开。民族语言文化是我们构建民族地区现代化的现代社会生活的重要因素之一。如果我们丢失了任何一个民族的语言文化，那么我们不仅失去了弥足珍贵的历史记忆，而且我们的文化和文明就会变得残缺不全，我们会愧对一个完整的历史和文明，同样愧对我们的子孙后代，愧对现代社会生活。保护和抢救民族语言文化，把它们融入现代社会生活，是历史和时代交给我们的使命，也是对未来和子孙后代负责任的做法。

中央现已明确强调，在民族地区的现代化建设中，必须尊重人与自然的和谐发展，要构建和谐社会，要以科学发展观为准绳审视民族地区的历史性变革和发展。在当今尊重人的个性和尊严的文明进程中，人的文化因素关系着社会的文明程度，而文化和文明又关系着人的思想道德和生活理念。也就是说，有什么样的文化，就会有什么样的文明和什么样的社会，有优秀的文化就会有先进文明的社会。优秀的文化一旦被愚昧落后的文化取而代之，社会就会倒退，就会走向黑暗和毁灭。因此，建设现代化的现代社会生活、构建和谐文明的社会、讲求科学发展观，就是要科学地看待人的生命、人的价值、人的作用，要提倡人的正确的生命观、价值观和思想道德观。然而，所有这些几乎都和我国各民族千百年积累的古老文明和优秀传统文化密切相关，我们知道文化来自人的生活和思想，反过来又服务于人的思想和生活，人的进步和文化的发展是相辅相成的关系。然而，在文化领域，像民族语言文字、民族文学艺术、民族宗教信仰以及不同民族的衣食住行等，均占据不可忽视的重要地位。不同民族的优秀的精神文明和物质文化，是由不同民族的不同自然环境、不同历史条件、不同社会背景、不同思维方式、不同表现手段、不同情感世界形成的特定产物。这就是人们常说的"一方山水养一方人"的道理所在。正因为如此,人们都对本民族语言和传承文化有着特殊感情,它使人们发自内心地感到亲切和仰慕,它是人们树立正确的人生观和世界观的不可忽视的重要组成要素。

总而言之,建设少数民族现代化和现代社会生活方式的高度文明的农村牧区,离不开各民族古老文明和优秀传统文化,这是我们现代化建设和现代社会生活方式构建的根基。尤其是,少数民族生活的广大农村牧区在日新月异快速发展的今天,更应该懂得保护和抢救以及充分发扬民族语言文化的必要性和重要性。同时,我们也应该清醒地认识到,保护和抢救民族语言文化及发挥它们的作用,与贯彻落实我国新时期的现代化建设的基本方针,实现科学发展的重要思想理念是不可分割的,也是实现民族地区的经济、社会、文化协调可持续长期发展,全面建设现代化和现代社会生活的关键举措,是构建和谐社会的重要步骤。对于那些人口较少民族的濒危语言文化来讲,在现代化建设和现代社会生活中更应该不失时机地去进行保护和抢救,使它们独具风格的语言思维以及古老文明和文化,在它们的现代社会生活中发挥应有的积极作用,推动它们现代社会生活更加健康、科学、理性而文明地繁荣发展,从而成为它们现代社会生活方式的重要文化内容。

参考文献

安柯钦夫等主编《中国北方少数民族文化》,北京,中央民族大学出版社,1999。
何星亮:《图腾文化与人类诸文化的起源》,北京,中国文联出版公司,1991。
李竹青:《民族现代化探索》,北京,民族出版社,1993。
刘烈恒主编《东北文化丛书》(5卷),沈阳,春风文艺出版社,1992。
〔美〕摩尔根:《古代社会》(上下册),杨东莼等译,北京,商务印书馆,1977。
祁庆富主编《民族文化遗产》,北京,民族出版社,2004。
张碧波、董国尧:《中国古代北方民族文化史》(上下册),哈尔滨,黑龙江人民出版社,2001。
赵锦元等:《当今世界的民族关系与民族问题》,桂林,广西师范大学出版社,1995。
中国社会科学院民族所与国家语委政法司编《国家、民族与语言》,北京,语文出版社,2003。
钟敬文:《民俗文化学梗概与兴起》,北京,中华书局,1996。
〔日〕角田文衛:《古代北方文化研究》(日文),东京,新时代社,1971。

Modernization and the Traditional Cultures of Chinese Ethnic Regions

Chao Ke[*]

I

China is well known as a multi-ethnic country with an astonishing variety of languages and cultures, which coexist with one another in peace, harmony and understanding. Today, in the 21st century, these ethnic groups are building their own modern social life with new ideas and technologies, while realizing the importance of preserving their own languages and cultures. Meanwhile, the increasing exchanges between borderland ethnic regions and developed hinterland regions are breathing new life into the modernization process in ethnic regions. Furthermore, minority groups are also launching a modernization drive under the guidance of a scientific outlook on development, so as to adapt their traditional lifestyles to modern social life, and to build a better and more dynamic new countryside. Here, we argue that the ongoing modernization taking place in ethnic

---

[*] Chao Ke was born in China in 1957. He was awarded his doctoral degree in 2004 in Japan. He is professor, director assistant and doctoral supervisor at the Institute of Ethnic Literature of CASS. His research interests focus on linguistic and cultural studies on Manchu-Tunguses language. His main publications include *Morphophonemics and Noun Morphology of the Ewenki Language* (in Japanese, 2009), *Manchu-Tunguses Language and Its Culture* (in Japanese, 2002), *Comparative Study on Manchu-Tunguses Language* (in Chinese, 1997), etc.

regions is to change those lifestyles that are no longer consistent with modern social development, while raising people's awareness of modern social life and improving the content of modern social life. However, the modernization drive and modern social life is highly conditional on a full respect for the will of ethnic groups, and for the existing languages and cultures that have been preserved with their lives and beliefs. That is to say, we must start from the specific demands of ethnic groups for modern social life, and adopt a prudent and sustained view of scientific development. Only by this can ethnic groups transform their homeland into a thriving haven of modern social life characterized by material and spiritual civilizations, without distancing themselves from traditional cultures or historical memories.

With the improvement of living conditions and the economic and political status of minority groups, the ethnic cultures that are essential to their spiritual life, especially those unique outlying cultures that remain immune from the influence of contemporary mainstream culture, are drawing increasing attention from all over the world. All these ethnic groups, be it a southern one inhabiting coastal or mountainous areas or a northern one inhabiting the vast Gobi desert or pastureland, or be it a big one or a small one, have their own languages and cultures handed down from generation to generation. These languages and cultures have become a mainstay of their spiritual life, a moral source for pursuing truth, beauty and goodness, and a spiritual bridge for dialogues with history and the future, for indeed, they trace the contours of history they have traversed, record their living states in different periods of time, and embody their thoughts, beliefs and pursuits from the far ancient past. Once we immerse ourselves in their specific social milieu and life, and communicate with them with our souls, we will discover many valuable ancient cultures and civilizations that have gone unnoticed by modern people. Today, we are glad that they have managed to preserve their ethnic cultures and civilizations with vitality and perseverance, defying the all-sweeping impacts of modern cultures and civilizations. Without them or their perseverance, we would have lost many historical memories and some earlier civilizations where we have descended from. The endangered languages and cultures of the sparsely-populated ethnicities appear particularly precious in the global context in which human civilizations and cultures are becoming increasingly similar. No doubt, these traditional cultures and civilizations have been playing a significant role in the modernization of ethnic regions and the formation of modern lifestyles, such as pastureland culture, snowfield culture, Gobi culture, forest culture, agrarian culture, just to name a few.

II

However, we must not overlook the fact that the modernization and modern lifestyle transformation have somehow bridged the gap between developed regions and less-developed ethnic regions, so that they are tending toward each other. Notably, some developed regions are bringing modern cultures and lifestyles into under-developed ethnic regions through various forms and levels of economic cooperation, which have rendered the most cherished cultures and civilizations particularly vulnerable to modern lifestyles and modernization. As such, ethnic languages and cultures as a whole are facing varying degrees of crisis, while those of less-populated ethnic groups are in imminent danger of extinction. To address this problem, the central and local governments have promulgated a set of policies on the preservation of ethnic languages and cultures, so as to bring the ethnic groups to realize the imminence and importance of preserving the endangered languages and cultures. China has also adopted effective and scientifically informed measures to adapt ethnic languages and cultures to modern civilization and modern social life, so that they can play a positive role in the socio-economic development of ethnic regions. Time and again, the history of human civilization has borne it out that modern cultures and civilizations cannot really revive until they are integrated with traditional ones. As a matter of fact, modern cultures and civilizations are inherently associated with traditional ones in that all modern cultures and civilizations can trace their origins to ancient times. The very diversity of ethnic cultures and civilizations presents us with a colorful world and a new thinking space. As we know, the vast northeast of China is home to over twenty ethnic groups, including the Mongolians, Manchus, Islams, Xibes, Sibos, Daurs,

Erwinks and Russians. For thousands of years, they have been settling here, along the greater and lesser Xing'an mountain ranges, at the foot of Changbai Mountain, by Dalai and Hulun lakes, on Hulunbeier Grassland, in Sanjiang River basin, near the underground forest in Mt. Changbai, in Pinus sylvestris and silver birch forests, on the Willow Island downstream Songhua River, in the nightless Mohe Village, and near the beautiful Nierji Reservoir. This area boasts a large number of scenic spots and historic resorts, including the world-famous Wokenhada Neolithic cave, Shibazhan Paleolithic cultural ruins, Pagoda State of Taizhou during the Liao and Jin dynasties, ruins of Puyulu Ancient City of the Jin dynasty, Yagou Rock Carvings by the Jurchens, ruins of Ningguta Ancient City, site of Acheng, ruins of Walihuotun Old City, Tomb of Wanyan Aguda, as well as ruins of Morigen Old City. In the long course of history, these ethnic groups have created, with labor and wisdom, an equally large number of cultures and civilizations of typical frigid and temperate zones. Among them are: the north-eastern agricultural civilization, the Korean paddy rice culture along Mt. Changbai, camel-herd culture of the Buriat Mongolians, shepherd culture of the Barhu Mongolians, Hezhe fishing and fish-skin culture, reindeer culture of the Ewenks, as well as the fishing and hunting culture of the Manchus. In food, clothing and everyday life, the ethnic groups also retain their distinctiveness, as seen in the Manchu Qipao and bone decorations, Mongolian robes and riding boots, Xibe embroidery, Korean hanbok gown and cobbies, Oroqen animal-hide clothing, and Hezhe fish-skin clothing; Manchu pickles and pork cooked in hot pot, Korean dog meat soup and cabbage in chili sauce, Mongolian roasted piglet and hand-served lamb meat, Xibe baked cake and oil tea, as well as Hezhe raw fish slices and side dishes.

The northern ethnic groups are more distinctive in the observation of fairs and festivals. These fairs and festivals include: Mongolian Aobao Festival in April and Nadam Fair in August; Korean Full Moon Festival, Manchu temple fairs, Western Migration Festival of the Xibe people, Fast-breaking Festival of the Kirgiz people, Salmon-harvest Festival of the Hezhe people, as well as Bun-fire Festival of the Oroqen people. Some of their representative recreations are: Kirgiz-style of horse racing, Hezhe dog-sledge racing and straw-ball forking, Boyiko of the Daur people, and reindeer chess of the Oroqen people. Spiritually, northern ethnic groups have also created splendid cultures and civilizations, such as Mongolian long tune and horse-head fiddle, Korean gayageum and fishermen's songs, Grain-sending song and Yang-ge dance of the Xibe people, as well as Mongolian cow-milking and falcon dances. Most of the northern groups believed in shamanism in earlier times, which holds that everything in the universe has a spirit. Their religious beliefs are: bear totem, mountain god worshipping, polytheism, snake god worshipping, Xili Mum worshipping, and so on. The main languages spoken here include: Mongolian, Korean, Manchu, Ewenki and Russian.

All these natural sceneries (mountains, rivers and forests) and historic resorts (ancient caves, city ruins, peculiar and multifarious ethnic languages, houses, cliff paintings, wood carvings, bone carvings, embroidery, festivities, songs and dances, myths and legends, recreations, wedding customs, etiquettes and religious beliefs) exhibit a strong local flavor, each with its own distinctiveness. Therefore, in the process of modernization and modern social life building, we should take particular care to preserve the unique and precious ethnic cultures and civilizations, including all those good elements in their material and spiritual life. It would be a great tragedy if we could only leave a unified world and thinking space for our future generations. However, we must recognize the fact that the current modernization and modern social life building in ethnic regions are affecting the preservation of traditional cultures and ancient civilizations. In those ethnic areas that are sparsely-populated and economically under-developed, and that are experiencing great leap-frog development, ethnic languages and cultures are facing the grave danger of extinction. Such phenomena have put the central government on high alert, which explicitly requires that 'The ethnicity of minority groups must be well preserved in the construction of new countryside.' Soon afterwards, the protection and preservation of ethnic/folk cultures was put on the agenda of The Law on Preserving Ethnic and Folk Traditions of the People's Republic of China (Draft), a legislation plan of the NPC Standing Committee, which laid a legal, theoretical and policy-oriented basis for the protection of ethnic/folk traditions and cultures.

Scholars and leaders from cultural sectors have also come to realize the imminence and importance of protecting and preserving endangered ethnic languages and cultures. Honestly, unless we are self-conscious of protecting ethnic languages and cultures in the process of modernization and building modern social life, we will lose, once and for all, an increasing number of ethnic heritages that used to be so dear, colorful and peculiar to us. While at the same time, the extinction of ethnic languages and cultures can also incur negative effects on the socio-economic prosperity of an ethnic region, for ethnic languages and cultures constitute an essential part of the survival and development of that ethnic group. Therefore, we should redouble our efforts in protecting these ethnic languages and cultures, taking them as part of modernization and the building of modern social life in ethnic areas.

III

For years, China has attached great importance to the protection and development of ethnic languages, cultures and civilizations, deeming them an important part of modern social life. For instance, in the 1950s – 1960s, the Chinese government sent a team of scholars and specialists on a comprehensive fieldwork on ethnic languages and cultures. The fieldwork resulted in a large quantity of materials arranged on ethnic languages and cultures, and a draft plan on the protection of ethnic languages and cultures. In the 1970s – 1980s, another large survey was conducted on the situation of languages and cultures in ethnic areas. Based on the survey, a wumber of books were compiled and published on Chinese ethnic languages, civilizations and cultures, which have greatly facilitated the protection and arrangement of ethnic languages and cultures in terms of field work and theoretical research. The survey also turned out a team of experts and scholars on ethnic languages and cultures, who have developed rich experience in fieldwork and strong analytical skills. Later, in the 1990s, the central government allocated special funds for a systematic and full-scale project on the survey, arrangement and preservation of ethnic languages and cultures in remote mountainous and border regions, and for the publication of a series of books on ethnic languages, cultures and religions. Now, the project has accomplished inspiring achievements, and has played a positive part in the process of modernization and the building of modern social life in ethnic areas. For example, in recent years, the northeastern region has successfully held a series of fairs and festivals, such as winter games among ethnic groups, ethnic ice and snow festival, ethnic bonfire festival, International Nadam Fair of Grassland Nationalities and Aobao Fair of Grassland Nationalities, and set up a number of folk gardens and museums, such as Mongolian Folk Garden, Manchu Rural Folk Garden, Korean Folk Garden, Russian Folk Garden, Urwenki Folk Garden, Daur Ethnic Folk Museum, Hezhe Ethnic Folk Museum, and Xing'an Forest scenic spot. Every year, various forms and scales of cultural revival activities are organized in the northeast, so as to boost the fame of these ancient ethnic civilizations and cultures and to improve their social status. In those multi-ethnic areas of the northeast, there are also some peculiar cultural activities with a strong ethnic flavor, such as Cultural Plazas, Cultural Parks, Cultural Stadiums, Cultural Exhibitions, Cultural Teams, Cultural Night Schools, Rural Ethnic Exhibitions, model Families and Households. All these cultural activities have played a significant role in protecting and preserving the northeastern ethnic languages, civilizations and cultures that are in imminent danger or face the danger of extinction.

Nevertheless, we are keenly aware that it is far from easy to bring ethnic languages and cultures fully in line with modern social life. To do this, the first and foremost thing is to raise people's awareness of protecting and preserving ethnic languages and cultures. Since the preservation work involves a great many factors, and since many ethnic groups inhabit mountainous and forest areas out of the way, we should increase our efforts in time, manpower and budget. Thanks to our continued efforts over the past half century, we have seen tremendous development in the protection, preservation, arrangement and research of ethnic languages and cultures in the vast rural/pastoral areas. In some better-conditioned areas, progress has also been made in the protection and preservation of ethnic languages and cultures in the process of economic development and modernization. These areas can serve as an example of the preservation of ethnic languages and cultures in the north-east, and invigorate the ongoing modernization drive and the building of modern social life in this region.

The vast rural and pastoral areas inhabited by ethnic groups are the best preserved ones in national languages and cultures. This is particularly true of those remote ethnic areas, where languages and cultures are better preserved and protected. Therefore, the Chinese government should place the protection of ethnic languages and cultures high on its agenda in the course of modernization and the building of modern social life, for it is crucial to the prosperity and development of these ethnic areas. The 16th NPC report required that 'We should uphold the good traditions of our national cultures, be commiffed to reform and opening up and modernization, and keeping an eye on the forefront of world cultural development.' While orienting themselves toward modernization and advanced cultures, the Chinese ethnic areas should also look inwardly at their own history, languages and cultures, so that all ancient civilizations can coexist harmoniously with modern ones, and that ancient Chinese civilizations can work together with contemporary science and technologies for common prosperity.

IV

We should bear in mind that all ethnic languages and cultures, different as they are, have contributed their bit in maintaining national eohesion, boosting national spirit and advancing national progress and development. These ethnic languages and orally transmitted literature, along with all spiritual and material cultures, have come together to create the profound and splendid Chinese civilization. The spiritual culture (as represented by ethnic languages and cultures, religious beliefs, as well as literature and arts) and material culture (as represented by food, clothing and everyday life) of each ethnic group constitute an important part of ancient Chinese civilization, serving as a nexus for maintaining national sentiments and feelings. It is exactly for this reason that we must take effective measures to protect and preserve ethnic languages and cultures. Furthermore, we should bring these civilizations and cultures into the framework of modernization and modern social life in a scientific and rational way, so that they can inject new elements into modern civilizations and cultures, and establish/improve rural and pastoral areas featuring a blend of ethnic and modern tastes.

We fully understand that all Chinese ethnic civilizations are closely interrelated, as is the case with the spiritual and material cultures of the less populated ethnic groups. When we view modern civilizations from the perspective of historical materialism, we will become aware of the historical relations, or even kinship ties, among them. Hence, we are duty bound to cherish, protect and preserve the ancient civilizations and good cultures of each member in our multi-ethnic family. We should treasure the labor, wisdom, creations and memories that have come down to us from the ancient past, as much as we do the earth and our lives. This requires us to uphold all those good cultures that meet the practical needs of national development and echo the demand of advanced thought, so as to contribute to a new sense of modern social life characterized by harmonious and scientific development, and open to all advanced civilizations and cultures. Only by combined with contemporary mainstream languages and cultures can Chinese ethnic languages and cultures regain new life, and display their peculiar cultural and economic values. In this sense, all ethnic languages and cultures, including those of less-populated ethnic groups, are equally important in their values and practical significance.

All ethnic groups, large or small, are unique in their spiritual and material cultures. For instance, from the different linguistic representations, linguistic structures and orally transmitted literature, we can learn a lot about the particular historical backgrounds, habitats, social structures and thinking patterns of different ethnic groups. Spiritual and material cultures are also important for implementing the scientific outlook on development, and for building a harmonious society in rural and pastoral areas. As we know, the ancient ethnic civilizations and cultures preserved in ethnic groups usually reflect their peculiar thinking patterns and linguistic representations that have arisen from their contact and communication with the nature, and typically demonstrate their virtues (such as diligence, unity and love), their harmonious coexistence with the nature, as well as their pursuit of truth, beauty and goodness. In other words, all these ancient civilizations and good cultures stem from and return to the nature, and stem from and return to their life. They highlight their steadfastness in aspiring for noble thought and better life; they help purify the material and spiritual world of the masses; and they empower them with spiritual and material forces. Meanwhile, they also play an important role in educating modern people, boosting their national self-confidence, self-respect, self-love, self-reliance and self-awareness, and promoting national solidarity and cultural exchanges across ethnic groups. In those ethnic groups with no written languages and smaller population particularly, their civilizations and cultures have bolstered their lives and spirit, enabling them to move peacefully and naturally to the modern society.

However, as mentioned above, in the era when technology and modern civilizations are developing fast, and when the modernization drive is well underway in rural and pastoral areas, it remains a serious challenge whether these ethnic languages and cultures can survive or not. If we cannot bear to see the disappearance of these ethnic languages and cultures, we will have to understand the importance and imminence of protecting and preserving the precious ethnic languages and cultures.

V

The ethnic languages and cultures preserved in rural and pastoral areas, including those endangered languages and cultures of groups with smaller population, not omly constitute an important part of China's modernization drive and the building of modern social life, but also reflect an inherent joint force that helps maintain national unity and prosperity of national languages and cultures. The splendid and remarkable history of China, as an ancient multi-ethnic country, lies as much in the common struggle, hard work and wisdom of all ethnic groups, as in the particular spiritual role played by these ancient civilizations and traditional cultures. Ethnic languages and cultures are a key element in the ongoing modern social life building in ethnic areas. Once we lose any of them, we will lose along with them some valuable historical memories, and our culture and civilization will become fragmented and incomplete. Therefore, we are charged by history and our times with the mission to protect and preserve ethnic languages and cultures, and to bring them organically into modern social life.

The central government has stressed that in the modernization drive in ethnic areas, we must show full respect for the harmonious development between human beings and nature, build a harmonious society, and view the historical transformations and development in ethnic areas from the point of view of the scientific outlook on development. Now, in the civilized course highlighting individuality and respect of man, man's cultural elements bear directly on the level of civilization of a society, while culture and civilization can also react to man's morality and conception. That is to say, a particular kind of culture can bring about a particular kind of civilization and society in that a good culture will bring about an advanced and civilized society. Once a good culture is replaced by a backward and ignorant one, the society will sink back into darkness and demise. In this sense, building modern social life and a harmonious and civilized society, and stressing the scientific outlook on development, are to treat life, human being's role and values with a seientifically informed attitude, and to adopt a right outlook on life, values and morality. Nevertheless, all these are closely related to ancient Chinese civilizations and traditional cultures that have accumulated over the past centuries. As is known, culture comes from people's life and thought, and conversely, serves people's thought and life. The progress of people is supplemental to the development of culture. And yet, ethnic languages, literature, religious beliefs and everyday life assume an important position in cultural spheres. The good spiritual and material cultures of all ethnic groups derive from different natural environments, historical conditions, social contexts, thinking patterns, ways of representation, and emotions and feelings. This is why we say: 'The unique features of the local environment always give special characteristics to its inhabitants.' It is precisely for this reason that people tend to harbor unique feelings for their own national languages and cultures, and show intimacy with and admiration for their languages and cultures. These languages and cultures are indispensable to helping people cultivate the right outlook on life and the world.

To sum up, the modernization drive and the building of modern social life in rural and pastoral ethnic areas impinge greatly on the ancient civilizations and traditional cultures of ethnic groups, which lie at the foundation of our modernization drive and the building of modern social lifestyle. Today, when ethnic regions are witnessing rapid changes, we should note particularly the necessity and significance of upholding national languages and cultures.

Meanwhile, we should be keenly aware of the fact that protecting and preserving ethnic languages and cultures and bringing their roles into play are indispensable to the implementation of China's modernization drive and scientific outlook on development during the new period. They are also crucial to a sustained and coordinated development of economy, society and culture, an all-round development of modernization and modern social life, and to the building of a harmonious society. As for those endangered languages and cultures of smaller ethnic groups, we should lose no time in protecting and preserving them, so that their peculiar languages, thinking patterns and cultures can play their due positive roles in the nationwide modernization drive and the building of modern social life, their modern social life can develop into a more healthy, scientific and rational way, and that their languages and cultures can constitutecan important part of their modern social life.

(Translated from the Chinese by Wang Wen'e)

References

He Xingliang (1991), *Totem Culture and Origins of Human Cultures*, Beijing: China Federation of Literary and Art Circles Publishing Corporation.

Liu Lieheng (1992), (ed.), *Series of Northeastern Culture*, Sheng Yang: Chunfeng Wenyi Press.

Qi Qingfu (2004), (ed.), *Heritage of National Culture*, Beijing: Ethnic Publishing House.

Li Zhuqing (1993), *Exploration of Ethnic Modernization*, Beijing: Ethnic Publishing House.

Institute of Nationalities Studies of CASS and National Language Committee (2003), (eds.), *States, Nations and Languages*, Beijing: Language and Literature Press.

Tsunoda Bunei (1971), *Research on the Northern Culture in Ancient Times*, Tokyo: Shinjidaisha.

Zhao Jinyuan et al. (1995), *Ethnic Relations and Ethnic Issues in Contemporary World*, Gui Lin: Guangxi Normal University Press.

Zhong Jingwen (1996), *Outline of the Study of Folklore Culture and Its Rise*, Beijing: Zhong Hua Book Company.

当代希腊社会中的文化自我觉识

斯特利奥斯·维尔维扎基斯[*]

一

当我最初对论坛的总的议题进行思考时,我的理解是要求探讨当代希腊社会生活方式的文化根源。但是,我很快意识到,这个涉及如此之广的任务可能需要将历史学家、社会学家、社会心理学家、政治学家或文化人类学家的概念工具和方法论综合起来。于是,我决定将研究的范围缩小,集中在当代希腊人的文化自我觉识这个问题上。此外,由于我不是一名社会科学家,没有关于整个希腊民族的信念、习俗以及习惯的近期演化的可靠经验数据可资利用,所以我的研究将限定于对某些著名希腊知识分子(大多是历史学家、艺术家、作家及哲学家)的文化自我觉识进行批判性评价。我尤为关注的是这样一种研究所关涉的自我觉识和自决这两个概念的哲学解释,但是我主要依据近现代希腊思想史,同时还以近代欧洲思想史的材料作为补充和影响因素,以此提供一个审视希腊及其历史的"外部"视角。

接下来,我将首先考量独特的希腊文化认同这个概念的含义。希腊文化

---

[*] 斯特利奥斯(斯蒂利亚诺斯)·维尔维扎基斯(Stelios (Stylianos) Virvidakis),男,1955年出生于雅典。1984年获美国普林斯顿大学博士学位。雅典大学哲学与科学史系教授。专业领域:认识论、元哲学、伦理学、近代哲学史等。主要著述有:《善的力量》(1996)、"关于行动的道德评价"(2006)、"康德《纯粹理性批判》中的哲学知识问题"(2007)等。2006年获法国政府颁发的"教育骑士勋章"。

认同产生于东地中海部分地区的长期历史发展之中，是一种整合若干基本要素和抵制外来文化同化的综合产物。然后我将着重谈一谈"希腊性"的特殊性，也即那些可能共有这种认同并以不同方式来表达这种认同的人们的一种品质。我尽力简略地描述一下对理论上把握这种品质但同时也是对这种品质在希腊社群和个人生活中的可能的具体表现形式所可能采取的几种典型的研究进路或态度。在本文的最后部分，我将就研究传统或当今意识形态趋向的知识分子如何采用其中某种或某些态度概述几点意见。这样一种研究可以帮助我们揭示他们在使民族和文化自我觉识成为可能的过程中，因而也是在一定程度上形成实际生活方式的过程中所起的最终作用。我在分析行将结束时坚持提醒人们关注所讨论的这些态度的实际影响和伦理意义。

二

事实上，探究可以认为属于 Greek（希腊）或 Hellenic（希腊）民族的人群的独特认同有几种可能的进路。[①] 20 世纪和 21 世纪的希腊社会科学家、艺术家和知识分子对于"当今的希腊人是谁？""他们与他们的过去及其余世界是怎样的关系？"这些关键问题提供了见仁见智的回答。所以，不妨尝试将促成希腊人形成或多或少的共同的自我认识的主观和客观因素分离开来，同时将决定外国人、远邻近邻、中立的观察家、敬仰希腊文化的人，以

---

① 有些希腊知识分子坚持使用原本词"Hellas"和"Hellenic"，而不使用"Greece"和"Greek"。后者源自拉丁文的"Graecia""Graeci"，由于某些语言和传统中的特殊用法而具有贬义，而前者凸显了与古希腊的关联。还应该提及口语词"Romioi"和"Romiosyni"的用法，它们指称的是拜占庭时期之后的希腊人，具有与奥斯曼帝国统治的痛苦经历相关的含义。拜占庭以东方"罗马"帝国而闻名，"Romaoi/Romioi"这个词是指称它的臣民。穆斯林将拜占庭帝国称为"Rum"，土耳其人称所有在伊斯兰的希腊人为"Rumis"，不过他们现在将希腊称为"Yunaniston"源自"Yunan"（"Ionian"）——他们称谓"古希腊"的词。关于"Romiosyni"这个概念的重要性及其正面和负面的细微差异，参见 Patrik Leigh Fermor, *Roumeli: Travels in Northern Greece*, London: John Murray, 2004 (1966): 96-125。弗莫谈到了一种"希腊—罗马两难"，即近代希腊思想中的"对立"或"分裂"。"Hellene"代表着亲西方的、苛刻的理想，符合与古典希腊相关的价值观，而"Romios"代表着一种更为大众化和现实主义的模式，体现了产生于拜占庭的历史经验和奥斯曼帝国占领时期（1453~1821）的善恶观。这些概念分别与下文所描述的探究希腊性的第一和第二种进路大致对应。关于另一位在希腊居住多年并对西方亲希腊者所赞同的希腊文化概念持批判态度的外国学者的观点，参见 Philip Sherrard, *The Wound of Greece. Studies in Neo-Hellenism*, London and Athens: Rex Collins & Anglo-Hellenic, 1978。

及以往和现在的同盟和敌人的认识变化的类似因素分离开来。如果你接受一种彻底的构建主义的而不是本质主义的民族认同概念，并且或许赞同本尼迪克特·安德森把民族视为"想象的共同体"的论述，[1] 那么你可能从事的是一项寻找构建想象的"希腊性"的元素的谱系研究。你似乎要面对一个在两种意义上的"困惑"，一种是说它是需要解释清楚的谜团，另一种是说它是需要以正确的方法拼合的拼图。本文中，我将提出这个困惑并且阐述过去两个世纪中所提供的主要"解决办法"。我的评判试图使可能不协调的视角综合起来，一方面这关联到我本人作为一个希腊人的主观觉识，这种觉识有意识或无意识地渗透着我所接受的各种程度的教育，另一方面关联到的可能是超然的哲学概念分析进路，这种进路是描述性的，但也是规范的。

确实，希腊的情况是相当特殊的。普通希腊人所采用的官方历史论述依据的是一种所谓的连续性，这种连续性跨越三千年，构成了古代时期、中世纪（拜占庭）时期以及近代时期。历史学家康斯坦丁·帕帕里戈普洛斯在其《希腊民族史》(1850~1874) 中详尽论述了这种连续性，以此来回应否认这种连续性的奥地利人雅各布·菲利普·法尔默赖厄提出的挑战。帕帕里戈普洛斯指出，法尔默赖厄的论点适用于种族连续性，而对文化而言是无效的。[2] 首先，由于显然有证据可以证明有一种共同语言经由各个不同时期从古代演化至今，所以可以去谈论相同的希腊民族。[3] 其次，人们也可以求助于所谓的拥有一种起源于独特的、多面的文明的核心认同的意识。这种文明最初在古代时期出现在巴尔干半岛，并且迅速在小亚细亚沿海、西西里以及南意大利蔓延。按照主流历史叙事，可以认为这种认同的核心部分存在于拜占庭时代，直到 19 世纪初期之前，它经历了各种各样的转变和奇遇。被视为尤为重要的是逐渐的民族"觉醒"，它被认为应该发生在 18 世纪，由法国大革命前后的欧洲意识形态气候促成。因此在反抗奥斯曼帝国的独立战争之后成为存在的近代希腊国家可以重扬它光荣的历史，恢复在四个世纪的被占领时期一直受压制的认同。

---

[1] 参见 Benedikt Anderson, *Imagined Communities: Reflections on the Origins and Spread of Nationalism*, 2nd ed., London: Verso, 1991。

[2] 关于希腊历史编纂学，参见 Alexander Kitroeff, "Continuity and Change in Contemporary Greek Historiography", in Martin Blikhorn and Thanos Veremis (eds.), *Modern Greece: Nationalism and Nationality*, Athens: Sage-Eliamep, 1990, 143-172。

[3] 实际上，希腊语本身的连续性问题仍然在争论中，并且具有明显的意识形态含义。我们将在下文回到这一点。

在过去的两个世纪，各种各样的知识分子努力去确立这种连续性概念，它抵制损伤性的断裂，最终以整合来自东西方的对立元素来达到成功的综合。希腊古俗志是一门相当原始和充满意识形态色彩的社会科学——一种当地的和经验的文化人类学形式，研究民歌、仪式和习俗，目的在于揭示可以追溯至古代时期的观念、风格主题，以及所有形式的社群生活。知识分子详尽阐述了不同时期的希腊思想的重构，旨在展示使多神论的希腊世界观与基督教—东正教世界观和谐起来的所谓综合。事实上，"希腊—基督教"文明这个概念——这种文明可能最初是在拜占庭帝国的文化体制中实现的——是由学者斯皮里宗·扎姆韦利奥斯明确提出并加以捍卫的。他属于"民族诗人"狄奥尼修斯·索洛莫斯那个圈子。这个概念作为近代希腊国家的官方民族意识形态的主要成分而流行一时。[1]

此外，艺术家、诗人及作家被认为在有意识或无意识地奋争，力图以新的表达式来表现一种希腊性品质。这里，应该首先提及属于"30一代"的作者的贡献。这些作者大多试图将关于一种特殊的希腊认同的美学和文化概念与现代主义、与对一种政治世界主义的承诺结合起来。[2] 某些思想家过去而且可能仍然认为希腊性体现了一种独有的精神经验的主要特征，这种精神经验以不同的方式反映在艺术以及更普遍的文化表现中，甚至反映在日常的生活方式中。[3] 这样，考古学家、艺术史学家以及文学批评家进行了各种各样的尝试来更精确地描述这种经验，某些哲学家和神学家也试图对它做

---

[1] 参见 Michael Herzfeld, *Ours Once More. Folklore, Ideology and the Making of Modern Greece*, New York: Pella, 1986。赫茨菲尔德特别强调了古俗志的意识形态特征，他称之为"国家级民俗学科"。（第13页）关于"希腊—基督教"文化综合，应该指出的是，许多哲学家认为，古典希腊的世界观不可能与基督教理想调和。关于民主与哲学之间的关系以及二者诞生在古希腊的意义的讨论，尤其参见 Cornelius Castoriades, *Ce qui fait la Grèce. I. D' Homère à Héraclite. Séminaires 1982 – 1983. II. La Création humaine*, Paris: Seuil, 2004。

[2] 后来以"30一代"而闻名的这批作家和艺术家包括多少受超现实主义启发的希腊诗人，如安德烈亚斯·埃姆维科斯、尼科斯·恩戈诺普洛斯和奥季赛乌斯·埃利蒂斯（1978年诺贝尔奖获得者）、受保罗·瓦莱里和T. S. 艾略特影响的乔治·塞费里斯（1963年诺贝尔奖获得者）以及散文作家，如乔治·塞奥托卡斯。

[3] "Greekness"（希腊性）一词一般是作为"hellinikotita"一词的译法而被接受的，不过那些想避免有"Greek"的派生词之嫌的人可能更愿用"hellenicity"。关于考古学在阐述希腊认同概念中的重要性，参见 Dimitris Damaskos and Dimitris Plantzos, *A Singular Antiquity: Archaeology and Hellenic Identity in twentieth-century Greece*, Athens: Mouseio Benaki, 3d supplement, 2008。

出界定①。更近一些，所谓的"新东正教"知识分子，即直接或间接受俄罗斯散居犹太人神学家影响的基督教思想家，形成了一个可与俄罗斯亲斯拉夫派相比的群体。②遗憾的是，由于他们不仅强调希腊民族性的独特性或独一性，而且强调对其他民族的所谓文化优越性，所以往往陷入以一种卓越的哲学观为伪装的恶毒的民族主义修辞。有时，他们毫无顾忌地谈论希腊人民的特殊历史命运，与德国哲学传统司空见惯的危险的浪漫主义思想形成呼应。

那么，以上论断的意思是说，存在一种三千多年几乎没有断裂的连续性，以及一种隐藏的"桑蚕"似的认同，虽经历变化却保持着同样的"深层"核心的认同。这些论断可能并且已经受到那些谴责其本质主义和目的论意义并担忧其政治后果的历史学家们的质疑。他们往往指出，这些观点显露出了应该从任何严肃的历史叙事中清除出去的无法证明的形而上学假定。甚至对相同的语言这个概念，主要根据语法、句法和语义方面的考虑而采取一种关于口头语言的严格认同标准的语言学家也有争议，因为这种相同语言从迈锡尼时代到当今经历了许多个发展阶段，采取了各种不同的形式。其实，大多数当代语言学家在研究古代、中世纪和近代希腊语时，更愿意谈论

---

① 这种特殊的"思维和感觉方式"得到了许多不同的而且往往是对立的描述，但被认为抓住了希腊人千百年来形成的国民性的特征。因此，这种方式被认为除了其他特质外主要关涉个人主义和善于心计，而且关联到希腊人国民性的各种缺陷（缺乏纪律性和不服从权威、争强好胜、懒散等），但是他们也信守一种"社会中心论"政治，这种政治承认人格的重要性、尺度感、人性、和谐、调和对立、尊重理性、对局限性和人的有限性的意识、对于生命的悲剧感、正义感、英雄行为、自决、热爱自由、对于感官愉悦的健康肯定、温暖、自豪与慷慨。诸如·奥季赛乌斯·埃利蒂斯这样的诗人坚持强调由于受益于对自然的希腊之光的特殊经验而获得的一种特殊的、伴随着"清澈""透明的深度"的"明朗"——不具有一种肤浅的、理性主义的性质。左派历史学家尼科斯·斯沃罗诺斯还谈到一种"抵抗精神"，据说这种精神激发了一系列同仇敌忾的英勇反抗，来对付外来威胁和觊觎东南欧洲要塞的入侵者。综上所述可被视为经由千百年而习得的文化特征，这可归因于希腊人所占据的特定地理区域的生活条件（与风景、自然资源、气候等有关），并主要归因于集体记忆和大众想象中保存的悠久的和充满惊险的历史经验。

② 这些"新东正教"和"希腊中心论"思想家当中最著名的是神学家和哲学家赫里斯托斯·伊安纳拉斯，他受像海德格尔这样的哲学家所影响，竭力主张克服西方形而上学传统，并且广泛地依靠东正教神秘神学。他对体现了一种存在的民族精神的社群主义政治——据说这种民族精神之楷模产生自希腊东正教的传统——提出了一种特殊的观点。伊安纳拉斯是一位多产作家，其已经译成英文的主要著作包括：*The Freedom of Morality*, New York: SVP, 1984, *Postmodern Metaphysics*, Brookline, MA: H. C. Press, 2004, *On the Absence and Unknowability of God: Heidegger and the Areopagite*. London: Continuum, 2005, *Orthodoxy and the West*, Brookline, MA: H. C. Press, 2006。

不同的语言。① 无论如何，被视为希腊文化千百年以来的常态的这种独特希腊性的特征，充其量不过是艺术和哲学想象的投射或创造，与之关联的往往是民众的定见，而这可以而且应该成为批判历史研究、社会学研究以及人类学研究的对象。从一种自由的道德和政治观点来看，显然不受欢迎的是其对民族主义话语的意识形态使用。

然而，人们可能不会反对最终承认并不诉求任何有争议的形而上学和评价假定的文化连续性所达到的相当程度。那么，一种独特的语言和文化"核心"发展成为一个多少是同质的希腊民族，可被视为是对"更早的民族和宗教认同的修剪"。② 而且，这种"修剪"需要民族实体的形成，这个民族实体最终将在巴尔干半岛的一部分地区确立其身份并构成一个民族国家，它所因循的构建模式远远超出了对所谓原初元素的发现。事实上，关于演化中的认同的性质和发展方向，关于它与其他为获得承认而奋争、力图在相同或邻近地理区域强行其存在的认同的对抗，存在许多微妙的问题。

三

我们不妨追随季米特里斯·齐奥瓦斯，将我们前面所归纳的研究希腊民族的出现和传承的主要传统进路的几个可供选择的态度或观念分离出来逐个进行分析。③ 它们是：（1）符号主义—考古学观念，它在很大程度上是从西

---

① 关于希腊语、其不同形态、共同要素以及千百年来的演化的语言和意识形态问题，有各种不同的研究进路，参见 Antonis Liakos, "'From Greek into Our Common Language': Language and History in the Making of Modern Greece", in A. F. Christidis (ed.). *A History of Ancient Greek: From the Beginnings to Late Antiquity*, Cambridge: Cambridge University Press, 1287 – 1295, Peter Mackridge, "A Language in the Image of the Nation: Modern Greeks and Some Parallel Cases" and Karen Van Dyck, "The Language Question and the Diaspora", in Roderick Beaton and David Ricks, *The Making of Modern Greece: Nationalism, Romanticism & the Uses of the Past (1797 – 1896)*, Farnham: Ashgate, 2009, 177 – 187 and 188 – 198。亦参见 Peter Mackridge, *Language and National Identity in Greece: 1766 – 1976*, Oxford: Oxford University Press。
② 参见 Costas Carras, "Greek Identity: A Long View", in Maria Todorova (ed.), *Balkan Identities: Nation and Memory*, London: Hurst and Company, 2004, 294 – 326, 294。
③ 季米特里斯·齐奥瓦斯是伯明翰大学教授，从事近代希腊研究。我以下的讨论主要依据他的文章（希腊文）"Greekness and the Generation of the 30s" ["Ellinikotita kai I genia tou 30"], *Cogito* 6 (May 2007): 8 – 10。亦参见他的著作（希腊文）*The Transformations of Nationism and the Ideology of Greekness in the Interwar Period* [*I metamorfoseis tou ethnismou kai to ideologima tis ellinikotitas sto Mesopolemo*], Athens: Odysseas, 1989。

方引入的，符合新古典理想，强调古希腊文化的"伟大性"，倡导对其价值的尊崇。持这种观念的人，如18世纪和19世纪的外国亲希腊者，往往因为当代希腊人不能效仿光荣的祖先而表示失望。[①] 希腊祖先的成就成为当今希腊人可望而不可及的楷模。（2）浪漫—有机观念，它要求我们追踪希腊民族的演化，从其古代起源经由千百年直至当今。这种观念奠定了主流历史叙事的基础，支持了希腊—基督教综合概念，将古典遗产与拜占庭传统结合起来，并且最终在奥斯曼帝国统治的黑暗时期从近代复兴引领了一个新欧洲国家的意识形态的形成。按照这一进路，希腊性不仅可以在历史纪念碑中找见，而且可以在普通人的集体记忆、民间文化和生活方式中找见，只要它们保存下来，不被当代技术进步和消费主义心态所毁灭。[②]（3）现代主义态度，关于它的阐述可与"30一代"的艺术文学运动联系起来。这种态度将希腊性视为一种动态的审美原型，渗透于所有那些分享希腊土地的自然资源的人们的表述中。通过关于共同的文化潜能遗产的意识可以达到对它的把握。它的主张者通常把它表述为一种关于与一个共同的希腊历史的可能关系的更为微妙、更为自由的观念，这种观念并不以一种关于希腊性的本质主义形而上学为预设。遗憾的是，它仍然可能导致一种不同版本的、但或许是同样有问题的保守的唯美主义神话学。[③]

不过，齐奥瓦斯更愿意选择一种后现代主义态度，也即第四种观念，他称之为批判的和反讽的态度。这种态度的痕迹可以在更早期的作者中找见，

[①] 持这样一种态度的学者的典型之例是阿托曼蒂奥斯·科雷斯，他是希腊启蒙运动的主要人物之一，18世纪末和19世纪初，也即在反抗土耳其人的独立战争之前和期间居住在法国。还可以研究那些探访希腊并记述了其经历的旅行者的日记和回忆录。关于新古典理想的不同研究进路，见前引书。

[②] 第一种观念强调希腊文化的"hellenic"维度的重要性，而第二种观念整合并强调"Romaic"方面。参见赫茨菲尔德的讨论，Herzfeld, *Ours Once More. Folklore, Ideology and the Making of Modern Greece*, 见前引书。亦参见 Beaton and Ricks, 见前引书。有一种研究近代希腊文学的批判进路值得关注，它展现了一种受惠于基督教—东正教信仰的浪漫—有机观念，参见 Zisimos Lorentzatos, *The Lost Center and Other Essays in Greek Poetry*, transl. by Kay Cicellis, Princeton: Princeton University Press, 1980.

[③] 关于这种进路的典型表现，参见塞费里斯的诸篇文章 in George Seferis, *On the Greek Style, Selected Essays in Poetry and Hellenism*, transl. by Rex Warner and Th. D. Frangopoulos, with an Introduction by Rex Warner, Athens: Denise Harvey & Company, 1982。亦参见塞费里斯在与哲学家康斯坦丁·察佐斯的争论中对现代诗歌所持的立场，察佐斯捍卫的是一种更为本质主义的关于一种希腊性品质的观念，认为这种品质是希腊人自古代到20世纪的艺术创造的特征所在，S. Seferis and C. Tsatsos (in Greek), *A Dialogue on Poetry [Enas Dialogos gia tin Poiisi]*, ed. by L. Kousoulas, Athens: Hermes, 1988。

比如康斯坦丁·卡瓦菲这位可能是最伟大的近代希腊诗人。[①] 按照这种观念，希腊性会被相对化，并且甚至唯美主义观念所特有的抽象和动态的统一也要明显地被剥夺。那么，希腊性可能被视为一种开放的、实际上是空洞的、与我们当代的多元认同相和谐的概念。这样，它就不可能再作为任何反动的民族主义意识形态的基础。问题在于这样一种观念是否等于彻底消解或解构希腊性这个概念，因而削弱对探究、阐释以及最终保护希腊性概念的关注。我们会愿意赞同这样一种彻底解构的企图吗？

四

我认为我们应该将着眼点落于以上可供选择的进路中第三和/或第四种的阐述和应用上。我们必须问我们自己，面对希腊认同这个困惑，这些进路可否作为可行的和有用的调节观念，以便达到一种更好的对于希腊遗产以及如今这种遗产在欧洲及其限制范围以外对希腊人和非希腊人的最终重要意义的批判性理解。不过，这是一个规范性建议，我们将在本讨论的最后再回到这个问题上来。就眼下而言，尽管在本文前面表达了一些异议，我们不妨尝试考察一下以上的所有进路仍然在决定文化自我觉识中起着重要作用的某些方式和所达到的程度，这种自我觉识不仅针对知识分子而言，而且是针对各种不同社会阶层的希腊人而言。此外，我们或许可以冒昧地就这种自我觉识如何反映在希腊人的生活方式中提出一个试探性的假设，以便思考其更广泛的伦理学意义。当然，这样一个复杂的任务不可能是几页文稿能承担的，我们这里所要说的更应该被视为对新的质问和进一步的研究指南的考虑。

的确，必须要考虑这样一个事实：对于希腊性的前两种态度即符号主义—考古学观念和浪漫—有机的观念仍然通过国家教育体系、希腊东正教会部分神职人员的布道以及大众传媒直接和间接地在不同层面上向年轻一代传递。第三种态度，即现代主义—唯美主义态度仍然在传播，尤其是通过艺术和文学文化，并且往往证实了一种更为雅致的教育。可以说，所有这些态度虽然不能被视为相互协调或补充的，但是到目前为止一直为官方保守意识形

[①] 当然，卡瓦菲的这种后现代主义读本包括其方法论预设颇有争议的解释性著作。关于卡瓦菲诗歌的这种解释，参见 Gregory Jusdanis, *The Poetics of Cavafy: Textuality, Eroticism, History*, Princeton: Princeton University Press, 1987。

态在不同阶段和不同程度上所利用。如今,可以认为第一种态度在一定程度上被搁置了,但是第二种态度仍然很活跃并且为教会卷入国家事务提供了一种意识形态基础。① 甚至某些守旧的左派思想家和政治家为了抵制全球化资本主义经济的强势,有时诉诸于一种爱国主义,而这种爱国主义求助于一个连续的、具有某种富有生气的有机统一形态的希腊民族的价值观。遗憾的是,他们与仇外的民族主义者的结盟也因此而终结。自由政治家和老于世故的知识分子更愿坚持现代主义的观点,他们想维系和捍卫一种受欢迎的和灵活的希腊性概念,从而可以适应当代欧洲认同的框架。

但是,思想更为激进的知识分子认为,避免或消除民族主义的唯一途径是采纳一种后现代主义的、反讽的立场,这样可以帮助我们去解构含混不清的希腊性概念,无论这一概念可能怎样被解释。在他们看来,我们作为一个开放的民主国家的公民的自我觉识要致力于促进一种真正世界主义、不断发展的文化,因而根本不需要一种封闭和同质的民族认同。我们会因此而充分认识到,我们需要以多元的、多形态的认同丰富我们的遗产。希腊不仅是诸文明的边界和汇合点,而且是一个活跃的、融合了不同民族、宗教和社会元素的熔炉,不存在要去寻求的明确而毫不含糊的希腊性。然而,至此问题可能已经清楚了,不仅为什么这种立场对于那些代表着官方国家意识形态、寻求纯正性、稳定性和一贯性的人们来说是难以接受的原因已经明了,而且为什么这种立场在大多数的希腊人中间同样不受欢迎的原因也已一目了然,他们担心其根深蒂固的关于他们是谁的自我概念这一心理上的重要维度会丧失掉。也许,希腊人并不愿意这样去颠覆这些根深蒂固的观念,毕竟它们渗透于支撑着他们无法逃脱的许多社会体制和教育实践的意识形态。更为重要的是,他们或许不愿意放弃一种安全感——无论它具有多大的误导作用,因为只有强烈地感到拥有一种共同的民族认同,感到归属于一种多少是有明确限定的文化传统,这种安全感才成为可能。事实上,特别是在严重的金融和道德危机时期,尤其可能如此,因为在这个时期国家发现接纳大多来自近东的数量不断增多的移民是困难的。

---

① 必须指出,有些神学家和神职人员对希腊东正教会所表现出的民族主义倾向进行了探讨,拒绝它对作为一种民族主义—种族主义异端的希腊文化的强调。就此而言,不妨提及希腊君士坦丁堡最高级主教和希腊阿尔巴尼亚大主教。反之,希腊—塞浦路斯东正教会所持的态度是特别民族主义的。实际上,许多保守的皈依者赞成这样一种观点,即基督教—东正教信仰和对教会生活的参与是近代希腊认同的本质特征。

那么，在希腊人的大众想象中繁衍的、由国家意识形态机制强化的民族和文化定见，不仅决定着个人的自我觉识，而且反映在当代希腊社会中盛行的共同生活方式中，就如我已经说过的，至于达到了什么程度我是无力评说的。这样一个任务要以极为细致的社会学和人类学田野工作为先决条件，并以关于这种定见在日常生活中的实际影响的心理学研究为补充。显然，占主导地位的四处流行的消费主义和物质主义价值观、影响社会各个方面促进世界范围的传播的快速技术进步、使用互联网和大众传媒实力的不断增长所产生的全球影响，使得保护和增强一种独特民族文化的遗产成为一件难事。而且，可以推测，某些习惯、习俗和时尚活动，对于"真正"传统价值的信念，对于外国影响的反应模式，现代城市和乡村中的建筑和人工制品所代表的表现形式，形成我们视为特殊的生活方式的审美品位和道德感受性，都可能显露出指向应该加以研究的特定历史起源的文化之根的存在。这样我们才希望能够确定，当今希腊人的"希腊性"——无论我们可能怎样看待它——是否具有一种共同历史的相同痕迹特征。[1]

在这个必定是不全面和简略的分析结束之前，我们短暂地回到我们在讨论过程中提出的规范性问题。什么是对于寻求一种希腊文化认同的正确立场？我们应该如何看待对阐述一种利用和整合从悠久的历史经验传承而来的分离元素、在很大程度上是想象的构建的心理需要？是否存在一种方法，我们可以而且应该借此去设法维系多少是纯正的传统生活方式的特殊性，而拒绝一种完全是世界主义的文化模式——它可能会带来一种只是把希腊人变成一个同质化的全球共同体的公民的枯燥乏味的社会齐一性？我们的人文教育可否将目标设定在一种复合的"全球本土化"社会生活理想，打造出一种维系多元认同、不断进步的传统、来自过去着眼未来的丰富遗产以及外向型的与国际共同体的合作模式的文化自我觉识和自决？并且这样一种教育理想如何付诸实践？

当然，我不可能在这篇短短的论文中对如此复杂的质问展开探讨。它们需要涉及哲学、历史及社会科学的合作，涵盖关涉许多国家和不同大陆的文化传统的相似关注的跨学科比较研究。我只不过是表示了一种态度，即尊重普遍的道德规范和价值观，同时允许批判地承认以特定的方式信守我们民族

---

[1] 关于知识分子所阐述的、在多少是广泛的大众叙事中繁衍的、与希腊性相关的种种定见。

文化遗产的某些方面的重要意义。① 换句话说，正如我所指出的，我不愿意从事一项将所有的希腊性观念都加以解构和抛弃的反讽活动，但又不选择恢复本质主义和目的论的观点或不允许以忠于一种真实原型的需要为基础的排他政治。② 这样一种研究进路的连贯性、稳定性以及实际效果应是从事另一项意义深远但十分辛苦的研究的理由所在。③

（萧俊明 译）

---

① 关于这一问题，我的立场接近于奎梅·安东尼·阿皮亚著作中阐述的观点。参见他的 The Ethics of Identity, Princeton: Princeton University Press, 2005 and Cosmopolitanism: Ethics in a World of Strangers, London: Penguin Books, 2006。
② 我意识到这样一个事实，为了探讨我们可能最终接受的开放的、无害的和灵活的希腊性概念，这种谨慎温和的立场需要加以解释和展开。无论如何，即便我们接受彻底的反现实主义甚至解构主义的民族和文化认同观念，但关涉到基本的认识和伦理规范时，如果这些概念导致某种有害的和自毁的虚无主义，我们可能拒绝它们。关于道德规范性的温和的现实主义论述，参见 Stelios Virvidakis, La robustesse du bien, Nîmes: éditions Jacqueline Chambon, 1996。
③ 本文的更早和更短的版本是以"欧洲及其希腊遗产"这个一般性论题在欧洲文化议会 2010 年 9 月在雅典召开的一届会议上提交的。我对与会者尤其是佩尔·斯登贝克的提问和评论表示感谢。对我的同事和朋友，特别是边文锡、弗拉基米尔·格拉杰夫、杰尼斯拉瓦·伊利耶瓦、瓦索·金迪、卡泰·帕帕里以及安娜·瓦西拉基表示感谢，感谢他们不无裨益的评论以及为我提供的重要文献资料。我还须感谢中国社会科学院论坛的参与者的提问和评论，我在对这些问题进行深入研究时会考虑他们的评论的。

Cultural Self-awareness in Contemporary Greek Society

Stelios Virvidakis[*]

I

When I first reflected on the general theme of the CASS Forum, I interpreted it as an invitation to explore the cultural origins of lifestyles in contemporary Greek society. However, I soon realized that such a broad task would probably require a combination of the conceptual tools and the methodological approaches of a historian, a sociologist, a social psychologist, a political scientist and a cultural anthropologist. So, I decided to engage in a more narrow study and focus on the problem of cultural self-awareness of contemporary Greeks. Moreover, since I am

---

[*] Stelios (Stylianos) Virvidakis was born in Athens in 1955. He was awarded his doctoral degree in 1984 at Princeton University. He holds a position of Professor of Philosophy at the Department of Philosophy and History of Science of the University of Athens. He has participated in many international conferences, given lectures in various Universities, in Europe, the U. S. A. and Japan, and has published a book in metaethics (*La robustesse du bien*, Nîmes: Jacqueline Chambon, 1996), a textbook of philosophy for Greek highschools and several articles in Greek, in French and in English, in scholarly journals, in conference proceedings, in philosophical dictionaries and encyclopaedias, mainly in the areas of ethics, epistemology and the history of philosophy. In 2006, he was awarded the title of *Chevalier dans l'Ordre des Palmes Académiques* by the French Government. His current research interests include issues in epistemology, metaphilosophy, metaethics, the history of modern philosophy and the philosophy of literature.

not a social scientist, and I don't have at my disposal reliable empirical data regarding the recent evolution of beliefs, customs and habits of the Greek people as a whole, my investigation shall be limited to a critical assessment of the cultural self-awareness of certain prominent Greek intellectuals, including historians, artists, writers and philosophers. I am especially interested in the philosophical construal of the very notions of self-awareness and self-determination involved in such an inquiry, but I shall mainly have to draw upon the history of ideas in modern and contemporary Greece, also influenced and complemented by material from the history of ideas in modern Europe, which provides an 'external' perspective on Greece and its past.

In what follows, I begin by considering the significance of the dominant conception of a distinct Greek cultural identity. This identity emerges out of a long historical development in a part of the Eastern Mediterranean as the product of a synthesis involving the integration of a few basic components and resisting assimilation by foreign cultures. I then concentrate on the peculiarity of 'Greekness', the quality attributed to those presumably sharing the identity at issue and expressing it in different ways. I try to describe briefly a few characteristic approaches or attitudes that could be adopted towards its theoretical grasp, but also towards possible forms of its concrete embodiment in the life of Greek communities and individuals. In the last part of my paper, I sketch proposals for a study of the appropriation and the use of one or more of these attitudes by intellectuals representing traditional and current ideological trends. Such a study could help us reveal their eventual role in making possible national and cultural self-awareness and thus in partly shaping actual lifestyles. I conclude my analysis by insisting on some reminders concerning the practical impact and the ethical implications of the attitudes in question.

II

In fact, there are various possible approaches to the distinctive identity of the people who could be said to belong to the Greek or Hellenic nation.[1] Social scientists, artists and intellectuals interested in Greece of the twentieth and the twenty-first centuries, provide diverging answers to the crucial questions: 'Who are the Greeks of today?' - 'How are they related to their past and to the rest of the world?' Thus, one could try to isolate subjective and objective factors contributing to the formation of a more or less common self-understanding of Greeks, as well as analogous factors determining the changing perceptions of foreigners, close or distant neighbours, neutral observers, admirers of Hellenism, past and present allies and enemies. Even if one accepts a thorough-going *constructivist* rather than an *essentialist* conception of national identities and perhaps endorses Benedikt Anderson's account of nations as 'imagined communities',[2] one may engage in a genealogical enterprise looking for the constitutive elements of the imaginary construction of 'Greekness' or 'Hellenicity'. One seems to be confronted with a 'puzzle', both in the sense of an enigma to be elucidated and of a jigsaw puzzle to be assembled in the proper way. In this section of the paper I

---

[1] Some Greek intellectuals insist on the use of the original terms 'Hellas' and 'Hellenic', rather than 'Greece' and 'Greek'. The latter, which are of latin origin ('Graecia', 'Graeci'), have acquired pejorative connotations through particular uses in certain languages and traditions, while the former highlight the link to Ancient Greece. One should also mention the use of the colloquial terms 'Romioi' and 'Romiosyni', which refer to Greeks after the Byzantine period and have connotations associated with the painful experience of Ottoman rule. Byzantium was known as the Eastern 'Roman' Empire and its subjects were designated by the word 'Romaioi/Romioi'. To Muslims the Empire was known as 'Rum' and Turks called all Greeks in Islam 'Rumis', while they now call Greece 'Yunanistan', from 'Yunan' ('Ionian') -their word for 'Ancient Greek'. On the importance of the notion of 'Romiosyni' and of its positive and negative nuances, see Patrik Leigh Fermor, *Roumeli: Travels in Northern Greece*, London: John Murray, 2004 (1966): 96 - 125. Fermor speaks of a 'Helleno-Romaic Dilemma', an 'antithesis' or 'split' in the Modern Greek mind. The 'Hellene' represents the pro-Western, austere ideal, conforming to values associated with classical Greece, while the 'Romios' stands for a more popular and realistic model, embodying virtues-as well as vices-emerging out of the historical experience of Byzantium and of the period of Ottoman occupation (1453 - 1821). These conceptions correspond roughly, respectively, to the first and to the second approaches to Greekness, described below (pp. 6 - 7). For the perspective of another foreign scholar who lived in Greece for many years and displays a critical attitude towards the conception of Hellenism espoused by Western Philhellenes, see Philip Sherrard, *The Wound of Greece. Studies in Neo-Hellenism*, London and Athens: Rex Collins & Anglo-Hellenic, 1978.

[2] See Benedikt Anderson, *Imagined Communities: Reflections on the Origins and Spread of Nationalism*, 2nd ed., London: Verso, 1991.

shall present the puzzle, and the main 'solutions' provided in the last two centuries. Here, my assessment attempts to combine probably incompatible perspectives, related on the one hand to my own subjective awareness of being a Greek, consciously and unconsciously informed by my education at various levels, and, on the other, to the presumably detached philosophical approach of conceptual analysis, descriptive, but also normative.

Indeed, the case of Greece is quite peculiar. The official historical account adopted by the average Greek appeals to a supposed continuity stretching over three thousand years and comprising an ancient, a medieval (Byzantine) and a modern period. It was elaborated in detail by the historian Constantine Paparrigopoulos in his *History of the Greek Nation* (*Istoria tou Ellinikou Ethnous-in Greek*) (*1850 – 1874*), as a response to the challenge put forth by the Austrian Jakob Philipp Falmereyer who denied any such continuity. Paparrigopoulos showed that Falmereyer's arguments, which applied to *racial* continuity, were ineffective as far as *culture* was concerned.[1] To begin with, one could speak of the same Greek nation since there is apparently evidence of a common language, evolving through different periods from antiquity to the present.[2] Then, one could invoke a supposed consciousness of possessing a *core identity* that originated in the unique, multifaceted civilization which first appeared in the Balkan peninsula in archaic times and soon spread in the coasts of Asia Minor, in Sicily and in Southern Italy. Following the dominant historical narrative, it could be argued that a central part of this identity survived in the Byzantine era and underwent various transformations and adventures until the early 19th century. What was regarded as particularly important was the gradual national 'awakening', which was thought to have taken place in the 18th century, encouraged by the ideological climate in Europe before and after the French revolution. The modern Greek State that came to existence after the war of independence against the Ottoman empire could thus reclaim a

---

[1] On Greek historiography see, Alexander Kitroeff, 'Continuity and Change in Contemporary Greek Historiography', in Martin Blikhorn and Thanos Veremis (eds.), *Modern Greece: Nationalism and Nationality*, Athens: Sage-Eliamep, 1990, 143 – 172.

[2] Actually, the issue of the continuity of the Greek language itself is still being debated and has clear ideological implications. We shall have to come back to this point.

glorious past and recover an identity which had been suppressed during four centuries of occupation.

Various intellectuals of the past two centuries worked hard to establish the conception of this continuity, which resisted traumatic breaks and culminated in a successful synthesis integrating opposed elements coming from East and West. Greek *laography* (*Volkskunde*) was a kind of a rather primitive and ideologically charged social science-a form of local and empirical cultural anthropology-which studied folk songs, rituals and customs, with a view to revealing ideas, stylistic motifs, and entire forms of communal life that could be traced back to ancient times. Intellectuals elaborated reconstructions of hellenic thinking at different stages, aiming at displaying the alleged synthesis which harmonized the pagan Greek with the Christian-Orthodox worldview. In fact, the notion of a 'Helleno-Christian' civilization, the possibility of which was first realized in the cultural institutions of the Byzantine empire, was explicitly put forth and defended by the scholar Spyridon Zambelios, who belonged to the circle of the 'national poet' Dionysios Solomos. This notion prevailed as a central component of the official national ideology of the modern Greek State.[1]

Moreover, artists, poets and writers were thought to be struggling, consciously or unconsciously, to achieve new expressions of a quality of *Greekness* (*Hellinikotita*). Here, one should mention mainly the contribution of authors belonging to the 'generation of the 30's', who, in most cases, tried to combine an aesthetic and cultural conception of a peculiar Greek identity with modernism

---

[1] See Michael Herzfeld, *Ours Once More. Folklore, Ideology and the Making of Modern Greece*, New York: Pella, 1986. Herzfeld lays particular emphasis on the ideological character of *laografia* which he describes as 'a national discipline of folkore' (p. 13). See also Herzfeld's more recent 'National Spirit or the Breath of Nature? The Expropriation of Folk Positivism in the Discourse of Greek Nationalism', in Michael Silverstein and Graig Urban (eds), *Natural Histories of Discourse*, Chicago: The University of Chicago Press, 1996, 277 – 298. Concerning the 'Helleno-Christian' cultural synthesis it should be noted that there are many philosophers who argue that the classical Greek *Weltanschauung* cannot be reconciled with Christian ideals. See, among others, Cornelius Castoriades, *Ce qui fait la Grèce. I. D'Homère à Héraclite. Séminaires 1982 – 1983. II. La Création humaine*, Paris: Seuil, 2004, for a discussion of the relation between democracy and philosophy and the significance of their birth in Ancient Greece.

and with a commitment to political cosmopolitanism.① Greekness was and may still be regarded by certain thinkers as embodying the main characteristics of a unique spiritual experience, reflected in different ways in artistic and more generally cultural expression, and even in everyday life-styles.② Thus, various attempts were made by archaeologists, art historians and literary critics to describe it more accurately, and by some philosophers and theologians to define it.③ More recently, the so called 'neo-orthodox' intellectuals, Christian thinkers directly or indirectly influenced by theologians of the Russian Diaspora, formed a

---

① The group of writers and artists who came to be known as 'the generation of the 30's' includes Greek poets inspired more or less by surrealism, such as Andreas Embirikos, Nikos Engonopoulos and Odysseus Elytis (Nobel prize of 1978), George Seferis (Nobel prize of 1963), who had been influenced by Paul Valéry and T. S. Eliot, and prose writers such as George Theotokas.

② The term 'Greekness' is generally accepted as a translation of 'hellinikotita', although those who want to avoid derivatives of 'Greek' may prefer 'hellenicity'. (See above, note 1) Concerning the importance of archaeology in the elaboration of conceptions of Greek identity, see Yannis Hamilakis, *The Nation and Its Ruins: Antiquity, Archaeology and the National Imagination in Greece*, Oxford: Oxford University Press, 2007 and Dimitris Damaskos and Dimitris Plantzos, *A Singular Antiquity: Archaeology and Hellenic Identity in Twentieth-century Greece*, Athens: Mouseio Benaki, 3d supplement, 2008.

③ This particular 'way of thinking and feeling' has been described in many different, and often conflicting ways that are thought to capture features of the national character of Greeks through the centuries. Thus, it has been presented as involving, among other traits, individualism and ingenuity, also related to defects of the Greek character (lack of discipline and insubordination to authority, propensity to discord and strife, laziness etc.), but also, a commitment to 'sociocentric' politics recognizing the importance of personhood, a sense of measure, humanity, harmony, reconciliation of opposites, respect for Reason, awareness of limits and of human finitude, a tragic sense of life, a sense of justice, heroism, self-determination, love of freedom, healthy affirmation of the pleasures of the senses, warmth, pride and generosity. Poets, such as Odysseus Elytis, also insist on a peculiar kind of 'clarity' -not of a superficial, rationalist nature-, which goes along with 'limpidity', 'transparent depth' and is achieved thanks to the peculiar experience of natural Greek light. The left-wing historian Nikos Svoronos also speaks of a 'spirit of resistance', supposedly motivating a set of common, brave reactions to external threats and invaders menacing the crossroads of South-Eastern Europe. Svoronos, who first wrote in French his short *Histoire de la Grèce moderne*, Paris: Presses Universitaires de France, 1972 (1955), develops this idea in an interview reprinted in his *The Method of History*, Athens: Agra Publications, 1995, 159 – 160 (*I Methodos tis Historias*- in Greek). All the above are usually regarded as cultural characteristics acquired through the centuries, which could be attributed to the living conditions in the particular geographical area occupied by the Greeks (related to the landscape, the natural resources, the climate etc.) and especially to that of their long and adventurous historical experience preserved in collective memory and in popular imagination.

group which could be compared to the Slavophiles in Russia. ① Unfortunately, emphasizing not only the distinctness or uniqueness, but also the alleged cultural superiority of the Greek nation to others, they often lapse into nationalistic rhetoric disguised under the pretentions of an outstanding philosophical outlook. ② Sometimes, they don't hesitate to talk about the particular historical *destiny* of the Greek people, echoing dangerous romantic ideas familiar from the German philosophical tradition. ③

Now, the above claims to the effect that there is an almost unbroken continuity of more than three thousand years, and a hidden identity of a kind of 'silkworm' entity, undergoing changes while maintaining the same 'deep' core, can and have been challenged by historians who deplore their essentialist and teleological implications and worry about their political consequences. It is often pointed out that such views betray unwarranted metaphysical assumptions which should be eliminated from any serious historical narrative. Even the notion of the *same language*, assuming different forms through the many stages of its evolution from the Mycenaean era to the present, is disputed by linguists who employ strict criteria of identity of a spoken language, based mainly on a set of grammatical, syntactic and

---

① The most prominent among these 'neo-orthodox' and 'hellenocentric' thinkers is the theologian and philosopher Christos Yannaras, who is influenced by philosophers such as Heidegger, preaching an overcoming of the Western metaphysical tradition, and draws extensively on Orthodox mystical theology He puts forth a peculiar vision of communitarian politics embodying an existential *ethos*, the model of which is supposedly derived from the tradition of the Greek Orthodox Church. Yannaras is a prolific writer. His main works translated in English include, *The Freedom of Morality*, New York: SVP, 1984, *Postmodern Metaphysics*, Brookline, MA: H. C. Press, 2004, *On the Absence and Unknowability of God: Heidegger and the Areopagite*. London: Continuum, 2005, *Orthodoxy and the West*, Brookline, MA: H. C. Press, 2006.

② On these issues, see Stelios Virvidakis, 'Les droits de l' homme à l' épreuve de la politique', *Rue Descartes* 51 (Janvier 2006): 47 – 58 and 'National Identities, Epistemic and Moral Norms and Historical Narratives', forth-coming in *Proceedings of the Fifth Balkan Philosophy Seminar* (Maltepe).

③ However, it should be noted that the word ; 'destiny' is often used without any commitment to a substantial metaphysical or teleological worldview. See Kostas Axelos, 'Le destin de la Grèce moderne', *Esprit* 7 (1954). Axelos' article provides perceptive remarks on contemporary Greek society that are worth taking into account in any investigation of the cultural self-awareness of *diaspora* Greeks. Later, Axelos developed a more speculative philosophical vision based mainly on Heideggerian ideas.

semantic considerations. Indeed, many contemporary linguists prefer to speak about different *languages*, when they study Ancient, Medieval and Modern Greek.① In any case, the features of a unique Greekness conceived as constants characterizing Hellenic culture through the centuries, are at best projections or creations of artistic and philosophical imagination, often related to popular stereotypes, which could and should become the object of a critical historical, sociological and anthropological scrutiny. What is clearly unpalatable from a liberal moral and political point of view is their ideological use in nationalistic discourse.

Nonetheless, one may not oppose the eventual recognition of a significant *degree* of cultural continuity, which doesn't appeal to any controversial metaphysical and evaluative assumptions. The development of a distinctive linguistic and cultural 'core' into a more or less homogeneous Greek nation could be then regarded as involving the 'cutting and pruning of earlier ethnic and religious identities'.② Still, the 'cutting' and 'pruning' required for the formation of the national entity which would finally establish its identity in a part of the Balkan peninsula and would constitute a national state, follows a pattern of construction that goes far beyond the discovery of the supposed original elements. In fact, there are many delicate issues pertaining to the nature and the direction of growth of the evolving identity and to its confrontation with other identities competing for recognition and trying to impose their presence in the same or adjacent geographical regions.

---

① For various approaches to linguistic and ideological issues concerning the Greek language, its different forms, their common elements and their evolution through the centuries, see Antonis Liakos, ' "From Greek into our Common Language": Language and History in the Making of Modern Greece', in A. F. Christidis (ed.). *A History of Ancient Greek: From the Beginnings to Late Antiquity*, Cambridge: Cambridge University Press, 1287 – 1295, Peter Mackridge, 'A Language in the Image of the Nation: Modern Greeks and Some Parallel Cases' and Karen Van Dyck, 'The Language Question and the Diaspora', in Roderick Beaton and David Ricks, *The Making of Modern Greece: Nationalism, Romanticism & the Uses of the Past* (1797 – 1896), Farnham: Ashgate, 2009, 177 – 187 and 188 – 198. See also Peter Mackridge, *Language and National Identity in Greece: 1766 – 1976*, Oxford: Oxford University Press.

② See Costas Carras, 'Greek Identity: A Long View', in Maria Todorova (ed.), *Balkan Identities: Nation and Memory*, London: Hurst and Company, 2004, 294 – 326, 294.

III

Following Dimitris Tziovas, we could isolate a few alternative attitudes or conceptions exemplified by the main traditional approaches to the emergence and to the heritage of the Greek nation that we summarized in the previous paragraphs.[1] These are: a) The *symbolist-archaeological* conception, largely imported from the West and conforming to neoclassical ideals, which focuses on the 'greatness' of Ancient Greek culture and promotes an admiration for its values; People who adopt it, like the foreign Philhellenes of the 18th and 19th centuries, often express their frustration because contemporary Greeks are unable to emulate their glorious ancestors.[2] The achievements of the latter serve as an unattainable model for the Greeks of today. b) The *romantic-organic* conception, which urges us to track the evolution of the nation since its ancient origins, through the centuries, to the present. This conception underlies the dominant historical narrative and sustains the notion of the Helleno-Christian synthesis, combining the Classical legacy with the Byzantine tradition, eventually leading, from the modern revival, during the dark period of the Ottoman rule, to the foundation of the ideology of a new European state. According to this approach, Greekness is not found only in past monuments, but also in the collective memory, the folk culture and the life-style of ordinary people, to the extent that these can be preserved and are not destroyed

---

[1] Dimitris Tziovas is a professor of Modern Greek Studies at the University of Birmingham. My discussion in what follows draws on his article (in Greek), 'Greekness and the Generation of the 30s' ('Ellinikotita kai I genia tou ' 30' -in Greek), *Cogito* 6 (May 2007): 8 - 10. See also his book, *The Transformations of Nationism and the Ideology of Greekness in the Interwar Period* (*I metamorfoseis tou ethnismou kai to ideologima tis ellinikotitas sto Mesopolemo* -in Greek), Athens: Odysseas, 1989.

[2] A characteristic example of a scholar who displayed such an attitude was Adamantios Korais, one of the main figures of Greek Enlightenment living in France in the late 18th and the early 19th century before and during the War of Independence against the Turks. One could also study the diaries and memoirs of travelers who visited Greece and described their experience. For different approaches to the neo-classical ideal, see the works cited above in note 7 and Sherrard, *op. cit.*

by contemporary technological progress and consumerist mentality.[①] c) The *modernist* attitude, the elaboration of which can be associated with the artistic and literary movement of the generation of the '30s. This treats Greekness as a *dynamic aesthetic archetype* informing the expression of all those who share the natural resources of the Greek landscape. It is supposed to be grasped through the consciousness of a common legacy of cultural potential. Its advocates usually present it as a subtler and more liberal conception of possible relations to a common Greek past, which does not presuppose an essentialist metaphysics of Greekness. Unfortunately, it may still lead to a different, but perhaps equally problematic version of a conservative aestheticist mythology.[②]

Now, Tziovas privileges the option of a postmodern, fourth, attitude that he qualifies as *critical* and *ironical*, traces of which could perhaps be isolated in earlier authors, such as Constantine Cavafy, arguably the greatest Modern Greek poet.[③] Greekness would be relativized and apparently deprived of even the abstract and dynamic unity characterizing the aestheticist view. It might then be regarded as an open and practically empty notion, compatible with our contemporary plural identities. Hence, it could no longer serve as the basis for

---

① The first conception emphasizes the importance of the 'hellenic' dimension of Greek culture, while the second integrates and stresses the 'Romaic' aspects. See above, note 1 and the discussion in Herzfeld, *Ours Once More. Folklore, Ideology and the Making of Modern Greece*, op. cit. See also Beaton and Ricks, op. cit. For an interesting critical approach to Modern Greek Literature which displays a version of the romantic-organic conception indebted to Christian Orthodox faith, see Zisimos Lorentzatos, *The Lost Center and Other Essays in Greek Poetry*, transl. by Kay Cicellis, Princeton: Princeton University Press, 1980.

② For a characteristic expression of this approach, see the essays by Seferis, in George Seferis, *On the Greek Style*, Selected Essays in Poetry and Hellenism, transl. by Rex Warner and Th. D. Frangopoulos, with an Introduction by Rex Warner, Athens: Denise Harvey & Company, 1982. See also Seferis' positions on modern poetry presented in a debate with the philosopher Constantine Tsatsos, who defends a more or less essentialist conception of a quality of Greekness, supposedly characterizing artistic creation by Greeks from ancient times to the twentieth century: G. Seferis and C. Tsatsos (in Greek), *A Dialogue on Poetry* (*Enas Dialogos gia tin Poiisi* -in Greek), ed. by L. Kousoulas, Athens: Hermes, 1988.

③ Of course, such postmodernist readings of Cavafy involve interpretative work the methodological presuppositions of which are quite controversial. For such a construal of Cavafy's poetry, see Gregory Jusdanis, *The Poetics of Cavafy: Textuality, Eroticism, History*, Princeton: Princeton University Press, 1987.

any reactionary nationalist ideology. The question is whether such a conception wouldn't amount to a complete dissolution or deconstruction of the very idea of Greekness, thus undermining interest in its detection, elaboration and eventual preservation. Are we willing to endorse such an attempt at a thorough-going deconstruction?

IV

I think that we should focus on elaborating and applying the third and/ or the fourth of the above alternative approaches. We have to ask ourselves whether these may be viable and useful as regulative ideas for confronting the puzzle of Greek identity, with a view to attaining a better critical understanding of the Greek heritage and of its eventual importance today, both for Greeks and non-Greeks, in Europe and beyond its limits. However, this is a normative proposal to which we shall come back at the end of our discussion. At this point, despite the reservations expressed in the introduction of this paper, we may engage in an attempt to examine some of the ways and the extent to which *all* of the above approaches still play an important role in determining the cultural self-awareness not only of intellectuals but also of Greeks of different social classes. Moreover, we could perhaps venture a tentative hypothesis concerning how this self-awareness is reflected in their life-style, with a view to pondering its broader ethical significance. Of course, such a complex task could not be properly undertaken in just a few pages and what we are going to say here should be regarded as the consideration of new queries and of guidelines for further research.

Indeed, one has to take into account the fact that the two first attitudes towards Greekness, the *symbolist-archaeological* and the *romantic-organic*, are still transmitted to the young generation in direct and indirect ways and at different levels, through the system of national education, the preaching of part of the clergy of the Greek Orthodox Church and the mass media. The third, *modernist-aestheticist* approach is also propagated especially through artistic and literary culture and usually testifies to a more refined education. One could say that all these attitudes, although they cannot be regarded as mutually compatible or complementary, have by now been appropriated at different stages and to various degrees by official conservative ideology. Today, the first may be considered to be partly superseded, but the second is very much alive and provides an ideological basis for the involvement of the Church in national affairs.① Even some old fashioned left-wing thinkers and politicians, who want to resist the imposition of a globalized capitalist economy, sometimes resort to a kind of patriotism which invokes the values of a continuous Greek nation possessing some form of vital organic unity. Unfortunately, they thus end up allying themselves with xenophobic nationalists. The modernist view is preferred by liberal politicians and sophisticated intellectuals who want to maintain and defend a palatable and flexible notion of Greekness that could be accommodated within the framework of a contemporary open European identity.

Nevertheless, more radically minded intellectuals argue that the only way to avoid or combat nationalism is by adopting the post-modernist, ironical stance that could help us deconstruct the fuzzy concept of Greekness, however it might be construed. According to them, our self-awareness as citizens of an open democratic state, committed to the promotion of a truly cosmopolitan, continuously evolving culture doesn't require a closed and homogeneous national identity at all. We would thus fully acknowledge the need to enrich our heritage with plural, multiform identities. Greece is not only a border and a meeting point of civilizations but an active melting pot of different ethnic, religious, and social elements and there is no definite and unambiguous property of Greekness to look for. However, at this point, it may become clear not only why such a position is difficult to accept for all those who represent the official national ideology, seeking

---

① It must be noted that some theologians and clergymen deplore the nationalist tendencies displayed by the Greek Orthodox Church and reject its emphasis on Hellenism as a version of a nationalist-racist heresy. Here, one could mention the Greek Patriarch of Constaninople, Bartholomaios and the Greek Archbishop of Albania, Anastasios. On the contrary, particularly nationalistic is the attitude displayed by the clergy of the Greek-Cypriot Orthodox Church. In fact, many conservative believers espouse the view that Christian Orthodox faith and participation in the life of the Church are essential features of modern Greek identity. See also the works by Yannaras mentioned above in note 9.

purity, stability and coherence, but also why it isn't very popular among the majority of Greek people, feeling threatened by the loss of a psychologically crucial dimension of their deeply ingrained self-conception of who they are. It could be argued that Greeks are not ready for such a reversal of well-entrenched assumptions informing the ideology that sustains many social institutions and educational practices to which they have been exposed. More importantly, they are perhaps reluctant to give up a sense of security-however misleading-, made possible by a strong feeling of possessing a common national identity and of belonging to a more or less clearly circumscribed cultural tradition. In fact, this may be especially true at a time of a serious financial and ethical crisis, while the country finds it difficult to accommodate a continuously increasing number of immigrants, mostly from the Near East.

Now, as I have already said, I am in no position to assess the extent to which the national and cultural stereotypes reproduced in the popular imagination of Greeks and reinforced by the ideological mechanisms of the State not only determine individual self-awareness, but are also still reflected in the common life-styles prevailing in contemporary society. Such a task would presuppose meticulous sociological and anthropological field work, complemented by psychological research concerning the real impact of such stereotypes in everyday life. It is obvious that the dominant consumerist and materialist values spreading everywhere, the rapid technological progress affecting all aspects of society and promoting world wide communication, the global impact of the use of the Internet and the continuous growth of the power of the mass media, make it very hard to preserve and enhance the legacy of a distinctive national culture. Still, it could be surmised that certain habits, customs and fashionable activities, beliefs and convictions about 'authentic' traditional values, familiar patterns of reaction to foreign influences, forms of expression exemplified in architecture and artifacts in modern cities and in the country, aesthetic preferences and ethical sensitivities shaping what we consider to be particular life-styles, may betray the existence of cultural roots pointing to specific historical origins which should be investigated in a systematic way. We could thus hope to be able to determine whether the 'Greekness' of the Greeks of today, however it may be conceived, bears the same characteristic traces of a common past.①

Before closing this inevitably incomplete and sketchy analysis, we should briefly return to the normative issues raised in the course of our discussion. What is the proper stance towards the quest for a Greek cultural identity? How ought we to treat the psychological need for the elaboration of a largely imaginary construction which appropriates and integrates disparate elements inherited from a long historical experience? Is there a way we could and should try to maintain the specificity of more or less pure, traditional life-styles, rejecting the model of a fully cosmopolitan culture that might bring about a bland and banal social uniformity, turning Greeks into mere citizens of a homogeneized global community? Could our humanistic education aim at a compound 'glocal' ideal of social life, forging a cultural self-awareness and self-determination which preserves identity in plurality and tradition in progress, a rich heritage coming from the past in a future-oriented, extrovert model of cooperation with the international community? And how practically effective would such an ideal of education be?

Naturally, I cannot even begin to explore such complex queries in the context of this short paper. They call for interdisciplinary and comparative inquiries involving the collaboration of philosophy, history and the social sciences and covering analogous concerns pertaining to many countries and cultural traditions in different continents. I shall simply gesture in the direction of an attitude which respects universal ethical norms and values and at the same time allows for a critical recognition of the significance of particularistic commitments to certain aspects of our national cultural legacy.② In other words, as I have already suggested, I am reluctant to pursue the ironical enterprise of deconstructing and jettisoning *all* conceptions of Greekness, without however opting for a revival of essentialist and teleological views, or condoning exclusionary politics based on requirements of

---

① For a list of characteristic stereotypes associated with Greekness, elaborated by intellectuals and reproduced in more or less widespread popular narratives, see above, note 7.

② On this issue, my position is close to the views elaborated and defended in the works of Kwame Anthony Appiah. See his *The Ethics of Identity*, Princeton: Princeton University Press, 2005 and *Cosmopolitanism: Ethics in a World of Strangers*, London: Penguin Books, 2006.

allegiance to an authentic archetype. ① The coherence, the stability and the practical fruitfulness of such an approach would be a matter for another far reaching and painstaking study. ②

---

① I am aware of the fact that this cautious, moderate position requires elucidation and development with a view to exploring the open ended, innocuous and flexible notion of Greekness which we may end up adopting. In any case, even if we accept thorough going antirealist or even deconstructionist conceptions of national and cultural identity, we may reject analogous approaches regarding basic epistemic and ethical norms, insofar as they lead to some form of pernicious and self-undermining nihilism. For an attempt to elaborate a moderately realistic account of moral normativity, see Stelios Virvidakis, *La robustesse du bien*, Nîmes: éditions Jacqueline Chambon, 1996.

② A much earlier and shorter version of this paper was presented at a session of the European Cultural Parliament with the general topic 'Europe and Its Greek Legacy', which took place in Athens, in September 2010. I would like to express my thanks to the participants and especially to Pär Stenback for their questions and remarks. I am also grateful to various colleagues and friends, especially to Moon Suk Byeon, Vladimir Gradev, Denislava Ilieva, Vasso Kindi, Kate Papari and Anna Vasilaki, for their useful comments on a much later draft and for providing me with important bibliographical material. I must also thank the participants in the CASS Forum for their questions and comments which I shall take into account while pursuing further research on these issues.

儒家政治及其矫正：从激进主义到渐进主义

陆建德[*]

儒家思想在中国当前的复兴恰逢其时，因为没有哪个国家能够在缺乏核心价值观的情况下单凭举国对于财富的不懈追求而得到治理。然而，这一复兴并未伴随着对儒家思想作为一种政治理论可能存在的缺陷的审慎意识，如果我们所说的政治指的是一门关于治理的科学与艺术或一种公共及社会伦理。

一

人们普遍认为道家与儒家作为中国文化中的一阴一阳是互补的。由于道家的两个主要文本《道德经》和《庄子》又是伟大的文学作品，因而在亚洲以外的国家道家更容易被接受，并且有时是许多优美的文学作品的灵感来源，比如 W. B. 叶芝的诗歌《蓝宝石》以及玛格丽特·尤瑟纳尔的《东方故事》。

可以说，尤瑟纳尔最喜爱的作家是庄子——社会习俗和偏见的主要反对者以及陌生化艺术的大师。当翟理斯的《庄子》译本于 1890 年问世时，奥

---

[*] 陆建德（Lu Jiande），男，1954 年出生。毕业于上海复旦大学，英国剑桥大学博士。中国社会科学院文学研究所所长、研究员、《外国文学评论》主编，著有《麻雀啁啾》（北京，1996）、《破碎思想体系的残编——英美文学与思想史论稿》（北京，2001）、《思想背后的利益》（上海，2005）。

斯卡·王尔德在《作为批评者的艺术家》（1969：221）中表达了一种由衷的欢迎，认为它是"对现代生活最为尖刻的批判"。这位无政府主义者、维多利亚时代的花花公子在内心深处被中国作家"恶毒的先验目的"所激发，而后者则体现在诸如"闻在宥天下，不闻治天下也""无为而万物化"的精彩语句中。王尔德生活在一个有序而稳定的社会，因而能有如此大度的赞赏。

对庄子而言，个体有权依照他自己的意愿规范他的全部行为。当亚里士多德将人定义为"政治动物"时，他认为与城邦隔绝的个体是"像跳棋游戏中孤子一般的非合作者"。但是，这一原则被不问政治的中国圣人完全颠覆。王尔德在极端个人主义上站在庄子一边，并采用庄子精微而具颠覆性的哲学来消解他所处社会中的一切"人道主义会社"、"慈善组织"以及"有关对邻人的义务的乏味说教"。任何一个当时到英国出游的中国人都不会认同王尔德的消解。他们会在方方面面注意到慈善的精神已经深深编织进了英国社会的经纬线之中，或者对存在诸如"皇家防止虐待动物协会"的志愿者组织大为惊喜。

我们也可以通过王尔德同时代人的视角来大致了解一下当时的中国。在20世纪初，G. E. 莫理循——出生在澳大利亚的英国殖民者以及《泰晤士报》驻北京记者——说过这样令人难堪的话："中国与其说是一个国家，还不如说是人间大杂烩。"最终，"他将整个国家嘲弄个遍，说爱国主义的分量还不足一盎司"（骆惠敏，1976）。李提摩太作为当时最具影响力的英国来华传教士之一，曾在《亲历晚清四十五年——李提摩太在华回忆录》（1916）一书中描述他自己如何在1880年前后几乎仅凭一己之力为山东饥民提供救济物资，而地方当局却袖手旁观。李提摩太既没有时间也没有兴致去谈论政府的无为主义。

的确，在环境危机和物质主义贪婪的时代，道家对人与自然间的和谐的强调可以作为对毫无节制的工业主义和唯发展主义的一个矫正。但是，对诗人或脱俗的哲学家来说的优点可能对政治家而言是缺点。如果将道家思想隐含的政治信息作为一条政治原则付诸实践，则必然招致灾难。牟复礼（1989：62~63）比较了西方人道主义与道家自然主义，敏锐地指出：西方的人本主义是在对宗教独裁主义的回应（或反对）中发展起来的，异教的自然出于历史及文化原因轻易地与人本主义联系到一起。在中国，道家对自然的理想化是对人类在社会中保有秩序和安全的能力的悲观主义的一部分；

它试图将自然作为躲避人类的避难所……道家因此将社会人看作一个被误导了的存在。它蔑视政府，害怕进步与文明，并且对所有的专门技能保持警惕。它将一切标准、定义、区分和等级（儒家正是于此寄托其价值）视作破坏原始自然健全状态的堕落手段。道家产生于一个社会秩序混乱的时代——儒家亦如此——因此它所执迷的就是对生命的保全。它退回到自然是因为它发现人类社会过于危险。

因此，道家也有一个世俗的方面，即通过不论任何手段来追求长生不死。

二

许多人都认为道家与儒家有着根本上的不同。儒家十分关注人民的福祉以及政府明显的终极目标。儒家政治对于现代人更具吸引力的原因是它包含一种民主元素："天视自我民视，天听自我民听"（《孟子·万章上》）。① 但仔细审视，这两个思想学派具有某种惊人的相似性：它们都接受弱政府的观念并且对作为政治基础的公共伦理都没有真正的兴趣。

《道德经》（60章）中有一句名言："治大国，若烹小鲜"。我们在别处找不到比这更生动的对政府不干涉信条的表述了。必须承认，自由放任主义也是儒家不可分割的一部分。在《论语》中，孔子以黄金时代贤君之一的舜作为"无为而治"的范例："'无为而治'者，其舜也欤！夫何为哉？恭己正南面而已矣。"（15.5）儒家政治世界——幸运或不幸地——摆脱了霍布斯的利维坦。政府的无为在孟子那里得到了进一步的确认："为政不难，不得罪于巨室"（《孟子·离娄上》）。国家的正当功能似乎已经委托于或者说屈服于豪门巨室。

孟子说，如果政府以仁政对待民众，那么惩处和罚金就会少得多，税赋和兵役也会很轻。这种父母般的仁爱被看作政治权力的源泉。孔子和孟子都认为人生来性善，而这种与生俱来的善使人能够追随一个品行更加高尚的人。管理一个国家的谋略几乎完全取决于个人的教养。一位君子的德性和教诲会在四海之内如水流冲涌般广为散播，各处人民也会像水流一样不可抗拒地向君子汇聚。

儒家区分了君子与小人。讽刺的是，道德范例的教化力量一经提出并被

---

① 这相应于拉丁语"民众的声音就是神的声音"。

绝对化，这两类人之间的界限就被粉碎了。孟子说："君仁莫不仁，君义莫不义"（《孟子·离娄上》）。在儒家文本中，"民"这个词看上去经常意指的是一个没有内部利益之争的统一整体。在孔子和孟子想象之中的政治世界里，明显缺失马基雅维利所谓的狮与狐。热爱并尊重他人的人总是被他人热爱并尊重；人人都按照别人友善对待自己的方式对待别人。一定存在一只看不见的道德之手将所有社会活动和关系带入幸福的和谐之中。

这种信念的一个出乎意料的结果是，由于来自低一级社会阶层的人们机械地去模仿君子的行为，他们无须为自己的行为负责。在中国有一句俗语"上梁不正下梁歪"，于是人们往往把百姓不端或严重罪过归罪于贪官，他们没有意识到百姓放弃对自己行为的约束的危险性。

儒家基本经典之一的《大学》开宗明义地说："正心修身齐家治国平天下"。从个人德性到公共之善的平滑转变在这句名言中得到实现。《蜜蜂寓言》的作者曼德维尔或许错误地认为个人之恶成就了公共之善，但是断言个人德性总是与公共利益相一致也是同样有误导性的。儒家关于实在的观点是一元论的，因为价值观是一致且相容的：存在一套支配一切的标准，所有的个人和公共行为都能据此得到评价。但是，正直之心与有序的家庭并非必然的共同伙伴。通过政治手段解决公共领域中各种可能的紧张和冲突纯粹是国家的事务。儒家社会理论某种程度上给人们这样的印象，即它不会踏入那个令人不快的世界。

认为真正的自爱等同于社会之爱也是西方的一种观点。正如亚历山大·蒲柏在《人论》中对自爱所赞美的：

> 上帝所爱由整及零；
> 而人类灵魂所爱
> 必然由零及整。
> 自爱却帮助唤醒道义之心，
> 犹如小石子搅乱平静的湖面；
> 紧随圆心的搅动，泛起一轮晕圈，
> ……
> 它将首先拥抱的，是朋友，父母，邻居，
> 接着是他的祖国，再下来是整个人类，
> 一波宽过一波，心灵的涌溢

环抱每一生灵,有爱无类;

大地的欢笑环绕四周,带着神赐的无限恩惠,

而上天注视着它在他胸中的形象。(第四章,第1273行至1284行)

这些同心圆就像蒲柏的奥古斯都时代英雄双行体一样有序。但在现实生活中,经常有不止一块小石子同时扰动镜面般的湖水,水面则随着晕圈的聚散而被搅乱。说时容易做时难。蒲柏自己的爱就不会从圆心平均地向四周波荡。在《愚人记》中,他把气出在他周围的文学机构上,同时又尽情地嘲笑他的作家同行。

儒学作为政治理论的弱点之一在于它经常在个人德性的领域内讨论政治或者说公共及社会伦理。如果我们指责孔子在个人与公共的区分上的无知,那么对孔子来讲是不公平的。当两者之间出现冲突,公共须让位于个人。在《论语》中,叶公对孔子说,在他们那里的正直之士是这样的人:如果他们的父亲偷了一只羊,他们会为这事作证。孔子斗胆用模棱两可的方式做了回答,他说在他们那里"父为子隐,子为父隐,直在其中矣"(13.18)。考虑到孝道是儒家道德结构中的基石这样的事实,孔子似乎赞成在民众中采用这一行为规范。

在基督教中,人们同样认为拥有美德的君主创造了拥有美德的人民,但人性却从来不受恭维。我们在这里发现了基督教与儒家的区分。可以说,儒家政治理论倾向于忽略人类弱点当中那些可耻的嗜好甚至是邪恶。儒家几乎完全是马基雅维利主义的反面。尽管孔孟区别君子与小人,他们不会认为,一般而言人会令人生厌、虚浮易变、虚妄无信、怯懦或贪婪;但是,一旦有人成功,其他人就会完全追随他,而这并不单纯出于对他的道德之善的追求。对这两位中国圣人而言,统治术几乎是没有必要的;狡诈奸猾和口是心非纯粹是道德犯罪。这种看法并不能断言他们是更好的人,而是说他们不被像马基雅维利对于他的国家的统一、和平和繁荣所怀有的那样强烈的富于远见的热情所驱使。T. S. 艾略特(1928:39~52)发现,正是那位佛罗伦萨人的热烈的爱国主义激励着他"泄露人性的秘密"。

这两位儒家大师用他们生命的大部分时间游历诸国来推行他们的道德哲学。和平与繁荣依赖于人民的德性,并反过来为后者提供支持。在那个时期,国家意识还没有定型。否则,他们的政治理论就会被为国家服务的集体理想和埃德蒙·伯克所说的"系于一地的公共感情"充实并充满活力。

"天下"的观念在一个被咄咄逼人的民族主义撕裂的时代可能值得赞扬,但它却无助于产生关于一个特定国家或民族的和平、昌盛与辉煌的强有力的理论。在这样的国家或民族中,诸如坚忍、英勇与公共精神这样的美德才有机会生长出来,民众也会兴旺,实现他们人生最美好的价值并对他们的共同体取得的成就感到骄傲。

三

综观整个中国历史,国家治理的实际过程并不总具有儒家政治理想的特点,法家的意义尤其不容忽视。然而,上述理想深深植根于集体无意识的背景之中,可以解释某些值得我们关注的现象:这个公共领域的特点在于弱政府、缺失公共空间以及缺少可在政府与人民中间起调节作用的志愿者或非亲属组织。作为一个整体的社会由家庭与宗族这样松散的单体组成。

地理疆域的广大也许使这个国家不便管理。尽管政府拥有经常是名义上存在的盐铁垄断,而由于交通与通信的不便,中国社会在经济上采用的是一种自由放任的政策。同样的政策也被应用在政治上。"天高皇帝远"就明言了在传统中国社会中政府干预的无效性与没有法纪的状态。在清朝覆灭三年后的1914年,一位日本历史学家将猖獗的匪祸归咎于政府的不作为。他提出,中国朝廷由于一直过于疲弱而无法维系最低限度的社会正义,就允许以强凌弱、以大压小。违法者似乎安全地超然于法律之上(史景迁,1978),逐渐地,那些被侮辱与被损害的人不得不借助极端手段来保护他们生存的权利(稻叶君山,1914,51章)。另一位日本学者渡边秀方在其著作《中国国民性论》中指出,日本人对来自国家的保护很有信心,而中国政府太弱,普通中国人则不得不依靠自己来保障人身安全。这种安全感的缺失侵蚀了公共世界的构造,并在某种程度上对于许多中国人的社会冷漠和自我中心的态度负有一定责任。我们可以从古典名著《水浒》中看到村民们是如何练习武术来防身对付土匪的。现代意义上的警力直到20世纪开端——在紧随八国联军之后的外国势力占领天津时期及其后——才刚刚建立。

在1949年中国共产党取得政权之前,中国百姓很容易受到黑帮、恶霸地主及地方流氓的威胁(明恩溥,1968,20章)。公共力量的缺失进一步损害了社会团结。因此就有了关于中国人缺乏互助的谚语:各人自扫门前雪,

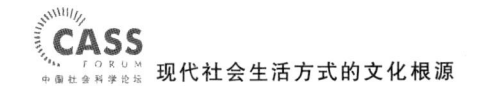

休管他人瓦上霜。讽刺的是，群策群力在中国历史背景中历来是生死攸关之事，举例而言，大禹曾带领人民治理黄河，但在百年前的现实中，中国的社会治理是如此混乱以至于中国人被贴切地形容为"一盘散沙"。

四

当时事态的确堪忧。在一种倾向于彻底变革的政治气候中，诸如"共和国"、"民主"、"革命"以及"解放"这样的词被引入中国，人们对于政治理论的兴趣也与日俱增。中国学生和知识分子对国家蒙受的屈辱深感受挫，而作为统治族群的满族顺理成章被人们当作中国失败的替罪羊。但是，自由和革命话语的发展异常地脱离了顽固的社会现实和根深蒂固的习俗（一些中国的政治科学家所警惕的正是这种为了营造气氛的修辞）。年轻的激进主义者就像18世纪法国的革命文人，钟爱宽泛的概括和满篇套话的法律体系而轻视铁的事实。当旧政权被推翻，他们说不出任何具体而富有建设性的东西，只是"一心想按照逻辑法则和一种先入为主的体系重建整个宪法而非试图纠正其错误之处"（托克维尔，1966：168）。

1911年清朝覆灭之后，是一个又一个临时政府和绵延几十年的内战。不同派系的军阀和民族主义者以及自封的皇帝都卷入了一场最不光彩但又不可避免的权力之争。他们出卖国家的重大利益换取外国列强的经济资助。诞生不久的"共和国"吸引了美国政治科学协会首任主席、常年任约翰·霍普金斯大学校长的古德诺的注意。当代政治科学家将古德诺看作历史制度主义者，因为他关注各种国家和社会制度对于一个国家的政治生活和公共管理的不可或缺性。对于那些将民主的复杂运作等同于投票站之类的表面文章以及"一人一票"原则的人，古德诺会刻不容缓地驳斥他们。

1913~1914年，古德诺作为"民国政府"的法律顾问在北京参与起草了国家的临时约法，在他看来这份约法故意低估了国家文化及政治遗产的负担。他敏锐地注意到，中国不具备西式民主必需的社会和政治条件，也不具备代议制的基本要素。他甚至赞同具有改良思想的清末官员，认为君主立宪制比"共和"体制更为现实，后者既不能带来责任政府也不能带来管理效率。

古德诺并不幻想有益于一个国家的东西也会有益于另一个国家。他对于向中国引进美国政治体系的迟疑使人们想起埃德蒙·伯克对那些难于处理的细节的注意。尽管伯克（1969：312）是法国大革命的坚定批判者之一，但他却不敦促法国人民直接效仿英国模式，以此表达他对法国人民的尊重："在我冒昧提出无论何种政治方案之前，我必须用我的双眼看，在某种意义上，用我的双手触摸，不只对于那些稳固的形势，对于那些暂时的形势也如此。"

辛亥革命发生10年之后，伯特兰·罗素访问中国并号召建立一个能够发展民族工业、普及教育的有序的好政府。为了保障这些目标的成功，他建议中国人应该培养政治意识、公共精神以及社会责任感（罗素，1922：15章）。他的时任妻子多拉记录了当时京郊百姓死于饥荒的场景。在华外国人组织了一些救援物资，而使他们震惊的是，中国人却明显表示出对灾民的漠不关心。"这里的人们对于救援是如此可怕的冷酷。他们竟置生重病的邻里于不顾，哪怕他们挣扎在垂死边缘"（多拉·罗素，1978：125）。

孙中山先生于1917年在规划他的现代中国的蓝图时曾痛惜这一不团结和冷漠的状态，却没有意识到他自己也许对这一悲剧也部分地负有责任。他逐渐看出——尽管为时已晚——中国所需要的是具有社会公德的公民以及一个强有力的中央集权政府。他的后任蒋介石曾经试图将权力集中，但由于日本侵华战争的干扰以及毛泽东领导的中国共产党的严峻挑战而失败。

在20世纪初期，年轻的激进分子拒绝接受运作期又长又慢的改良。他们理想化地认为人类生而性善且可以被完善，一切罪恶都源于非理性以及随之而来的不好的社会和政治安排。他们并不熟悉或者说抗拒一种渐进式的思想路线。温和被贬损为怯懦的标志。现在可以为一个遥远的未来做出牺牲，头可断血可流，但是决不能向现实让步、妥协或者有任何和解的姿态。胜者为王。幸运的是这种挑战和对抗的语言现今已经不再具有影响，但它毕竟广为流传了几十年。

在很长一段时间里，中国政治正确性的标志就是：最美的图画是在一张白纸上画的图画。毛泽东是不能忍受龟速的。在他的一首诗中，他要求他的追随者远离渐进主义的方法："一万年太久，只争朝夕"。因此才有了诸如"大跃进"、一时的奇迹以及所有不切实际的计划。

与儒家政治试图将个人与公众视作同一不同，毛泽东直率地坚持认为存在个人道德和公共组织的两个世界，有着两种冲突的价值体系。在这方面，他与国家主义的爱国者马基雅维利十分相像。毛泽东以这样的观念教育青年一代：一个国家的伟大是出于公民和集体的道德而非个人的道德。的确，有失必有得。像马基雅维利一样，毛泽东打破了太多的常规，但终于取得了回报。毛泽东曾以自嘲的口吻夸耀道，他在许多方面都超越了秦始皇。这当然并非夸大其词。

我们可以以一种新的角度解读毛泽东在 20 世纪 50 年代之前的活动。以下是以赛亚·伯林——一位犹太复国主义者同时也是 20 世纪自由事业领头人之一——赞成马基雅维利的一种解释："一旦你着手一项旨在改造社会的计划，那么你无论付出何种代价都要坚持到底：摸索、退却或被顾虑击倒都是对你选定事业的背叛。作为一名医生就要专业，就要准备烧灼、腐蚀或截肢；如果这正是治疗疾病所需的，那么出于个人的顾虑或某些与医术无关的规定就使治疗半途而废就是糊涂和软弱的标志，并将总是带给你两个世界最坏的部分"（伯林，1997：59）。这些言论也正可以应用到毛泽东的事业以及他与儒家政治的分歧上。毛泽东最大的功绩就在于最终建立了一个前所未有的强大而集权的政府并且实现了相当程度的管理有效性。也许在中国的历史长河中这是政府第一次彻底剿灭土匪，这是毛泽东的贡献，尽管是以（有时不必要的）极高昂的人力代价换来的。但是，这个发射台是为渐进主义的改革者们预备的。邓小平具有改革思想的管理方式只有用一种复杂的行政机构才能承担在分权与重组的过程中大规模管理复杂经济的任务。

五

如今，许多研究政治学的中国学者都是谨慎而务实的现实主义者，他们宁愿相信实践智慧而非理论明晰性或意识形态上的正确性。他们开始发现人类的真理具有相对性和悖论性，发现妥协的政治才应该是指导原则，发现人类有瑕疵并易错，是由非常弯曲而不能建造任何完全笔直之物的材料造就的。这些学者不大相信历史总在进步或存在指导历史发展的铁的定律。如果现存体制不能很好地发挥作用或不能紧跟时代，他们的现实感就会告诉他们这只能以一种温和的方式来改变，以防发生严重的副作用。改革者们——而非革命者们——更倾向于世俗的、一点一滴的调整以及局部的改正，而不是灵机一动的推倒重建计划。渐进主义改革者的信念乃是，现实而成功的改革是长久且可持续的逐步推进的过程；如果说一个极端教条主义者会嘲笑说这是"裹足不前"，那改革者也不会为他的信念感到羞愧。他们会紧密关注每个步骤的效果，以便从第一步的成败中找到对第二步的启发。中国的一句谚语恰当地总结了这一经验主义的立场——"摸着石头过河",也即在走出一步后仔细打量再迈下一步。

"天堂立现"的观念再也不能轻易激起这些政治学家们的兴趣,他们开始严肃地质疑无论是 19 世纪还是后现代的一切宏大叙事。这并不意味着他们满足于中国的现状,相反,在面对无数社会问题时,他们怀有一种紧迫感,且从不谴责人们的义愤。他们从其他国家的艰辛历程中汲取了教训,懂得了像中国这样的国家长期积累下来的问题或灾祸是错综复杂的,为了解决这些问题需要大量努力,醉醺醺的谴责和煽动性的街头政治毫无用处。他们在社会实践中已经适应了多元主义,因为他们发现不一贯的以及表面上不相容的价值观其实可以——尽管并不总是和平地——共存。

在美国和欧洲国家,大规模的公共事务项目、社会保险以及农业补贴主要是在私有经济的范围之内进行。认为必须在纯粹的资本主义和纯粹的社会主义之间做出严格的、基要主义的选择是误导性的。对抽象理论的沉溺已经过时,并且存在这样一种坚持,即认为个别问题应该个别解决,对具体论题的扎实研究比起对"主义"的空谈更有价值。建立中国版的能够设置食品及药物标准并检测其安全性的美国食品药品监督管理局,可能比草率引进在历史和文化背景完全不同的国家中发展起来的社会和政治理论更加有用。那么什么是中国当前最需要全力解决的问题?不胜枚举:对法治的普遍忽视、执法能力的低下、劳动权利保护的缺失、逐渐加大的贫富差距及沿海内陆省份的差距、前所未有的环境污染、国家医疗服务和适应于全球化速度的金融体系的欠缺等。要应对这些挑战,最重要的是公共机构的逐步建立和加强。

人们经常说,中国的经济繁荣并没有伴随着政治的民主化。这种抱怨可能有点道理。但是,可以争论的是,那些对中国的批评对以下一点察觉得有些迟缓,即中国经济上的繁荣正是适应于中国需要的政治制度的直接后果。正在进行着的大规模的社会改革具有深远的经济和政治意义。另外,人们阅读并公开讨论弗里德里希·冯·哈耶克、卡尔·波普、迈克尔·欧克肖特、约翰·罗尔斯和萨缪尔·亨廷顿(尤其是他对政府统治程度的强调)等来自盎格鲁-撒克逊世界的政治思想家的著作,所有法国后现代主义学者更是讨论的对象。简而言之,中国的政治学家们随"参照结构"(借用爱德华·萨义德的说法)的改变而以不同的方式看待世界和他们自身。了解托克维尔对(比如说)法国大革命的批评和分析的人,都会无可避免地将其对中国现代的激进主义的理解置于一个新的视野中。儒家的名誉恢复了，但是儒家政治思想的局限性也得到充分的关注。

与以往不同的是抽象的自由受到怀疑。自由通常被认为与和平、秩序和法治联系在一起。伯克对于社会生活之瓦解的警告十分贴切："如果谨慎和告诫是智慧的一部分，那么当我们仅仅与无生命的事物打交道时，它们当然也会成为我们责任的一部分；当我们推倒和建设的主体不是砖石与木料而是有知觉的存在时，由于其状态、条件和习惯的突然改变，可能会使大众的处境变得悲惨。"在伯克看来，一位优秀立法者的资格就是拥有一颗富有感受力的心与一种怀疑的自信。"他应该热爱并尊重他的同类，同时畏惧他自己……由于政治制度是一项用于社会目的的工作，它只能通过社会的手段来形成……我们的耐心将比我们的力量收获更多"（伯克，1969：281）。在当前的社会政治环境中，对这些言辞的热烈回应显示了一个更为人性化、在政治上更为成熟的中国，一个愿意谴责任何可能使普通的中国民众服从于宏大社会实验的一切危险政策的中国。

越来越多的中国人将社会秩序置于首位，正利用大众传媒参与关于广泛的公共议题的讨论和辩论。不时能够听到对于社会底层之无助的义愤的表达、对制衡以及对决策制定过程中的透明性的要求。中国人在现代及西方含义上比他们的先辈们对政治更感兴趣，他们正通过他们自己独立的努力迎接一个公共领域以及一个开放的社会。与此同时，这些政治上的新参与者正在认真学习如何正确使用语言，并且对于表述和解释的话语、在虚伪的语汇中隐藏的利益十分敏感。他们认识到，很多事情原因复杂，但是有人出于政治的动机，不愿意了解复杂的原委，热衷于运用或滥用一些意识形态上的空泛术语来遮蔽关于中国的事实。

在30年的时间跨度中，几乎三分之一的中国人已经脱离了极端贫困，同时一项巨大的城市化工程正在进行之中。最重大的成果可能是这样一个事实，即尽管存在对官僚腐败以及地方对于贫困人员坐视不管的政策的严厉批评，但是绝大多数中国人仍然支持现行的政治体制，这也是这一体制能令几十年来关于它的崩溃的预言一再破灭的原因。

（杜　鹃译）

参考文献

伯林，Berlin, I. (1997), "The Originality of machiavelli", In *Against the Current: Essays in the History of Ideas*. London: Pimlico。

伯克，Burke, E. (1969), *Reflections on the Revolution in France*, ed. Conor Cruise O'Brien. Harmondsworth: Pelican Books。

艾略特，Eliot, T. S. (1928), "Niccolò Machiavelli", in *For Lancelot Andrews: essays on style and order*. London: Faber and Gwyer。

稻叶君山，Kimiyama, I. (1914), *A History of the Qing Dynasty*, transl. Dan Tao. Beijing: Commercial Press。

莫理循，Morrison, G. E. (1976), *The Correspondence of G. E. Morrison*, 2 vol., Lo Hui-min (ed.). New York: Cambridge University Press。

牟复礼，Mote, F. W. (1989), *Intellectual Foundations of China*, 2nd edn. New York: Knopf。

骆惠敏编《清末民初政情内幕：莫理循书信集》，1976。

李提摩太，Richard, T. (1916), *Forty-Five Years in China*. London: Unwin。

罗素，Russell, B. (1922), *The Problem of China*. London: George Allen & Unwin。

罗素，Russell, D. (1978), *The Tamarisk Tree: My Quest for Liberty and Love*. London: Virago。

史密斯，Smith, A. H. (1968), *Village Life in China*. New York: Haskell House。

史景迁，Spence, J. D. (1978), *The Death of Woman Wang*. New York: Viking Press。

托克维尔，Tocqueville, A. de (1966), *The Ancien Regime and the French Revolution*, transl. S. Gilbert. London: Fontana。

王尔德，Wilde, O. (1969), *The Artist as Critic: Critical Writings of Oscar Wilde*. New York: Random House。

Confucian Politics and Its Redress: From Radicalism to Gradualism

Lu Jiande[*]

The current revival of Confucianism in China comes at a timely moment, for no country can be governed by a relentless nationwide pursuit of wealth without core values. This revival, however, is not accompanied by a careful awareness of possible defects in Confucianism as a theory of politics, if by politics we mean a science and art of government or public and social ethics.

I

It is widely believed that Taoism and Confucianism, the yin and yang in Chinese culture, are mutually complementary. As the two primary Taoist texts, Tao De Ching and Zhuang Zi, are great pieces of literature, Taoism has enjoyed a more favorable reception in countries outside Asia and is sometimes the source of inspiration for beautiful literary works like W. B. Yeats's poem 'Lapis Lazuli' and

---

[*] Lu Jiande was born in China in 1954. He received his education from Fudan University, Shanghai, and was awarded his doctoral degree at Cambridge University. He is professor and Director of the Institute of Literature, Chinese Academy of Social Sciences. He contributes to China's leading intellectual journals and is also the author of *Dr Zhivago and Other Essays* (Beijing, 1996), *Fragments of Broken Systems: Studies in British and American Literature* (Beijing, 2001) and *Interests Behind Ideas: Essays in Cultural Politics* (Shanghai, 2005).

Marguerite Yourcenar's Oriental Tales.

Arguably Yourcenar's favorite writer was Zhuang Zi, the arch rebel against social habits and prejudices and also a master of the art of defamiliarization. When Herbert A. Giles's translation of Zhuang Zi appeared in 1890, Oscar Wilde heartily welcomed it in The Artist as Critic (1969: 221) as 'the most caustic criticism of modern life'. At the bottom of his heart an anarchist, this Victorian dandy was intrigued by the Chinese author's 'wicked transcendental aim', which is spelt out in snappy sentences like 'All modes of government are wrong' and 'Do nothing, and everything will be done.' Living in a society of order and stability, Wilde could afford such appreciative generosity.

For Zhuang Zi, an individual is entitled to regulate the whole of his conduct by his own will. When Aristotle (Politics, 1253a) defined human beings as 'political animals', he considered the individual cut off from his polis as 'a non co-operator like an isolated piece in a game of draughts'. But this principle is turned upside down by the apolitical Chinese sage. Wilde sided with Zhuang Zi as regards extreme individuality and used Zhuang Zi's subtle but subversive philosophy to dismiss all the 'humanitarian societies', 'philanthropist organizations' and 'dull lectures about one's duty to one's neighbours' in his society. Hardly any Chinese visitors to Britain at that time would have found Wilde's dismissal congenial. Here and there they would have noted that the spirit of charity was woven deeply into the warp and weft of British society, or expressed their delighted amazement at the very existence of volunteer organizations such as the 'Royal Society for the Prevention of Cruelty to Animals'.

We might also take a brief look at China through the eyes of Wilde's contemporaries. At the turn of the 20th century, G. E. Morrison, an English colonial and correspondent for The Times in Beijing, made the embarrassing remark that China was a hodge-podge of humanity rather than a nation. As a result, 'he jeered all over the country, patriotism weighed not more than an ounce' (Lo Hui-Min, Introduction to Morrison, 1976). For his part Timothy Richard, one of the most influential British missionaries to China at that time, described in Forty-Five Years in China (1916) how, around 1880, he almost single-handedly provided relief to famine victims in Shandong province, with the local authorities standing idly by. Richard had neither the time nor the taste for prattles about governmental do-nothingism.

Indeed, in a time of environmental crisis and materialist greed, Taoist emphasis on harmony between man and nature could serve as a corrective to unbridled industrialism and developmenta-lism. But what in a poet or unconventional philosopher is a merit may well be a vice in a statesman. If the implied political message in Taoism is put into practice as a social principle, disasters will no doubt ensue. Comparing Western humanism with Taoist naturalism, Frederick W. Mote (1989: 62 -3) perceptively pointed out:

Humanism in the West developed in response to (or against) religious authoritarianism, and pagan nature was readily associable with its humanism for historical and cultural reasons. In China Taoist idealization of nature was part of a pessimism about humanity's capacity to keep order and safety in society; it sought nature as a refuge from humanity… Taoism therefore came to regard social man as a misguided being. It scorned government, feared progress and civilization, and was wary of all kinds of technical skills. It came to see all standards, definitions, distinctions, and classifications (in which Confucianism placed such value) as degenerating devices destructive to the healthy state of pristine nature. It emerged in an age of social disorder-as did Confucianism-and its obsession came to be the preservation of life. It withdrew to nature because it found human society too hazardous.

Consequently Taoism has a mundane aspect-the pursuit of longevity through whatever means.

II

It is believed by many that Taoism is fundamentally at variance with Confucianism, which cares very much about people's well-being, the manifest final objective of government. What makes Confucian politics more attractive to the modern mind is thatit has an element of democracy: 'Heaven sees according as my people see; Heaven hears according as my people hear' (Mencius, 5a. 5).[1]

---

[1] This corresponds with 'Vox populi, Vox dei'.

But looked at closely, the two schools of thought share something surprising in common: both accept the concept of weak government and neither is really interested in public ethics, the very foundation of politics.

There is a famous doctrine in Tao De Ching (ch. 60): the art of governing a large country is like cooking a small fish-leave it alone (otherwise it will fall apart). Nowhere could we find a more vivid expression of the gospel of governmental non-interference. Laissez-faireism, it must be admitted, is also an integral part of Confucianism. In The Analects, Shun, one of the two renowned leaders of the Golden Age, was instanced by Confucius as 'having governed without exertion' (无为而治). 'He did nothing but gravely and reverently occupy his royal seat' (15. 4). The Confucian political world is free from a Hobbesian Leviathan, fortunately or not. Governmental inaction was further confirmed by Mencius, who argued that 'the administration of a state is not difficult; it lies in not offending the great families' (4a. 6). The proper functions of state seem to have been delegated or surrendered to households of power.

If a benevolent government treats its people very well, Mencius says, it is sparing in the use of punishment and fines, and the taxes and levies are light. This parental kindness is considered the source of political power. Both Confucius and Mencius believe that man is born good, and this innate goodness enables him to follow a more virtuous person. The tricky business of managing a state depends almost solely upon the cultivation of the private individual. If you are a good man, your virtue and teachings will spread everywhere within the four seas like the rush of water, and people in all places will flock to you irresistibly, also like the rush of water.

Confucianism differentiates the superior man from lower people. When the edifying power of moral example is asserted and made absolute, the boundaries between the two categories ironically crumble. Mencius says, 'If the sovereign be benevolent, all will be benevolent. If the sovereign be righteous, all will be righteous' (4a. 20). Often the term 'people' in Confucian texts seems to refer to a unified whole with no internal conflicts of interests. In the imaginary political world of Confucius and Mencius, lions and foxes are conspicuously absent. He who loves and respects others is constantly loved and respected; everybody does unto others as he/she would be done by. There must be an invisible hand of morality that brings all social activities and relations into happy harmony.

An unexpected result of this belief is that people from lower social orders, since they are automatically drawn to copy the behavior of the superior man, do not have to be responsible for their own conduct. There is a customary saying in China that if the upper beam is not straight, the lower beams will go aslant. Unfortunately there is no shortage of corrupt officials to account for the commonality's misdemeanors or serious offences.

The Great Learning, one of the basic Confucian texts, opens with the theme that once you rectify your heart, cultivate your person and regulate your family, then you can order your state well. A smooth transition from private virtues to public good is effected in this celebrated statement. Mandeville is perhaps mistaken in believing that private vices make public good, but it is equally misleading to assert that privatevirtues are always consistent with public interests. The Confucian visions of reality are monist, for values are coherent and compatible: there is a set of overarching standards in terms of which all private and public conduct can be evaluated. But righteous hearts and well ordered families are not necessarily common bedfellows. It is purely the state's business to deal with possible tensions and conflicts of various kinds in the public sphere through political means. Confucian social theory somehow gives the impression that it would not enter into that unpleasant world.

It is also a Western view that true self-love and social love are the same. As Alexander Pope lauded self-love in An Essay on Man:

> God loves from Whole to Parts: but human soul
> Must rise from Individual to the Whole.
> Self-love but serves the virtuous mind to wake,
> As the small pebble stirs the peaceful lake;
> The centre mov'd, a circle strait succeeds,
> Friend, parent, neighbour, first it will embrace,
> His country next, and next all human race,
> Wide and more wide, th'o' erflowings of the mind

Take ev'ry creature in, of ev'ry kind;

Earth smiles around, with boundless bounty blest,

And Heav'n beholds its image in his breast. (iv, 1273 –1284)

These concentric circles are as orderly as Pope's Augustan heroic couplets. But usually in real life there is more than one pebble simultaneously stirring the mirror-like lake and the surface is thrown into confusion as the circles meet and collide. Easier said than done. Pope's own love would not ripple out evenly from the center to the periphery. In The Dunciad he vents his spleen on literary institutions around him and so heartily holds up fellow-writers to ridicule.

One of the weaknesses of Confucianism as political theory is that politics, or in other words public and social ethics, is often discussed within the realm of private virtues. It would do injustice to Confucius if we accuse him of being ignorant of the difference between the private and the public. When conflicts between the two arise, the public has to give way to the private. In The Analects, the Duke of Sheh informs Confucius that in their part of the country, there are those who may be styled upright in their conduct. If their father has stolen a sheep, they will bear witness to the fact. Confucius risked ambiguity in replying that among his people, 'the father conceals the misconduct of the son, and the son conceals the misconduct of the father. Uprightness is to be found in this.' (13.18) Considering the fact that filial piety is the keystone in a Confucian moral structure, Confucius seems to endorse this norm of behavior among his people.

In Christianity it is also assumed that virtuous rulers create virtuous men, but human nature is never flattered. Here we find the divide between Christianity and Confucianism. It can be said that Confucian political theories tend to overlook the disgraceful indulgences of human frailties or even wickedness. Confucianism is almost exactly the opposite of Machiavellianism. It would never occur to Confucius and Mencius that people could be ungrateful, fickle, false, cowardly or covetous; but once a person succeeds others will follow him entirely, not simply because of his moral goodness. Statecraft to the two Chinese sages is hardly necessary; and cunning and duplicity are outright moral offences. This outlook does not assert that they were better men, but that they were not driven by a clear-sighted passion as strong as that of Machiavelli for the unity, peace and prosperity of his country. T. S. Eliot (1928: 39 – 52) discovered that it was the Florentine's passionate patriotism that urged him to 'blow the gaff on human nature'.

The two Confucian masters spent much of their life traveling through quite a number of states to promote their moral philosophy. Peace and prosperity depend upon, and in turn support, the virtues of the citizen. At that time national awareness was not crystallized, otherwise their theory of politics would have been enriched and enlivened by collective ideals of service to the state and by what Edmund Burke would call 'locality of public feeling'.

The idea of 'all under heaven' might be praiseworthy in an age torn by militant nationalism, but it is not conducive to the birth of robust theories about the peace, glory and splendor of a particular state or nation, where virtues like fortitude, valor and public-spiritedness have a chance to thrive, and citizens are able to prosper, to realize the best of their selves and to feel proud of the achievement of their community.

III

Actual processes of governance throughout Chinese history have not always been characterized by Confucian political ideals. However, these ideals, deeply rooted in the background of collective unconsciousness, could have been responsible for phenomena worthy of our attention: a public domain characterized by weak government, lack of public space, no volunteer or non-kinship organizations mediating between government and people. Society as a whole was composed of loose monads of families and clans.

Geographically the country was perhaps too big to rule. Despite government monopolies over salt and iron, which however often existed only in name, economically Chinese society had adopted a laissez-faire policy because of poor communication and transport. Politically the same policy also applied. The aphorism 'the sky is high and the emperor far away' speaks loudly of the lawlessness and ineffectiveness of government intervention in traditional Chinese society. In 1914, three years after the collapse of the Qing Dynasty, a Japanese historian attributed the widespread scourge of banditry in China to government inaction. He put forward the view that the Chinese imperial court, because it had been too weak to maintain a basic level of social justice, had allowed the strong to oppress the weak and the great to tyrannize the small. Lawbreakers seemed safely beyond the reach of law (Spence, 1978, only one of the myriad stories of absolute misery). Eventually the insulted and injured had to resort to extreme means to protect their rights to subsistence (Kimiyama, 1914: ch. 51). Another Japanese scholar Watanabe Hideyoshi pointed out in his Chinese Characteristics that the Japanese would feel confident in state protection, whereas ordinary Chinese had to rely upon themselves for personal security. This lack of a sense of security ate into the fabric of the public world and may well have been responsible for a certain degree of social indifference and self-centeredness among many Chinese. We learn from the classical novel Water Margin how villagers were practising martial arts for self-protection against gangsters. Police forces in the modern sense were only established at the very beginning of the 20th century, during and after the foreign occupation of Tianjing following the Boxer Rebellion.

Before the Communists came to power in 1949, Chinese neighborhoods could easily be terrorized by criminal mafias, despotic landlords and local ruffians (Smith, 1968: ch. 20). The absence of a public force further undermined social solidarity. Hence the proverbial Chinese incapability of mutual help: each one sweeps the snow from his own doorsteps and doesn't bother about the frost on his neighbor's roof. The irony is that in China concerted collective effort has been a matter of life and death in their historical context: for instance Great Yu leading his people in the fight against the flooding of the Yellow River; but in reality a hundred years ago the country was so poorly organized in a social sense that its people were adequately described as 'a sheet of loose sand'.

IV

The state of affairs was indeed dismal at that time. In a political climate favorable to radical change, terms like 'republic', 'democracy', 'revolution' and 'liberty' were introduced into China and there appeared a surge of interest in political theories. Chinese students and intellectuals felt frustrated at their country's humiliation and the Manchus, the ruling ethnic group, were conveniently used as scapegoats for China's failure. But the development of a discourse of liberty and revolution was strangely separated from stubborn social realities and deep-rooted customs. (It is this kind of atmospheric rhetoric that some Chinese political scientists have come to be vigilant against.) The young radicals, like those revolutionary men of letters in 18th century France, had a fondness for broad generalizations, cut-and-dried legislative systems, and a contempt for hard facts. When the old regime was toppled, they had nothing concrete and constructive to say, except their 'desire to reconstruct the entire constitution according to the rules of logic and a preconceived system instead of trying to rectify its faulty parts' (Tocqueville, 1966: 168).

The fall of the Qing Dynasty in 1911 was followed by one makeshift government after another and decades of civil wars. Warlords and nationalists of different stripe as well as a self-appointed emperor entered into a most disgraceful but inevitable struggle for power. They traded vital national interests for financial support from foreign powers. The newly created 'republic' caught the attention of Frank J. Goodnow, the first president of the American Political Science Association and for many years the president of Johns Hopkins University. Contemporary political scientists think of Goodnow as a historical institutionalist because of his interest in the indispensability of the whole range of state and societal institutions for a country's political life and public administration. Goodnow would dismiss offhand those who equated the complicated working of democracy with formalities of polling stations and the doctrine of 'one-person, one-vote'.

Serving as legal advisor to 'the Republic of China' in Beijing from 1913 to 1914, Goodnow took part in drafting a provisional constitution for a country that in his view willfully underestimated the burden of its cultural and political inheritance. He shrewdly observed that China did not possess the social and political conditions necessary for Western-style democracy, or the 'nuts and bolts' of a representative system. He even agreed with the reform-minded mandarins towards the end of the Qing Dynasty that a constitutional monarchy was more practical than a 'republican' framework incapable of securing either responsible government or administrative efficiency.

Goodnow did not harbor the illusion that what is good for one nation must be good for another. His hesitation at importing the American political system into China recollects Edmund Burke's attentiveness to stubborn details. Burke (1969: 312) expressed his respect for the French people by not urging upon them a direct imitation of the British model, even though he was one of the most staunch critics of the French Revolution: 'I must see with my own eyes, I must, in a manner, touch with my own hands, not only the fixed, but the momentary circumstances, before I could venture to suggest any political project whatsoever.'

Ten years after the Nationalist Revolution of 1911, Bertrand Russell called for a good and orderly government that could develop national industry and popularize education. To secure success for these objectives, he suggested, the Chinese should cultivate political consciousness and a public spirit, as well as a sense of social duty (Russell, 1922: ch. 15). His (then) wife Dora Russell recorded her observations when people outside Beijing were dying of famine. The foreigners had organized some relief and were shocked at the apparent indifference of the Chinese. 'People here are horribly callous about relief. They leave their severely ill neighbours alone, even when they are dying' (Russell, 1978: 125).

Dr Sun Yat-sen deplored this state of disunity and apathy when drawing up his blueprint for a future modern China in 1917, without realizing that he himself might be partially responsible for this tragedy. He came to see, albeit belatedly, that what was needed were citizens with civic virtues and a strong and centralized government. His successor Jiang Kai-shek attempted to centralize power, but he failed, because of the interruption of the Japanese war and the severe challenges from the Communist Party led by Mao Zedong.

In the 1920s young radicals of leftist conviction refused to accept reform as being too long and slow an operation. They idealistically believed that human beings were naturally good and perfectible; all evils arose from irrational and therefore bad social and political arrangements. They were unfamiliar with or resistant to a gradualist line of thinking. Moderation was stigmatized as the trademark of cowards. The present could be sacrificed for a remote future, heads could be severed and blood shed, but there should be no concessions to reality, no compromises or reconciliatory gestures of any kind. The winner took all. This language of defiance and confrontation has fortunately come to a peaceful end, but for several decades it enjoyed widespread currency.

It was for quite a long time the trademark of Chinese political correctness: the most beautiful picture is one drawn on a clean sheet of paper. Mao would have no patience with the plodding speed of the tortoise. In one of his poems he asked his followers to stay away from the gradualist approach: 'Oh no, ten thousand years? It's too long. / Make it, here and now.' Hence, the Great Leap Forward, miracles of a moment and all the unrealistic plans for never-never land.

Unlike Confucian politics that tends to identify the private with the public, Mao candidly insisted that there were two worlds, that of personal morality and that of public organization, two conflicting systems of value. In this aspect he was like Machiavelli the nationalist patriot. Mao inculcated in the young the idea that what makes a nation great are civic and collective virtues rather than private virtues. Indeed, 'one cannot make an omelette without breaking eggs'. Like Machiavelli, Mao broke too many eggs, but the omelette was finally prepared. In a moment of self-irony, Mao boasted he had outdone the First Emperor in many aspects. He was surely not saying something too far-fetched.

The activities of Mao before the 1950s can be interpreted from a new perspective. The following is a sympathetic account of Machiavelli given by Isaiah Berlin, a Zionist and also one of the leading champions for the cause of liberty in the 20th century. 'Once you embark on a plan for the transformation of a society you must carry it through no matter at what cost: to fumble, to retreat, to be overcome by scruples is to betray your chosen cause. To be a physician is to be a professional, ready to burn, to cauterize, to amputate; if that is what the disease requires, then to stop half way because of personal qualms, or some rule unrelated to your art and its technique, is a sign of muddle and weakness, and will always give you the worst of both worlds' (Berlin, 1997: 59). These words may well also apply to Mao's enterprise and his departure from Confucian politics. His greatest merit was that an unprecedentedly strong and centralized government and a considerable degree of administrative efficiency were finally achieved. Perhaps for the first time in China's long history the government wiped out banditry completely. This was Mao's contribution, though made at (sometimes unnecessarily) great human cost. But the launching pad had been laid for gradualist reformers. Only with an intricate administrative machinery could the reform-minded government of Deng Xiao-ping assume the task of regulating on a grand scale a complex economy in the process of decentralization and re-structuring.

V

Nowadays many Chinese students of political science are prudent and pragmatic realists believing in practical wisdom rather than theoretical clarity or ideological correctness. They have come to see that human truths are relative and paradoxical, and that the politics of compromise should be the guiding principle; that human beings are flawed and fallible, made out of timber so crooked that nothing entirely straight can be built. They are not very confident that history is ever in progress or that there is an iron law governing historical development. If the existing system is not working very well or in keeping with the times, their sense of reality tells them that it can only be changed in a gentle manner, just in case grave side effects should arise. Reformers rather than revolutionaries, they prefer mundane piecemeal readjustments and local corrections to inspired programs for demolitions and reconstructions. If a radical doctrinaire would laugh at the 'minced steps of an old lady with bound feet', a gradualist reformer does not feel ashamed of his belief that reforms of the practical and successful kind are long and well-sustained step-by-step processes. The effect of each step is closely watched, so that the success or failure of the first gives a hint of the second. A Chinese saying sums up this empiricist position very well: 'Wade across the river by feeling out for stones' -take one step and look around before taking another.

No longer easily aroused by the idea of 'paradise now', they tend to have serious doubts about all the grand narratives, whether of the 19th century or post-modern. This does not mean that they are satisfied by the status quo in China. Instead, they have a sense of urgency in the face of numerous social problems and would never decry righteous indignation. Taught by the bitter experiences of other countries, they understand that long-growing problems or evils of a country such as China are a tangled business, asking for a good deal more than drunken denunciations and demagoguery in order to be got rid of. In their social practice they have been accustomed to pluralism in the sense that they have found that incoherent and apparently incompatible values can actually coexist, though not always peacefully.

In the United States and European countries, large-scale programs of public works, social insurance and farm subsidies were carried out within the framework of predominantly private economies. It is misleading to believe that stark and fundamentalist choices have to be made between pure capitalism and pure socialism. Addiction to abstract theory has been outgrown and there is an insistence that individual problems should be individually solved, and that solid studies of concrete issues are more valuable than empty talk of 'isms'. The creation of a Chinese version of the American FDA that can establish standards for foods and drugs and test their safety would be perhaps more useful than hasty importations of social and political theories developed in countries which have totally different historical and cultural contexts.

What are the issues that need to be tackled at the present time in China? They are legion: the pervasive disregard for the rule of law, the deplorable implementation of justice, the need for protection of labor rights, the increasing disparity between rich and poor, between coastal areas and inland provinces, and unprecedented environmental pollution, the lack of a national health service and of a financial system compatible with the speed of globalization. To meet these challenges, the gradual establishment and consolidation of public institutions is of vital importance.

It is often said that the economic boom in China has not been accompanied by a democra-tization of politics. This complaint perhaps carries a grain of truth. But it could also be argued that critics of China are slow to perceive that the boom is the direct result of a political arrangement suitable for China's needs. The kind of extensive social reforms underway have far-reaching economic and political implications. On the other hand, Friedrich von Hayek, Karl Popper, Michael

Oakeshott, John Rawls and Samuel Huntington (especially his emphasis on degree of government) from the Anglo-Saxon world as well as all the French postmodernist pundits are read and publicly discussed. In a nutshell, Chinese political scientists see the world and themselves differently as their 'structure of reference' (to borrow Edward Said's phrase) has changed. An acquaintance with Tocqueville's critique and analysis of the French Revolution, for example, will ineluctably put one's understanding of modern Chinese radicalism in a new perspective.

Liberty is generally perceived as associated with peace, order and the rule of law. Burke's warning against the disruption of social life is very apt: 'If circumspection and caution are a part of wisdom, when we work only upon inanimate matter, surely these become a part of duty too, when the subject of our demolition and construction is not brick and timber, but sentient beings, by the sudden alteration of whose state, condition, and habit, multitudes may be rendered miserable.' The qualification of a good legislator, according to Burke, is a feeling heart and a doubting confidence. 'He ought to love and respect his kind, and to fear himself… Political arrangement, as it is a work for social ends, is to be only wrought by social means… Our patience will achieve more than our force' (Burke, 1969: 281). Warm responses to these words in the current sociopolitical environment tell of a humane and politically more mature China, a China that is ready to decry any policy that might subject ordinary Chinese to all the hazards of grand social experiments.

Prioritizing the social order, more and more Chinese are now participating in discussions and debates about a wide range of public issues in the mass media. Articulate indignations at the helplessness of the underprivileged, demands for checks and balances, and for more transparency in the decision-making process, are heard from time to time. Far more political than their forefathers in a modern and Western sense, the Chinese are ushering in a public realm and an open society through their own independent efforts. Meanwhile the politically initiated are carefully learning the business of using language properly and have become very sensitive to discourses of representation and interpretation, to hidden interests couched in a deceptive vocabulary, to ideologically convenient (ab)uses of blanket terms at the expense of not easily digestible facts.

Within the span of 30 years, almost one third of the Chinese population has been lifted out of extreme poverty and a huge project of urbanization is going on. The greatest achievement is perhaps the fact that, despite unsparing criticisms of bureaucratic corruption and local hands-off policies towards the poor and needy, an overwhelming majority of Chinese support the current political system and this is the only reason why the system has defied predictions of its collapse for several decades.

References

Berlin, I. (1997), 'The Originality of Machiavelli', in *Against the Current: Essays in the History of Ideas*. London: Pimlico.

Burke, E. (1969), *Reflections on the Revolution in France*, ed. Conor Cruise O'Brien. Harmondsworth: Pelican Books.

Eliot, T. S. (1928), 'Niccolò Machiavelli', in *For Lancelot Andrews: Essays on Style and Order*. London: Faber and Gwyer.

Kimiyama, I. (1914), *A History of the Qing Dynasty*, transl. Dan Tao. Beijing: Commercial Press.

Morrison, G. E. (1976), *The Correspondence of G. E. Morrison*, 2 vol., Lo Hui-min (ed.). New York: Cambridge University Press.

Mote, F. W. (1989), *Intellectual Foundations of China*, 2nd edn. New York: Knopf.

Richard, T. (1916), *Forty-Five Years in China*. London: Unwin.

Russell, B. (1922), *The Problem of China*. London: George Allen & Unwin.

Russell, D. (1978), *The Tamarisk Tree: My Quest for Liberty and Love*. London: Virago.

Smith, A. H. (1968), *Village Life in China*. New York: Haskell House.

Spence, J. D. (1978), *The Death of Woman Wang*. New York: Viking Press.

Tocqueville, A. de (1966), *The Ancien Regime and the French Revolution*, transl. S. Gilbert. London: Fontana.

Wilde, O. (1969), *The Artist as Critic: Critical Writings of Oscar Wilde*. New York: Random House.

韩非子与现代性

白彤东[*]

一 韩非子的时代：中国向"现代化"之转变？

为了论证传统中国哲学的重要性，有些人常常强调传统中国思想于西方思想之独特。但是一些批评者常常反驳说，中国思想只是不同于西方近现代（Modern）思想，而与古代西方思想非常相似（中医与古希腊医学、中国的天人感应思想与西方中世纪的思想，等等）。由此，中西思想之分就被描绘成了古今思想之别。在这篇文章里，通过对韩非子（约公元前280～公元前233年）的一些初步研究，笔者希望展示：第一，在所谓"春秋战国"时代（约公元前722～公元前222年），中国已经在某种意义上经历了向"现代性"（Modernity）的转变（这一转变在西方发生在15世纪之后）。春秋战国时期的诸子百家中很多学派实际上都在以不同的方式在应对"现代性"问题，尽管它们中的大多数也许并没有意识到这一点。第二，与其他同时代的思想家相比，因为韩非子最好地理解了中国的"现代化"转变的性质，他可能是人类历史上第一个"现代"思想家。如果这些猜测成立的话，那么春秋战国时期的"古代"中国思想可以很容易地与现代相关，因为那时的

---

[*] 白彤东（Bai Tongdong），男，1970年出生。2004年获波士顿大学哲学博士。现为复旦大学哲学学院教授，美国中国哲学家协会副主席。主要研究领域：中国哲学、政治哲学、科学哲学等。主要著述有：《旧邦新命——古今中西参照下的古典儒家政治哲学》（2009）、《实在的张力——EPR论争中的爱因斯坦、玻尔和泡利》（2009）等。

思想家和我们都在处理一样的问题，即现代性问题。这些讨论也会加深我们对现代性本质的理解。第三，通过对韩非子的批评，我们也许能够意识到今天一些主流思想的问题。

韩非子生活在战国时代末期。春秋战国时代充斥着社会与政治上的混乱和转变。在这一时代之前的西周的政治架构是一个封建的、金字塔般、扩张的系统。周王（尤其是最初几代的周王）分封他们的亲戚、忠实和能干的臣下（很多人同时也是周王的亲戚）、前朝的贵族等（"封土建国"）。这些人成为他们诸侯国的统治者。这些诸侯国中的一些是在周帝国的边远地带，因此可说它们是向这些"蛮夷"之地军事殖民（钱穆，1996：57）。这些事实上的殖民地的建立有助于帝国的势力扩张。当这些诸侯国通过蚕食其周围的"蛮夷"之地得以扩张后，它们的统治者常常会做与周王所做类似的事情，即分封他们的亲戚与亲信。就周帝国来说，周王统领诸侯，诸侯统领大夫，大夫统领家臣，而家臣统治他们属地的民众（因而这些属地地小人少）。因此，在每个层级上都是一个主子统领有限的臣属。这一现实使得统治者通过个人影响与接触来统治成为可能。但是，部分因为宗族的纽带经过几代以后被削弱，部分因为帝国已经扩张到当时的极限从而使得内斗变得不可避免，这种等级系统在春秋战国时期渐趋瓦解。在春秋时代，与从前不同，周王只被给予了名义上的尊重。最终，他实质上变成了诸侯之一（并且是实力很弱的一个）。诸侯国的疆界不再被尊重，通过吞并战争七雄终于产生，也带来了中国历史上的战国时代。在春秋战国时代，诸侯国乃至后来七雄的统治者不得不直接统治领土越来越大、人口越来越多的国家，而这些国家的存亡以及这些君主在其国内的存亡完全依赖于他们的实力。

上述这一转变与欧洲从中世纪到（西方的）现代的转变有很多奇妙的相似之处。欧洲中世纪的政治架构也是封建的、金字塔般的，这一架构在欧洲的现代化转变中也渐趋瓦解。从中产生的广土众民的国家试图通过战争获得统治地位。当然，中西的转变还是有不同的。比如，中世纪欧洲没有世俗君主享有如周王那样高和长久稳定的地位。教皇的位置相对稳定，但是它是否有公认的天下共主的地位是有争议的。中国的转变的一个驱动力量是农业革命，这使得它也许不像西方转变之始的商业革命，并且也肯定远不如西方转变后期的工业革命那么剧烈。欧洲的"春秋战国"也没有能够达到中国所达到的统一（尽管它们确实成功地打了两场"世界"大战和很多较小规模的战争)。但是,中国春秋战国与西方现代化的转变的相似性是清楚和深刻的。与封建制度一起消失的是贵族阶级和他们的生活方式。比如,如钱穆先生指出的,与封建等级摇摇欲坠但还没有坠落的春秋时代的战争相比,战国时代的战争是彻底地残忍与丑恶的(钱穆,1996:88~89)。军队被平民化了,因此贵族的行为准则也消逝了。战争服务于对资源的争夺,并成为砍脑袋的残忍运动。相应的,欧洲产生了拿破仑和他的人民战争。某种意义上讲,我们还在处理着这一变化的结果。比如,日内瓦公约可以被看作骑士之间的行为准则,因此这就解释了它为什么难以被应用到人民战争中的所有士兵身上,以及为什么到今天它还不能被普遍遵循。人民战争中,每个人都卷入进来,因此使军事人员与"无辜"平民的区分(及其相关问题)就变得很模糊。春秋战国的另外一个重大变化是土地的贵族专有继承和旧有的公田系统的废除,以及土地自由买卖的兴起。在西方则出现了臭名昭著的英国圈地运动。

现在,我们的问题是:这些相似意味着什么?它们也许意味着中国在春秋战国时代已经经历了某种形式的现代化。这一猜测也许会对我们理解现代化和现代性的本质、理解"古""今"之别有所启示。在中国与欧洲的封建制中,在它们的金字塔的每一层级上都只有几百或几千个人。也就是说,每一级都是一个实质上的寡民之小国。而在现代化转变之后出现的国家都是广土众民的。这似乎是个不重要的变化,但是,在政治里,大小很重要。比如,当一个共同体(Community)很小的时候("小国寡民"),基于一种对善的整全和相互分享的理解的道德和行为准则是可能的,但是,当这个共同体太大时,这种道德与准则就不能再普遍适用,因而就有了不可避免的价值多元。这是现代性的一个基本事实,一个为一些西方近现代思想家和韩非子所共同把握的事实。这里,我们的问题就变成:什么可以替代道德,成为一个国家的黏合剂?这是一个西方近现代与中国春秋战国时的思想家都努力回答的问题。一个相关的共同问题是:当金字塔式的封建架构消失了,我们如何能有一个统治阶层和新的统治结构?对这个问题的回答,于西方(比如支持平等和大众教育的启蒙思想家)、于"古代"中国(比如认识到所有人潜能上平等和支持某种形式的大众教育的儒家),似乎也很相像:一种向上的可流动性(Upward Mobility)使得以前的平民在官僚阶层中的升迁成为可能。但是这些思想家对如何实现这种向上流动性有不同的想法[比如,韩非子反对儒家教育,而偏向于以军事和(农业)生产为基础的贤能政治

(Meritocracy)]。因此，春秋战国时代中国思想家与西方近现代思想家在思想上的相似也许反映了他们面对类似问题的事实。比如，笔者在一篇文章中展示了《老子》（一个成书于春秋战国时代的有政治哲学向度的文本）与近代西方思想家卢梭思想的相似。他们都看到了"现代化"的问题，认为现代化的结果会很糟糕，并因此都呼吁回到小国寡民的时代（白彤东 2009）。

笔者至此论述了中国在春秋战国时期所经历的可能是西方现代化的一个预演。笔者在这篇文章里会进一步论证因为韩非子是春秋战国时代第一个意识到他的时代变化本质的思想家，所以他可能是人类历史上第一个现代思想家。如果我上述论点的前一半是对的，那么说中国春秋战国的思想在古今之分上属于古代就是错的。在这个意义上，黑格尔和马克斯·韦伯对中国"古代"思想的评判（因为它是古代的而贬低它）也是错的。一些中国当代的（以及西方的）思想家可能更糟，因为他们将中国古代思想标为"两千年封建专制的糟粕"。我们撇开"糟粕"这个情绪性字眼不谈，中国自秦以降的两千年的历史既不封建也不纯然是专制的。[①] 并且，雅思贝尔斯这样的思想家把中国春秋战国时代的思想和与其近乎同时的古希腊、古印度思想放到一块，称之为"轴心时代"的思想，这种说法也忽视了中国传统思想与其他这些思想的一个关键不同。在这个意义上，同情儒家的当代学者，如罗哲海，也以轴心时代的思想来理解儒家，因而也就犯了与雅思贝尔斯一样的错误。

需要澄清的是，中国与欧洲的现代化变革是历时长久的和混乱的。在春秋战国时代，多数国家都停留在过去的方式里。只有秦国实行了一个明显的现代化计划，而韩非子本人的属邦韩国没能做到这一点可能是韩非子政治观形成的重要因素之一。[②] 在欧洲，封建因素在俄国直到20世纪早期还有残留。[③] 有些人可能反驳说，上面提到的欧洲的有些现象是在近现代欧洲晚期甚至是当代欧洲发生的。但也许这只是意味着从古代到现代的转变要经历很长时间。毕竟这种变化在中国花了五百年（春秋战国），并且，我们甚至可以说中国春秋战国之后的很多历史事件仍然是对现代性挑战的回应。

[①] 春秋战国之后，传统中国的政治制度可能是专制君主（皇帝）与精英阶层（在中国历史中，这个阶层由大部分儒士组成）的张力的结果。见钱穆《中国历代政治得失》（2005）中的详细论述。

[②] 笔者感谢 Peter Moody 提醒我这一点的重要。

[③] 笔者感谢 Al Martinich 提醒我这一点的重要。

二 韩非子的政治哲学?

在我们考察《韩非子》这部著作以发现其对现代性的洞见之前,让我们首先回应一个问题:《韩非子》这部著作是不是一部政治哲学著作,其作者是不是一个政治哲学家?海外中国思想研究者葛瑞汉将韩非子思想描述为"非道德的统治国家之技艺的科学"(Amoral Science of Statecraft),美国学者保罗·戈丁批评了这个说法(Goldin, 2011)。在他的批评中,他正确地指出了韩非子与西方政治哲学家比如霍布斯与洛克的区别。比如,韩非子有时给统治者甚至大臣教授无耻的自我防卫的技术,而这种厚黑之学似乎是在霍布斯与洛克的著作里找不到的。但是,在另一部通常被认为是政治哲学的著作中(有些人会说它是西方近现代政治哲学的奠基之作),即马基雅维利的《君主论》中,我们可以找到类似的教授。并且,在其他一些西方政治哲学的著作中,我们也可以找到类似于上述的厚黑教导的踪迹。

但是,不可否认的是,《韩非子》与中国思想史上的很多文献确实与西方传统中的政治哲学文献多有不同。前者常常不是为了纯粹的理论讨论而写,而是对统治者的具体建议或是与其他大臣与政策顾问的争论之记载。如钱穆先生指出的(2005:21),在秦以后的时代,也许是因为儒家的向上流动思想的贡献,士人常常成为统治精英的一部分。这与春秋战国之前和中世纪(乃至近现代的大部分时期)的欧洲不同。因此,过去中国的知识精英就可以把他们的政治思想和理论付诸实践,而没有太多需要将它们变成脱离现实的理论。钱穆先生没有指出的一个事实是,中国士人于政治的深深卷入,也使得他们没有理论探讨的闲暇。实际上,卢梭说的一段话可以用来支持钱穆的说法。在《社会契约论》的第一段里,他指出:

> 人们要问我,我是不是一位君主或一位立法者,所以要来谈论政治呢?我回答说,哪个也不是;而且这是我为什么来谈论政治。假如我是个君主或者立法者,我就不应该浪费自己的时间来谈要做什么事了;我会去做那些事情或者保持沉默(Rousseau, 1978:46)。

与此不同,中国历史上的很多政治思想家是居于政治的核心。这一点在春秋战国时代已经发生了。比如,西方与权力核心最接近的思想家之一马基雅维利，他的政治地位也不及身为韩国诸公子的韩非子。如果我们可以相信《史记》里的记述的话，秦王（即后来的秦始皇）在读了韩非子的著作以后，与韩国打了一场仗，就是为了能把韩非子弄到他的身边来（"秦王见《五蠹》、《孤愤》之书，曰：'嗟乎，寡人得见此人与之游，死不恨矣！'李斯曰：'此韩非之所著书也。'秦因急攻韩"）（《史记·老子韩非列传》）。对这种重视，马基雅维利和其他西方政治哲学家恐怕只有嫉妒的份儿了。

当然，这一辩护只是解释了为什么中国很多思想家的作品与西方不同，并暗示，如果被给予机会（或者，更准确地说，被剥夺参与现实政治的机会），中国这些思想家会写出与西方政治哲学著作更相像的作品。但它并没有展示中国传统中的这些文献是政治哲学文献。但是，如果我们把哲学当作反思的工作，从而把政治哲学当作对政治事务的系统反思，我们可以看到《韩非子》确实含有这样的思考。韩非子和传统中国的很多其他政治思想家有对最高层的政治实践的亲身经历，并因而可以凭借它对政治进行反思。这就有可能弥补了他们于建筑在闲暇之上的思辨的缺失（我们已经看到，西方政治哲学家的闲暇可能是非自愿的）。笔者这里并非要否认《韩非子》包含厚黑术。实际上，这部书可能是这类书籍的上乘之作。笔者这里只是论证它包含了应当是属于政治哲学领域的思想。

三 韩非子之死与"法家"思想的命运

另一个对韩非子思想的重要性的攻击集中在韩非子及分享他的想法的人与国家的命运上。尽管韩非子对政治有着深刻的理解，他最终还是成了政治斗争的牺牲品。与韩非子一样曾求学于荀子的李斯当时在秦国居高位。他也许感到自己的地位被韩非子所威胁，因此说服秦王去逼迫韩非子"自杀"。有反讽意味的是，据《史记·老子韩非列传》记载，李斯所给出的论辩（"韩非，韩之诸公子也。今欲并诸侯，非终为韩不为秦，此人情也"），有着儒家而非法家的味道。看起来李斯并不相信韩非子在他的书里面所论证的，统治者可以通过赏罚使臣下变得忠诚。李斯自己的命运也好不到哪去。他被秦二世残酷地杀害了。通过韩非子会支持的政策来使秦国强大的关键人物商鞅也在支持他的秦王死后未得好死。实践着韩非子会支持的政策的秦国最终统一了中国，但它也没有延续多久。所有这些历史事实给那些不喜欢韩非子思想的人（比如儒家）以无限的欢乐。他们用这些事实来展示韩非子政治思想的邪恶本质与不足。①

笔者虽然高度同情儒家的政治哲学，但是我不得不说这种对韩非子及其政治哲学的批驳太过廉价。韩非子在《韩非子·难言》与《韩非子·说难》中展示了他对能让君主听从正确建议的困难的深刻理解，因此有些人就说他不能遵循他自己的理解。② 但是他的悲剧结局也许只是展示了让君主听从的巨大困难，这一困难在某些情形下超越了此种技艺的大师的掌控。③ 一般地讲，一个人不能遵循自己的哲学虽然很反讽，但是并不能证明其哲学是错的。至于秦国（秦朝）的命运，也许秦所带来的政治变动太过剧烈，以至于不能为它在短时间内消化。"暴秦"确实在它建立不久就被推翻了。接下来的汉朝试图回到封土建国的老路，但是这招致了七王之乱。它最终回到了含有很多《韩非子》中建议安排的秦制，同时对其有所修改。秦制后来实际上也为中国历史上的大多王朝所遵循。事实上，一些看起来是儒家的政治安排，比如科举，可能也包含着韩非子的遗产。过去很多思想家对韩非子的政治哲学及其在中国传统政治中的角色多有反思，而对这些反思的评价是个重要而艰巨的工作。这里，笔者只是希望，在我们处理韩非子的哲学与其在传统中国的命运时，我们能多有些同情（Charity）。

四 韩非子：第一个现代思想家

下面，我会给出与现代性问题相关的一些韩非子主要思想的概述。这里需要澄清的是，下面的仅仅是一个概述，而对人类历史上深刻有如韩非子这样的思想家的细致研究所需的远远超过一篇文章所能处理的。首先，像在第一节中提到的，我认为现代性的一个关键特征是，由于人口膨胀、封建诸侯向"蛮夷之地"扩张接近极致，以及因此而带来的对日渐有限的资源的争夺，这些导致了封建的、金字塔般的政治结构的瓦解，替代它的是广土众民的大国。在著名的《五蠹》篇里，韩非子展示了他对这些变化的理解。比

---

① 比如，明张鼎文写道："非之书未行，止于狱司；斯之术已用，遂至车裂。天道之报昭昭哉！"（陈奇猷，2000：1224）。
② 参见司马迁在《史记·老子韩非列传》里的说法："余独悲韩子为《说难》而不能自脱耳"。后人赵用贤也指出："韩非子非死于不自免于说难，而死于悖其术"（陈奇猷，2000：1226）。清梅曾亮指出，韩非子不知道他不应该挑明君主不想为人所知之术，因而招致身死（陈奇猷，2000：1257）。
③ 比如，王世贞指出，管仲与韩非子的命运之别在于时机的不同（陈奇猷 2000，1228）。

如，他指出"古""今"的一个关键区别在于，"古者……人民少而财有余，故民不争。是以厚赏不行，重罚不用，而民自治。今人有五子不为多，子又有五子，大父未死而有二十五孙。是以人民众而货财寡，事力劳而供养薄，故民争，虽倍赏累罚而不免于乱"。这是为什么今天人民必须辛苦工作，乃至需要与人争斗才能活下来，这种争斗的蔓延使厚赏重罚变得必要。因此，"夫古今异俗，新故异备。如欲以宽缓之政，治急世之民，犹无辔策而御悍马，此不知之患也"。他所指的危险的无知的人可能是被他列为五蠹之一（甚至是之首）的儒。如我们这里可见及他处可见，韩非子的关注焦点明显不是道德是否存在与真实，而是道德是否有效。事实上，他承认我们人类是能够善待他人的。在《五蠹》篇里，他指出："穰岁之秋疏客必食"。但在这句话前，他指出："饥岁之春幼弟不饷"。在本文中，韩非子有力地展示了道德的无效，并论述说，为了管理民众的行为，法律方式和制度安排是关键，而专注于道德培养是危险的误导。为了让法律与制度的安排有效，民众必须被平等地对待，而他们的贵贱与亲疏不应被考虑。官爵的授予应该纯粹基于一个人在农、战中的成就。通过这些，韩非子支持一个建立在平等基础上的国家（君王除外），以及一个基于具体、实在的成就（割了多少脑袋和割了多少庄稼）的、允许向上流动的贤能政治。用这些成就而非道德来衡量贤能是因为，道德不仅无效，它还很混乱，会被任意解释，从而也就制造了不同的权力中心因而使国家不稳定。这里包含着韩非子的另外一个反对儒家德治的论辩。道德在大的共同体里不可避免地会变得多元，因此就不可避免地变得无效。在《显学》一章中，韩非子指出孔子、墨子死后，"儒分为八，墨离为三"。儒墨两家"俱道尧舜"，但是"取舍不同"，给出的政治建议常常截然相反。可是我们无法审核三千年以前尧舜的原意，而在这种无参验的情况下，我们也无法断定哪一家的解读（或每家里哪一派的解读）是必定对的。在《韩非子·五蠹》中，韩非子也指出，"微妙之言上智之所难知也"，因此它（比如儒家的道德形上学或后来的宋明理学乃至新儒家所看重的心性之学）无法"为众人法"，因为"民无从识"这些"上智之所难知"的道德论说。与此相对，智慧德行有如孔子这样的"天下圣人"不过有"服役者七十人"而已，而"下主"的鲁哀公"南面君国，境内之民莫敢不臣"。

在笔者上面提供的概述里，我们已经可以看到韩非子有很多洞见是为后来的西方近现代乃至当代的思想家所分享的。他给出了大的共同体里为什么道德价值之多元不可避免的原因（这种理解可能不充分），也解释了使用简单与普遍可理解的东西（比如赏罚）的必要。[①]由于他有这种理解，他可以说与当代自由主义思想家罗尔斯是比肩的。[②] 与之相对，很多西方近现代思想家简单地歌颂那些通常认为是卑微的东西（比如短期的物质利益），而没有理解我们为什么不得不求助于它们的原因，而有些人甚至走向极端，否认价值的实在。与他们意见相左，但是可以说是与他们一样头脑简单的是很多现代道德保守主义者，他们哀叹现代人的道德沦丧、道德相对主义、道德虚无主义，并攻击那些他们以为推动和歌颂了这些潮流的近现代思想家，好像这些所谓的推动者造就了今人的道德沦丧，好像如果这些"推动者"能被保守主义者的圣战所摧毁的话，那么世界的秩序就会得以重建。但是，尽管韩非子与那些比较复杂和深刻的自由主义思想家的论述有相近之处，然而韩非子并没有给自由与权利留下太多空间。相反，他论辩说统治者需要用那些每个人都不得不听从的东西（即赏罚）来控制所有人。（当然，他关注的是控制人的可以参验的行为，但并不在意控制人内在的想法。这反而比那些"狠斗私字一闪念"的道德学派还要宽容些。）但是，如果我们想想西方近代早期政治哲学家比如马基雅维利和霍布斯对控制的强调，他的这种取向也许会显得不那么扭曲。[③] 更重要的是，他确实有一个合理的担忧，对他来讲，价值的多元似乎会带来国家的不稳定。他的这一担忧似乎也为他所处的时代乃至中国（及世界）历史的大部分现象所支持。如果是这样的话，那么不是韩非子，而是自由主义思想家欠我们一个解释，解释我们为什么现在可以同时有多元性和稳定。这恰恰是罗尔斯在他的晚期哲学里试图回答的（Rawls, 1996）。但是，他的回答是否充分是需要考究的。比如，罗尔斯也许忽视了一点，即现代技术的发展（比如通信）使得国家紧紧控制地方乃至个人事务（以防止动荡）成为可能。也就是说，当今自由民主国家所享有的自由与多元也许是建立在韩非子渴望的但是无法想象的高度中央集权的基础上的。因此，自由可能确实是西方现代性的一个独立贡献，但是我们可

[①] 参见 Jeremy Bentham, *An Introduction to the Principles of Morals and Legislation*, New York: Hafner Press, 1949。该书开宗明义的说法，即痛苦和快乐是人类的唯一的和最高的主子（Bentham, 1949: 1）。

[②] 参见 Rawls, John., *Politisal Liberalism*, New York: Columbia University Press, 1996。

[③] 马基雅维利是不是一个现代思想家、是不是第一个现代思想家，这是一个有争议的问题。参见 Ivantoe, "Han Fei Zi and Meral Self-Cultivation," *Journal of Chinese Philosophy*, forthcoming, 2011。

以拥有自由的这个事实同时也是对韩非子的驳斥与辩白。只有在韩非子的担忧被他所不能预见的技术发展解决了以后，他所忽视的自由才成为可能。类似的，他没有给出对统治者的（除了国家兴亡之外）的任何制约，这使得他不同于自由主义思想家。但是，与西方很多近现代思想家类似，韩非子为法律的绝对权威和法律面前（除了统治者之外）人人平等辩护，因此为现代的宪政种下了种子。①

五 韩非子、儒家以及韩非子与自由主义者边缘化道德的问题

因为韩非子的思想对我们理解现代性是如此的关键，所以考察他的思想如何与其他学派的思想互动就可能是一个卓有成效的工作。一个有趣且重要的问题是它与《老子》的关系。但是这个问题应该单独处理，并且也不与本文主题紧密相关。在这一节里，我会专注于韩非子与儒家政治哲学的关系问题。

像上面提到的，韩非子曾向儒家学派的重要思想家荀子学习过（他还可能向很多其他学派的学者学习过）。《韩非子》中的有些段落明显有《荀子》的影子。但是，儒家是韩非子批评的主要对象。与《老子》的世界观一致，韩非子也论辩说统治者应该遵循自然（"法"或者"道纪"），并且认为人为的东西（包括儒家的道德）只会毁了一个国家。韩非子也令人信服地论证了在一个广土众民的国家里，基于微妙与深刻的哲学教导的道德不可避免地是多元的，因此就不能成为统一一个国家的政治系统的基础。也就是说，儒家的建立一个道德国家的理想虽然美好，但却是彻底地不切实际与无效。这里的结论似乎是，如果我们希望保持他思想的完整，我们就无法用儒家思想改造韩非子。但是，儒家思想里有无空间来采取韩非子的一些主张，并加以修正呢？

对于这个问题，笔者认为，儒家不仅可能吸收韩非子的一些主张，并且儒家还有必要这么做。如上所述，春秋战国时的一个关键问题在于基于出身的封建等级制度的消逝与能够直接管理一个领土越来越大、人口越来越多的

---

① 参见 Schneider, Henrique, "Legalism: Chinese-Style. Constitutionalism?", *Journal of Chinese Philosophy*, forthcoming, 2011。

国家的政体的需要。对这个问题，儒家的解决办法是重建等级社会，但是这个等级社会不再基于出身与血缘，而是基于儒家道德（包括官员的能力）。但是，在韩非子看来，儒家德治或礼治的理想是基于已经消逝的政治现实之上的，因此就不再在一个新时代里相关。我想，儒家对这个一针见血的挑战有两种回答。儒家可以鼓吹回到小国寡民时代（与《老子》和卢梭的建议类似）。但是，如果我们不认为让韩非子所处的或我们所处的现代社会回到小国寡民状态是可能的或可欲的（Desirable），并且如果我们还想让儒家的一套政治哲学在现有大多数国家广土众民的现代世界还适用，我们就必须正面回答韩非子的挑战。我的一点初步的想法是儒家可以采纳韩非子的一些处理广土众民的大国不可或缺的制度上与法律上的设计，但是儒家会以儒家理想做这些设计的指引。比如，虽然在理想状况下，孔子希望不用刑罚，但是在非理想的世界里，他并不反对刑罚的应用。①

综观中国历史，与韩非子的初衷（以及他的思想体系）相违，儒法互补可能是历朝政府的指导哲学。比如，儒家从支持更适合"小国寡民"的举孝廉到接受更适合大国的科举就是对韩非子思想的一个整合的努力。传统中国所采用的官僚体系源自韩非子的设计，但是，这个体系又有不可否认的儒家色彩。那么，我们可以问：这个混合有多成功？如果它是成功的话，韩非子的政治哲学就必然有缺陷。特别是，他认为，在大国里支持儒家价值就不可避免地毁了这个国家，这个信念就会成问题。但是我们也看到了他的价值多元与德治无效的论辩的力量。儒家因素可以渗透到传统中国政治制度中，并且能为持有不同的整全（Comprehensive）观念（比如佛道）的人们所接受，也许就暗示着有些儒家因素足以成为拥有多元价值的民众的"重叠共识"（Overlapping Consensus）的。有如儒家因素也许修正了只用韩非子的想法的局限，从而强化了中国传统社会一样，发展类似的因素也许对今天自由民主社会的局限也会起到有用的修正。

---

① 在《论语》的2.3、12.19与13.6节和《大学》的第三章中，孔子讨论了理想的或规范性的案例。在这些案例中，刑罚变得或应该变得不必要。但是，在13.3节中，他指出法律手段应被礼乐所指导，这就暗含了他并不反对应用法律手段。对他在13.3节中的表面上不同的态度的一种解释是说孔子在这节中是在讲一个现实的案例。在这个现实世界中，众人还没能够在没有约束的情况下自愿地遵循礼乐教化。

参考文献

Bai, Tongdong (2009), "How to Rule without Taking Unnatural Actions (无为而治): A Comparative Study of the Political Philosophy of the Laozi", *Philosophy East and West*, Vol. 59, No. 4/October, 2009, 481-502. 【其中文修改版收于《旧邦新命——古今中西参照下的古典儒家政治哲学》(第五章)】。

Bentham, Jeremy (1949), *An Introduction to the Principles of Morals and Legislation*. New York: Hafner Press.

陈奇猷 (2000),《韩非子新校注》,上海古籍出版社。

Goldin, Paul (2011), "Persistent Misconceptions about Chinese 'Legalism'", *Journal of Chinese Philosophy*, forthcoming.

Ivanhoe (2011), "Han Fei Zi and Moral Self-Cultivation", *Journal of Chinese Philosophy*, forthcoming.

钱穆 (1996),《国史大纲》,商务印书馆。

钱穆 (2005),《中国历代政治得失》,三联书店。

Rawls, John (1996), *Political Liberalism*. New York: Columbia University Press.

Rousseau, Jean-Jacques (1978), *On the Social Contract with Geneva Manuscript and Political Economy*. Edited by Roger D. Masters and Translated by Judith R. Masters. New York: St. Martin's Press.

Schneider, Henrique (2011), "Legalism: Chinese-Style Constitutionalism?", *Journal of Chinese Philosophy*, forthcoming.

Han Fei Zi and Modernity

Bai Tongdong[*]

I Han Fei Zi's Times: A Period of China's 'Modernization'?

On the issue of the significance and relevance of traditional Chinese philosophy, those who value Chinese philosophy often claim the distinctiveness of Chinese thought from Western thought. But some critics often counter this claim by saying that Chinese thought is only distinctive from modern Western thought, and is in fact quite similar to ancient Western thought. Thus, the distinction between Chinese and Western thoughts is portrayed as a distinction between ancient and modern ones. In this article, through some preliminary studies of Han Fei Zi (c. 280 −233 B. C. E.), I will argue that, during the so-called Spring and Autumn and Warring States Periods (for short SAWS) (roughly from 722 B. C. E. to

---

[*] Bai Tongdong was born in China in 1970. He was awarded his doctoral degree in 2004 at the Philosophy Department of Boston University. He holds a position of professor of philosophy at the School of Philosophy of Fudan University. He has published two books and numerous book chapters and research articles including *A New Mission of an Old State: The Contemporary and Comparative Relevance of Classical Confucian Political Philosophy* (2009) and *Tension of Reality: Einstein, Bohr, and Pauli in the EPR Debates* (2009). He is now the vice president of Association of Chinese Philosophers in America His current research interests include issues in philosophy of science, Chinese philosophy and political philosophy.

222 B. C. E.), China already experienced the transition to (some form of) 'modernity', a transition that happened after the 15th century (if not later) in the West. Many of the 'hundred schools' of SAWS were actually addressing the problem of 'modernity' in various ways, although most of them might have not been conscious of it. I will then argue that Han Fei Zi was perhaps the first 'modern' thinker in human history in that, among thinkers of SAWS, he understood the nature of China's transition to modernity the best. If these speculations are true, then the "classical" thoughts of SAWS in 'ancient' China can be easily relevant to today's world, as both they and we are dealing with the same problem, the problem of modernity. The discussion here can also shed light on the nature of modernity. Then, by criticizing some of Han Fei Zi's ideas, I hope to offer criticisms of some dominant ideas of today.

Han Fei Zi lived toward the end of the so-called 'Warring States Period' of Chinese history. This period, together with the earlier 'Spring and Autumn Period', were times of social and political turmoil and transformation. Before these periods, in the so-called Western Zhou dynasty, the political structure was a feudalistic, pyramid-like, and expanding system. The kings of Zhou (especially of the first generations) enfeoffed their relatives, loyal and competent ministers (many of whom were also the king's relatives), nobles of the past Shang dynasty, etc. These people had become the princes of their own principalities. Some of these principalities were in the remote areas of the empire, and, in a way, they were colonies in otherwise 'barbaric' areas (Qian 1996, 57). The establishment and expansion of these de-facto colonies thus helped to broaden the imperial reach. When the principalities expanded (by encroaching on the surrounding 'barbaric' land), their rulers did the same as the kings did, enfeoffing their own relatives and ministers. In the entire empire, the king ruled over princes (of various ranks), princes over lesser lords, and these lords over people in their fiefs. These fiefs were small in terms of both their sizes and their populations. On each level, one master ruled over a limited number of subjects, and this makes it possible for the master to rule through personal influence and personal contact. But this hierarchical system was collapsing during the aforementioned periods, partly because the familial bounds had been weakening after so many generations, and partly because the empire expanded to its then limit and infighting became inevitable. In the Spring and Autumn period, the king of Zhou was given nominal homage only, unlike how the throne was treated before, and eventually he became one local lord, a very weak one at that, among many. Finally, the boundaries of each principality were not respected anymore, and, through wars and conquests, seven large states emerged. This was the beginning of the Warring States period. In these periods, the rulers (former princes under the king of Zhou) had to rule directly over states that kept becoming larger and more populous, and the survival of these states and their rulers within their own states depended upon their physical strength alone.

The transitions these Chinese states experienced have some uncanny similarities to the European transitions from the Middle Ages to (Western) modernity. The political system of the Middle Ages was also a feudalistic, pyramid-like structure, and it was collapsing during the transitions. The emerging large and populous states were fighting ('warring') for domination. Of course, differences remain. For example, there was no secular throne in medieval Europe that enjoyed a status as high, longstanding and stable as the kings of Zhou. The Papacy was relatively stable, but whether it was an explicit overlord-ship is debatable. A driving economic force in China's transitions was agricultural revolution, which might have been less drastic than the commercial revolution that happened around the beginning of the Western transitions and is certainly dwarfed by the Industrial Revolution that came toward the end of the Western transitions. The European 'Warring States' didn't manage to achieve the kind of unity the Chinese states achieved (although they did manage to wage two 'World Wars', among many other, smaller-scale wars). Nevertheless, the similarities between the transitions in SAWS and the Western modernization are clear and profound. Gone with the feudal system were the noble classes and their ways of life. For example, as the Chinese historian Qian Mu (钱穆) pointed out, compared to wars in the Spring and Autumn period, where the feudal system was tottering but still in place, the wars in the Warring States period were downright brutal and ugly (Qian 1996, 88 -89). The military became plebeianized, and so codes of conduct of the nobles vanished. Wars served the need of an economic struggle for resources, and became a brutal sport of head-chopping. In Europe rose Napoleon and his people's war. In a way, we are still dealing with the aftermath of this change. For example, the Geneva Convention can be compared with codes of conduct among the knights, and it is thus difficult to apply it to all soldiers in the wars of people, which might help to explain the difficulty for its being followed universally even today. In people's war, everyone is involved, thus making the distinction between the military and innocent civilians (and the related issues) very murky. Another major change in SAWS was the abolishment of the exclusive inheritance of land by the noble class and the old communal system, and the emergence of free market of land. In the West, there was the notorious English enclosure movement.

The question now becomes: what do these similarities mean? They may have suggested that the changes China experienced in SAWS were a form of 'modernization'. This speculation may shed some light on the nature of modernization and modernity, and on the divide between 'the ancients' and the 'moderns'. In the feudal systems of China and Europe, on each level of the pyramid, there were only a few hundred or a few thousand people. That is, on each level, there was a de facto small community of few people. The states that emerged after the transitions, however, are large and populous. This might appear to be an insignificant change, but in politics, 'size matters'. For one thing, the noble codes of conduct and virtues that are based upon a comprehensive and shared conception of the Good—which are possible when the community is small—cannot be universally applicable to a large community anymore. Here comes an inevitable pluralism of values, a fundamental fact of 'modernity' both some Western modern thinkers and Han Fei Zi insightfully grasp. Then, the question becomes: what can replace virtues as a glue of the state? This is a question both Western modern thinkers and Chinese thinkers during SAWS try to answer. A related question common to both is that, with the pyramid-like feudal structure gone, how do we have the ruling class and a new ruling structure? The answers to this question, both in the West (for example, the Enlightenment thinkers who advocate equality and mass education) and in 'ancient' China (for example, the Confucians who recognize the equal potentials of all human beings and also advocate some form of mass education), seem to be quite similar: an upward mobility that makes it possible for former commoners to rise through the ranks. But thinkers differ on how this upward mobility is realized (for example, Han Fei Zi doesn't like the idea of Confucian education, and prefers a military-and farming-based meritocracy). Thus, similarities of thoughts between Chinese thinkers of SAWS and Western modern thinkers may reflect the fact that they are facing with similar problems. For example, in an article, I argue that there are profound similarities between the Laozi, a work of political philosophy (among other things) of SAWS, and Rousseau. They both see the consequences of 'modernization', which they consider very bad, and thus call for a return to a stage where there are only small states with few people (Bai 2009).

To sum up, I have argued that what China experienced during SAWS (a few hundred years before the common era) may have been a forerunner of Western modernization, and I will argue later in this article that Han Fei Zi is perhaps the first 'modern' thinker in that he was the first thinker during SAWS who was consciously aware of the nature of the change of his times. If the first half of my thesis holds, then it is simply false to say that Chinese political thoughts of SAWS belong to the ancient in the ancient-modern divide. In this sense, Hegel and Max Weber are wrong about their dismissive evaluation of traditional Chinese thought. Many contemporary Chinese thinkers have done even worse when they dismiss traditional Chinese thoughts as 'garbage from two thousand years of feudalism and authoritarianism'. For leaving the emotionally charged term 'garbage' aside, the past two thousand some years of Chinese history since Qin Dynasty (the first dynasty after SAWS) was neither feudalistic nor purely authoritarian. ①Moreover, even thinkers such as Karl Jaspers are missing a crucial difference of traditional Chinese thought from their contemporaries in India, Greece, and elsewhere in the world when they lump them together as thoughts of the 'Axial Age', so are contemporary sympathizers of Confucianism such as Heiner Roetz who also label Confucianism during SAWS as thoughts of the Axial Age.

---

① The political regimes of ancient China since SAWS may have been a result of tension between an authoritarian ruler (the emperor) and an elite ruling class of—for much of Chinese history—Confucians. See Qian 2005 for more detailed discussion.

To be clear, the transitions, both in China and in Europe, are long and messy. During SAWS, many states still stuck in the old ways. It was only the state of Qin that carried out a distinctive modernization program, and the state of Han (Han Fei Zi's home state)'s failure to do so was a major factor shaping Han Fei's outlook on politics.① In Europe, feudal elements existed in Russia into the early twentieth century.② It might be objected that some aforementioned phenomena in Europe happened in late modern Europe or even in contemporary Europe. But this might have meant that the transitions from the ancients to the moderns take time. After all, it took about 500 years for China to go through the transitions, and we can even argue that many historical events in China after SAWS are still responses to challenges posed by 'modernity'.

II Han Fei Zi's Political Philosophy?

Before we go into the studies of the book Han Fei Zi in order to see if it contains insights into modernity, let me first address a question: Is the book Han Fei Zi a work of political philosophy and its author a political philosopher? In his criticisms of A. C. Graham's description of Han Fei Zi's thoughts as an 'amoral science of statecraft', the American scholar Paul Goldin correctly points out the differences between the writings of Han Fei Zi and those of Hobbes and Locke (Goldin 2011). For one thing, the former sometimes offers brazen advice to rulers or even the ministers about how to protect their welfare, something, presumably, one can't find in Hobbes's and Locke's writings. But we can find similar advice in another text that is commonly considered a text of political philosophy—maybe even a founding text in modern political philosophy, Machiavelli's The Prince, and traces of advice like the aforementioned one can be found in other texts in Western political philosophy.

It cannot be denied, however, that the Han Fei Zi and many other texts in the history of Chinese thoughts are often different from texts of political philosophy in

---

① I thank Peter Moody for reminding me of this point.
② I thank Al Martinich for reminding me of this point.

the Western tradition. The former are often written not for the purpose of purely theoretical discourse, but are concrete advice to the rulers or policy debates with other ministers or counselors. As Qian Mu pointed out (2005, 21), in the post-Qin imperial times, perhaps thanks to the Confucian heritage of upwardly mobile meritocracy, the intellectual elite (shi ren 士人) often become part of the ruling elite, sharply different from the pre-SAWS times and the Middle Ages (as well as much of European modernity) in Europe. The Chinese intellectual elite in the past could thus put their political thoughts and theories into practice, and have little need to put them into theories that are detached from practice. (What Qian Mu didn't point out is that this reality (the deep political involvement of the Chinese intellectual elite) also made them lack of leisure that is instrumental to theoretical pursuit.) In fact, Rousseau made a point that supports Qian Mu's. He wrote in the opening paragraphs of On the Social Contract,

I shall be asked if I am a prince or a legislator, to write on politics. I answer that I am neither, and that is why I do so. If I were a prince or a legislator, I should not waste time in saying what wants doing; I should do it, or hold my peace. (Rousseau 1978, 46)

In contrast, many political writers in Chinese history were in the center of politics, and it was already the case during SAWS. In particular, while Machiavelli wrote The Prince for a prince, Han Fei Zi was a prince! If the account in the Shiji (史记) can be trusted,[1] the king of Qin who later unified China and became 'the first emperor', after reading works by Han Fei, even waged a war against the Han Fei's home state just for the sake of having him in the king's company—a fortune that might be the envy of Machiavelli and many other Western political philosophers.

Of course, this defense only explains why the writings of many Chinese political writers are different from those in the Western tradition, and implicitly suggests that, if given opportunity (or, more accurately put, the lack of opportunity in real-world politics), these Chinese writers could have written works that bear more resemblance in style to the writings in the Western tradition. But it doesn't

---

[1] Sima Qian (司马迁), *Shiji* (史记), Vol. 63 (老子韩非列传).

show that these writings in the Chinese tradition are those of political philosophy. However, if we take philosophy as a reflexive enterprise (and political philosophy as a system of reflections on political matters), we can see that the Han Fei Zi does contain this kind of thinking. To make up his lack of leisurely speculations (as we have seen, this leisure Western political philosophers enjoy might have been involuntary), Han Fei Zi and many other political writers of ancient China had first-hand experiences of the political reality on the highest level and could thus use these observations in their reflections on politics. I am not denying that the Han Fei Zi contains a lot of 'dark arts' of politics—indeed, this book might be a masterpiece of this genre, but am only arguing that it also contains thoughts that rightfully belong to the realm of political philosophy.

Ⅲ Death of Han Fei Zi and the Fate of the 'Legalist' Teachings

Another attack on the significance of Han Fei Zi's ideas is centered around his fate and the fate of the people and the state that shared his thoughts. In spite of his profound understanding of politics, Han Fei Zi eventually became a victim of political intrigue. Li Si (李斯), a former fellow student of Han Fei Zi under the Confucian master Xun Zi (荀子) and a high official of the state of Qin at that time, probably felt threatened by the presence of Han Fei Zi. He persuaded the king of forcing Han Fei Zi to commit 'suicide'. It is somewhat ironic that the argument Li Si gave, according to Shiji, is not 'Legalistic' but more Confucian in tenor. For he argued that Han Fei Zi was a prince of the state of Han, and it is only human (and natural) that in wars for dominance, Han Fei Zi would always vie for the state of Han. It seems that Li Si didn't believe, as Han Fei Zi argued in his book, that people can be made loyal through rewards and punishments. Li Si himself didn't fare much better. He was brutally executed by the Second Emperor of Qin. Indeed, Lord Shang (商鞅), a crucial figure who made the state of Qin the strongest among all warring states through policies Han Fei Zi may have approved of, also died an unnatural death after the king who appreciated him died. The state of Qin that also practiced policies of Han Fei Zi's liking eventually unified

China and became the Qin dynasty, but it didn't last long. All these historical facts have given infinite pleasure to those who don't particularly like Han Fei Zi or the 'Legalists', in particular, the Confucians. They use these to show the inadequacy or just the evil nature of Han Fei Zi's political philosophy.①

Although highly sympathetic to Confucian political philosophy, I must confess that I find these shots at Han Fei Zi and his political philosophy a bit cheap. Han Fei Zi showed his deep understanding of the difficulty of having the king's ears (Chapters 3 and 12 of the Han Fei Zi), and some argue that his actions failed to follow his understanding.② But his tragic death may have merely shown the sheer difficulty of having king's ears that, under certain circumstances,③ even transcends the mastery of a master of this art. Generally speaking, the failure of one's following one's own philosophy, ironical as it is, doesn't falsify one's philosophy. As for the fate of Qin, it is possible that the political changes which the Qin dynasty brought about were too drastic for the country to digest at a short period of time. It is true that the 'tyrannical Qin' (baoqin 暴秦) was overturned shortly after its founding. But the following dynasty, the Han dynasty, first tried to go back to the 'good old ways' of feudal system, and this attempt led to its own trouble (the revolt of the seven kings (qi wang zhi luan 七王之乱)). It eventually went back to the political system, with some revisions, of the Qin dynasty, a system that bears a lot of arrangements suggested in the Han Fei Zi. This system had been largely followed throughout Chinese history. Indeed, many apparently Confucian arrangements, such as keju (科举), may have contained the legacy of Han Fei Zi.④ There are many insightful reflections on the merits and problems with Han Fei Zi's political philosophy and the role of his political teachings in the history of Chinese politics by Chinese political thinkers in the past,⑤ and the evaluations of them are a demanding project. I am here only

---

① See, for example, Zhang Dingwen (张鼎文)'s remark in Chen 2000, 1224.
② See Sima Qian, op. cit., and Chen 2000, 1226 and 1257.
③ See, for example, Wang Shizhen (王世贞)'s account in Chen 2000, 1228.
④ Ivanhoe in Ivanhoe 2011 seems to share my evaluation on this matter.
⑤ In the volume edited by Chen Qiyou (2000), there is an excellent collection of this kind of reflections.

calling for charity when we are dealing with his philosophy and its fate in traditional China.

Ⅳ Han Fei Zi: the First Modern Thinker?

Now, let me give an outline of some main ideas of Han Fei Zi's that are related to the issues of modernity. To be clear, the following is merely an outline, and a closer study of Han Fei Zi, a profound political thinker of human history, demands much more space than this article contains. First, as I mentioned in the first section, I think that a key feature of modernity is the collapse of the feudal, pyramid-like structure due to the increase of population, and expansion of feudal states into 'barbaric' areas being near the limit of the time and thus the increase of infighting over increasingly limited resources. In its place is the rise of populous and large state (s). In the famous 'Five Vermin' chapter (Chapter 49 of the Han Fei Zi), he demonstrated his understanding of these changes. For example, he points out a crucial difference between the "ancients" and the 'moderns:' 'In ancient times … the people were few and there was a surplus of goods,' while in 'modern' times, due to the natural growth of human population ('today it is not too many for one father to have five sons … so when the grandfather is not dead yet, he already has twenty-five grandsons'), 'the people are numerous and the goods and wealth are scarce'.[①] This is why in "modern" times people have to work hard, and even struggle for survival, against others, a situation which makes rich rewards and harsh punishments necessary. Failing to appreciate this and other differences between the ancients and the moderns, those who 'wish to use the government of generous and relaxed times to rule the people of chaotic times are like wishing to stop a runaway horse without using reins and whips. This is the danger of ignorance'. The dangerously ignorant people he has in mind may have been the Confucians (who are one of the five vermin, and perhaps the most vicious one of the five, according to Han Fei Zi). As is seen

---

[①] The translations of the *Han Fei Zi* in this article are mine. For another English translation, see Watson 1964.

here and many other places in the Han Fei Zi, his focus is clearly the effectiveness of (Confucian) virtues, and not their reality. In fact, he acknowledges that we human beings are able to be kind to each other. Again, in the 'Five Vermin' chapter, he says, 'in the fall of a year of plenty, it is considered necessary to feed even a stranger' (Chapter 49 of the Han Fei Zi). But right before this claim, he says, 'in the spring of a year of famine, even one's little brother is not fed'. Throughout this and other chapters, Han Fei Zi forcefully demonstrates the ineffectiveness of morality, and argues that, to regulate people's behaviors, legal means and institutional arrangements are the key, and the obsession with moral cultivation is a dangerous distraction. In order for these arrangements to be effective, people have to be treated equally, with no regard to their social status and relations to the ruler and ministers. People should be offered various ranks purely based upon their achievements in wars and in farming. Through these, Han Fei Zi advocates a state of equality (minus the ruler who is above all) and a meritocracy that allows upward mobility strictly based upon concrete achievements (how many heads one cut off in wars and how many crops one 'cut off' in farming). For virtues are not only ineffective, but they are also confusing and subjected to arbitrary interpretations, thus creating different centers of powers and destabilizing the state. Here lies another argument Han Fei Zi offered against Confucian rule of the virtuous. For virtues will inevitably become pluralistic in large communities, and thus inevitably become ineffective. In the 'Eminent Schools of Learning' chapter (Chapter 50), Han Fei Zi points out that after Confucius and Mozi (the founder of another eminent school of his times, the Mohist school) died, their schools were divided into eight and three factions respectively. These two competing schools (Confucian and Mohist) both claim to follow the teachings of the sage rulers Yao and Shun, but they offer opposite teachings. But there is simply no evidence which people can agree on and is used to determine the thoughts of which school are genuine followers of the teachings of sage kings, who died thousands of years ago. In the previous chapter, Han Fei Zi also argues that the words of the wise are so subtle that even the wisest can't fully understand. Then, how can they be used to guide and regulate the masses? In contrast, while wise and virtuous as Confucius could only have some seventy followers, a less than mediocre ruler of Confucius's home state of Lu could commend the obedience of his whole state (through the political institution under the ruler's control).

In the sketch I've offered about Han Fei Zi's arguments, we can already see many insights later shared by Western modern thinkers and even today's liberal thinkers. He offers reasons—adequately or not—for the inevitable pluralism of values in large communities and for the necessary use of things simple and universally understandable, such as reward and punishment.[1] Because of this understanding, he is a sophisticated thinker on par with contemporary liberal thinkers such as John Rawls.[2] In contrast, many Western modern thinkers celebrate what is commonly considered base (such as short-term material interests) without understanding why we have to appeal to them, and some even go to the extreme to deny the reality of virtues. Opposite to them but on par with them in terms of simplicity are many modern moral conservatives who bemoan the moral decadence, relativism, and even nihilism of the moderns, and attack those modern thinkers who they believe promote and celebrate these trends, as if these alleged promoters were the driving force of modern moral decadence, and as if the order of the world would be restored if these promoters were crushed by the conservatives' moral and philosophical crusades. But in spite of the fact that he might be close to the more sophisticated and profound liberal thinkers of Western modernity, Han Fei Zi didn't leave much room for freedom and liberties that are valued by liberal thinkers, and argued that, instead of tolerating different views of life, the rulers should use what everyone must bow down to—that is, rewards and punishments, especially the latter—to control all. (Of course, he is only keen on controlling people's actions, which are observable, and are rather indifferent to their inner thoughts. In this sense, he might be more tolerant than the moralists who wouldn't allow a flash of bad thoughts.) But his direction may appear less devious, if we considered the directions Machiavelli, Hobbes, and some other

---

[1] C. f. Jeremy Bentham's opening statement in his *An Introduction to the Principles of Morals and Legislation* that pain and pleasure are the sole and supreme masters of human beings (Bentham 1949, 1).

[2] C. f., among others, Rawls 1996.

early modern Western thinkers offered.① More importantly, he did have a legitimate concern: it seems to him that pluralism of values brings about instability of the state, and his observation was well supported by the facts of his times and perhaps much of the Chinese (and world) history. If this is the case, it is the liberals that owe us an explanation of why we can have diversity and stability at the same time in the contemporary world. This question is the central concern of Rawls's later philosophy (c. f. Rawls 1996). But whether his answer is adequate or not is open to questions. For one thing, Rawls might have ignored the role of modern technology (communications, etc.) that makes it possible for the state to control the local affairs and its citizens' personal affairs tightly (so as to prevent instability). That is, the liberties and pluralism today's liberal democracies enjoy may have been built upon, ironically, the centralization of power the level of which was unthinkable for and desired by Han Fei Zi. Therefore, the idea of freedom and liberties might indeed be a new contribution by moderns from the West, but the fact that we can have it today is both a rebuttal to Han Fei Zi and, meanwhile, a vindication of Han Fei Zi. Liberties become possible only after his concern with stability is answered with technological developments he couldn't foresee at his days. Similarly, he didn't offer any check and balance against the ruler (other than the success and failure of the state), which made him different from liberal thinkers, but, like many Western modern thinkers, Han Fei Zi argued for the absolute authority of laws and the equality before laws (minus the ruler), thus planting seeds for contemporary constitutionalism.②

V Han Fei Zi, Confucianism, and Problems with Han Fei Zi's/Liberals' Sidelining of Virtues

Since Han Fei Zi's thought is so central to our understanding of modernity, it may be fruitful to see how his thought interacts with (challenges and is challenged

---

① Whether Machiavelli is a modern thinker, or even the first Western modern thinker who introduced the modern concept of the state is debatable. C. f. Ivanhoe 2011.
② C. f. Schneider 2011.

by) thoughts of other schools. An intriguing question is its relation to that of the Laozi.① But it deserves a separate treatment and is not closely related to the theme of this article. In this section, I will focus on the relations between Han Fei Zi's philosophy and Confucianism.

As was mentioned, Han Fei Zi studied with, probably among others, Xun Zi, an important figure in the Confucian school, and there are passages in the Han Fei Zi which echo well with some passages in the Xun Zi. But Confucianism is a main target of Han Fei Zi's criticisms. Consistent with the worldview in the Laozi, Han Fei Zi argues that rulers should follow what is natural (fa 法 or daoji 道纪), and thinks that what is human, including Confucian virtues, can only doom the state. As is discussed in the previous section, Han Fei Zi also convincingly argues that in a large and populous state, virtues that are based upon subtle and profound philosophical teachings are inevitably pluralistic and thus cannot be the basis of the political system that unifies a state. That is, the Confucian dream of building up a virtuous state, though beautiful, is totally ineffective and unrealistic. The conclusion seems to be that there is no place of Confucian revisions in Han Fei Zi's political philosophy if we wish to hold onto the integrity of his philosophy. But what about the other way around? That is, is there room for Confucianism to adopt suggestions by Han Fei Zi and improve on them?

My own idea on this question is that, not only is there a possibility for Confucianism to assimilate suggestions by Han Fei Zi, but also there is a need for Confucians to do so. As is previously mentioned, a key issue during SAWS lies in the disappearance of the feudal hierarchy based upon birth, and the emerging need of a new polity that can directly govern an ever larger and ever more populous state. The Confucian solution to this problem is to re-establish a hierarchy that is not based upon birth, but upon Confucian virtues (including the competence of the officials). But Han Fei Zi challenged this solution by arguing that the Confucian ideal of rule by virtue or rule by rituals (li zhi 礼治) is based upon a political reality that had disappeared, and was thus no more relevant in his times. I think that Confucians could offer two answers to this incisive challenge. First,

---

① C. f. Bai 2009.

Confucians can call for a return to the earlier stage of 'small states with few people' (xiao guo gua min 小国寡民), as the Laozi (and its Western counterpart Rousseau) did. ① If, however, we don't consider it possible or desirable for the society at Han Fei Zi's times or the society we have today to return to this primordial stage, and if we wish Confucianism to be politically relevant at a time when states are large and populous (which, as is argued in the first section of this article, is a fundamental fact of modern states) we must directly answer Han Fei Zi's challenge. I think that Confucians can adopt some of the institutional and legal mechanisms devised by Han Fei Zi, mechanisms indispensable to handling the political affairs of a large and populous state, but guide them with Confucian ideals. For example, although, ideally, Confucius wished to do without the use of punishment, he would nevertheless be open to the use of it and other legal and ritual tools in a non-ideal world. ②

Throughout Chinese history, this hybrid of Confucianism and Han Fei Zi's philosophy (contrary to the wish of Han Fei Zi and perhaps inconsistent with his philosophical system) may have been the guiding political philosophy of the government. For example, from advocating the political selection process based upon 'recommending the filial and the uncorrupt' (ju xiao lian 举孝廉) that is more suitable to a small state, Confucians later accept the national civil exam system (ke ju 科举) that is more suitable to a large and populous state. Indeed, the bureaucratic structure of China's past comes from the design of Han Fei Zi and, at the same time, has an undeniably Confucian touch. Now, the question becomes: how successful is this hybrid? If it is successful, then there has to be something wrong with Han Fei Zi's political philosophy. In particular, his conviction that the advocacy of Confucian virtues in a large state will inevitably doom the state has

---

① See Bai 2009.
② In 2. 3, 12. 19 and 13. 6 of the *Analects* and Chapter 4 of the *Great Learning*, Confucius discussed the ideal or normative case, in which punishments become or should become unnecessary. However, in 13. 3, he pointed out that legal means should be subjected to appropriate conducts and music, implying that he wouldn't object to the use of legal means. One way to interpret the apparently different attitude toward legal means shown in 13. 3 is to say that, in 13. 3, Confucius was talking about a realistic case, in which common people are not yet able to follow the codes of appropriate conducts without some form of legal and institutional enforcement.

to be questionable. But we also see the power of his argument of the inevitable pluralism of virtues and the ineffectiveness of rule by virtues. Then, maybe there is a thinner version of virtues that can be universally adopted and is critical to the well-being of the state. If this is a case, it will also post a challenge to Western liberals (for example, Rawls) who insist on the distinction between the private virtues (virtues of the ancients) and the public virtues (virtues of the moderns) and on restricting the former to the so-called 'background culture'. That is, there can be thinner virtues of 'the ancients' that exist in public arena, don't lead to oppression of pluralism, but are important to the functioning of the state. The fact that Confucian elements could permeate political regimes of 'ancient' China and be adopted by people with different comprehensive worldviews (Chinese Buddhists, Daoists, etc.) suggests that there might be Confucian elements thin enough to become 'overlapping consensus' among people with pluralistic values. Moreover, to counter Han Fei Zi's challenge that Confucians are trying to use subtle words even the wisest can't understand to guide the lives of the masses, Confucians from the very beginning have developed practices even the least educated and most disadvantaged could adopt. As Confucian elements might have strengthened China's societies in the past by correcting the excesses of strictly following Han Fei Zi's teachings, the development of these elements might offer useful corrections of the limits of liberal societies today.

Reference

Bai, Tongdong (2009), 'How to Rule without Taking Unnatural Actions (无为而治): A Comparative Study of the Political Philosophy of the Laozi', *Philosophy East and West*, Vol. 59, No. 4/October, 2009, 481 - 502。

Bentham, Jeremy (1949), *An Introduction to the Principles of Morals and Legislation*, New York: Hafner Press.

Chen, Qiyou (2000), *Han Fei Zi Xin Jiao Zhu* (《韩非子新校注》), Shanghai: Guji.

Goldin, Paul (2011), 'Persistent Misconceptions about Chinese "Legalism"', *Journal of Chinese Philosophy*, forthcoming.

Han Fei Zi (1991),《韩非子集解》,王先慎编,收于《诸子集成》,上海书店出版社。

Ivanhoe (2011), 'Han Fei Zi and Moral Self-Cultivation', *Journal of Chinese Philosophy*, forthcoming.

Qian, Mu (1996), *Guo Shi Da Gang* (《国史大纲》), Beijing: Shangwu Press.

Qian, Mu (2005),《中国历代政治得失》, Beijing: Sanlian Shudian.

Rawls, John (1996), *Political Liberalism*, New York, NY: Columbia University Press.

Rousseau, Jean-Jacques (1978), *On the Social Contract with Geneva Manuscript and Political Economy*, Edited by Roger D. Masters and translated by Judith R. Masters, New York, NY: St. Martin's Press.

Schneider, Henrique (2011), 'Legalism: Chinese-Style Constitutionalism?', *Journal of Chinese Philosophy*, forthcoming.

Watson, Burton (tr.) (1964), *Han Fei Tzu: Basic Writings*, New York, NY: Columbia University Press.

关于佛教与文化的反思

素旺那·沙他－阿南德[*]

引　言

当我们想要探寻佛教与文化的关系的时候，我们首先需要区分出佛教的至少三个主要时期。

第一个时期：佛陀涅磐之前的"佛教"；

第二个时期：佛陀涅磐之后直到阿育王以前的佛教；

第三个时期：阿育王以后的佛教。

我们都知道，佛教是一个"跨文化"或者说"跨习俗"工程，它的终极目标并不限于任何一种文化。生老病死的现象是普遍存在的。佛教使苦难终止（"灭"）的终极目标对所有人来说都有意义。但是，当我们想对佛教与文化的论题做进一步考察的时候，我们需要注意到在佛教传统的长期发展中的不同历史时期。

专业地讲，佛陀涅磐之前的佛教并不真的存在，而是只存在一种由乔达摩·悉达多提出的生活和修行方式。我们可以将这一时期的佛教看作一种改革主义运动，它为公元前500年左右盛行的印度教体系提供了另一种选择。

---

[*] 素旺那·沙他－阿南德（Suwanna Satha-Anand），女，1955年出生。在美国夏威夷大学获得博士学位。朱拉隆功大学人文学院哲学系教授，前主任。专业领域：佛教哲学、宗教与社会变迁。撰写、编辑和翻译了10部著作。泰国哲学和宗教学会前主席。

第二个时期的佛教是僧团佛教，在佛陀涅磐后约三个月之后的第一次结集上，众信徒集体做出这一决定，不要"对佛陀定下的任何规则做出改变"。这种对佛陀涅磐的保守反应在小乘佛教内部创造了它自己的遗产。[1]

第三个时期的佛教是在国家资助下成为制度化意识形态的佛教。[2] 佛教在这个时期传播到了亚洲大陆的其他地区，成为了南北两派。在中国大陆、中国西藏、韩国、日本以及越南发展的佛教属于北派；而在泰国、缅甸、柬埔寨以及老挝的佛教属于南派。换句话说，当我们想要探寻佛教与文化的关系的时候，我们需要对佛教的不同形式做一区分，即区分作为改革主义运动的佛教、作为保守反应的佛教以及作为国家意识形态的佛教。佛教的这三个不同阶段和面貌与佛教的文化环境直接相关。[3]

在本文中，佛教这个词被用来指称佛教的第一个时期，即佛陀涅磐之前的佛教。本文的最后部分会触及佛教的一个特殊形式，即深受佛教第二时期和第三时期影响的泰国佛教。

佛教对不同文化领域的反思

在佛教背景中，将"文化"一词用作通称似乎是行不通的。笔者的理解是，佛教针对文化生活的不同领域提出了不同的态度。本文提出五个主要的文化领域并探寻针对每个领域的不同态度。这一分析意在提示而非结论。

第一个领域——泛灵论和神话

笔者认为，佛教对业已存在的泛灵论以及神话的信仰和实践持一种温和告诫的态度。苦行修炼、树木崇拜、河流崇拜、大山崇拜、神话神祇、天人、仙人以及地方神灵等其他形式都被早期佛教普遍地承认。佛陀只是简单地告诫说，这些崇拜和修行将不会引导人们走向真正的解放或苦难的终止。

---

[1] 参见 Edward Conze, *A Short History of Buddhism*. London and Boston: Unwin Paperbacks, 1982 中对第一次结集的重要意义所做的概述。亦参见 Mettananto Bhikkhu, *Founding Events of B. E. 0001*, Bangkok: Saeng Arthit, BE. 2545 中对第一次结集的政治主张所做的批判性的和有争议的描述。

[2] 参见 Steven Collins, *Nirvana and Other Buddhist Felicities: Utopias of the Pali Imaginaire*. Cambridge: Cambridge University Press, 1998, pp. 1-120 中对佛教在东南亚从权威佛教演化为教化佛教的形态和形式所做的不无启发的解释。

[3] 本文尚需以一种颠倒的因果条件秩序来探讨佛教与文化之间的关系。按照这种框架，关键的问题应该是："佛教是怎样受不同的当地文化所影响，而不仅仅是佛教影响当地文化？"

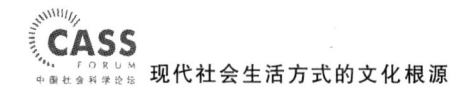

并不存在公开的谴责或彻底的反对。①

第二个领域——印度教

笔者认为，佛教对于印度教信仰和修行的各种形式持极度批判的态度。佛陀对以下事实提出了批判性的意见，即如果恒河之水能像很多印度人修行和信仰的那样涤净罪恶，那么所有的鱼龟就都能上天堂了。他还指出，婆罗门们全都忘记了他们是从婆罗门母亲的子宫中而非从大梵天王生出的。印度教创世神话曾被用于证明婆罗门最高种姓的地位的正当性，即婆罗门从大梵天王口中生出而其他种姓的人们则从大梵天王宇宙身体的其他"低一级"的部分生出。这个创世神话说明了古代印度社会对不同种姓的社会区分的神学/神话辩护。

第三个领域——语言

佛教将语言看作一种用于交流的约定工具。佛陀据载曾反对过他的门徒之一提出用吠陀语言（梵文的一种形式）教学的建议，而坚持使用方言来传播他的教导。② 对他的意图的一个重要解读是，佛陀想让他的教导使不同的人群都"感到自然"，而不是将一种"神圣性"元素归于他的教导，就像在他之前的婆罗门曾做的那样。佛陀也创造出了一个崭新的第一人称代词来称呼自己。他称自己"如来"，这个词是指某个"如此而去"的人。③ 这个人称代词不断提醒人们注意"无我"状态，即在一个人的经验和记忆背后并不存在永恒的自我。笔者认为佛陀对语词的这种创新性的使用说明了他对于语言的态度。语言是用于交流的，但当人们能够轻易地对语言约定中的"自我"产生依附时，对语言的使用就应该小心了。使苦难终止的道路是超越语言之上的，同时语言也不能充分表述觉悟的状态。④

第四个领域——家庭

佛教对家庭持一种矛盾的妥协态度。通过简单地分析乔达摩王子离开他

---

① 关于泰国社会中佛教对精神崇拜的宽容的文化例证，参见 Stanley J. Tambiah, *Buddhism and the Spirit Cult in North-east Thailand*, Cambridge: Cambridge University Press, 1970。

② 关于这一问题的讨论，参见一部关于佛教史传世之作 Sathien Bhotinantha, *Lectures on the History of Buddhism*. Bangkok: Council of Mahamakut-Rajavidyalai, B. E. 2496。佛教正典中的准确引证可在 *The Tripitaka*. Bangkok: Mahachulalongkorn-Rajavidyalai, B. E. 2539（Vinaya Cullavagga, volume 7/No. 285 in Khuttagawattu, Khantaga）中找见。

③ 参见任何关于佛教哲学的标准解释，它们通常把"如来"当作佛陀用来称谓自己的词。然而，据我所知，我尚需找到关于这种用法的哲学解释，正如我在文中所暗示的。

④ 关于禅宗对于语言的约定俗成以及语言在表达觉悟体验的局限性所持的观点，参见 Thomas P. Kasulis, *Zen Action Zen Person*, Honolulu: University Of Hawaii Press, 1981。

的妻子和孩子追求觉悟来评价佛教关于家庭的立场是十分困难的。在佛陀觉悟之后，他教导僧侣离开家庭生活，作为僧侣去修行法（Dhamma），由此指示出家庭需要被抛在身后。但是，他最初拒绝为其三度请求出家而被拒的姨母剃度似乎指示出他并不希望鼓励女性离开家庭生活。这也许是那时与世俗社会的一种必要的妥协。① 并且，第一条戒律表述得十分清楚，那就是两性生活与僧侣生活不能混合。最终，觉悟带来从轮回中的解脱。这指示出的不仅是对家庭的超越，还有对生命本身的超越。

第五个领域——技艺与技术

佛教对于过分关注技艺与技术问题持谨慎态度。有一次，追随佛陀的僧众们热烈地辩论技艺问题，他们自问："谁才对技艺真正有知？谁应该研习哪类技艺？哪类技艺才是全部技艺的精华？"有些僧侣说驯象术是精华，有些更倾向于驯马术，其他人则提出驾车术、射箭术、武器研制、指算、数学、统计学、做诗、讲述神奇故事以及法律实践。后来，这些辩论被佛陀知道了，他说："剃度的僧侣讨论这些事是不合适的。当你们聚在一起，你们只应该做两件事情，或者论法或者像佛陀一样静坐"，他接着说，"没有生活负担的僧侣们应该集中精力奉献社会。控制六处以便摆脱轮回。永远不要对某一特定地点、某一特定关系、某一特定希望产生依附。摆脱无明，独自云游。这些才是僧侣所为。"② 笔者认为，佛陀并不是反对技艺和技术，而是告诫僧侣们集中精力在其他他们分内的事务上，也就是修法。人们可能会说，技艺和技术并不指向佛教的终极目标，也就是对苦难的终止。

从文化的以上五个领域中我们可以看到，从佛教终极目标的角度看，文化可以被看作"规约"的一种表达，而这可能成为对达到终极目标的妨碍。"真理"以及这种规约的目的需要在终极目标的视野下持续地加以重新检验。但是，如果我们不得不将文化生活的所有不同领域都放入同一层面，我们可能就会看到下列图景。

---

① 参见拙作 "Women's Spiritual Life and the Family," forthcoming in Korean to be published by Ewha Woman University, Seoul, Korea。

② 关于佛教对于技术问题的讨论及正典出处，参见 Suwanna Satha-Anand, "Buddhist Reflections on Technology, Reason and Human Values," in Philip Cam, Rainier A. Ibana, Pham Van Duc (eds.) *Philosophical Perspectives on Globalization*, Korea; The Korean National Commission for UNESCO and The Asia-Pacific Network for Education for Democracy, 2006. pp. 59–76。

印度教的神话神学以及社会学是一个主要的障碍。第一，这可能是因为印度教提供了一个与佛教不一致的终极目标。第二，家庭是一个不能割舍的依附。这是因为家庭是将人们最有力地与今生联系在一起、由规约所规定——通过两性关系、婚姻、财物管理、宗族、继承、社会及政治秩序等——的一种制度。第三，技艺和技术会使注意力偏离正确的佛教目标，因为对这些技艺的掌握要求在不同技能的培养上投入很多注意力以及献身精神。第四，语言和泛灵论很大程度上是人们日常生活及实践的一部分，而人们的日常生活和实践又需要被重新导向佛教的目标。

总而言之，我们可以说，佛教提出批判性的反对、温和的告诫以及宽容的共存作为对待在人类生活的各领域业已存在的文化实践的三种可能态度。

佛教与泰国文化

我们或许也需要探讨佛教与泰国文化的关系的问题。我们首先不要忘记，泰国历史中的佛教的形态和形式属于佛教第二个以及第三个时期。换句话说，作为改革主义运动的佛教在泰国文化世界中从未成为主导力量。泰国的上座部佛教是佛教历史中的保守时期在文化上的产物，并且它基本上是一种被国家调解过的佛教形式。佛教通过与泰国国家的庇护关系在超过700年间充当了对国家和国王统治的文化辩护。

在斯蒂文·柯林斯教授看来，《帕峦王的三个世界》一书中的佛教为以每人业报积累的不同程度为基础的社会等级体系提供了一种宇宙论。这个业报的概念在佛教的第一时期是对一个业已存在的印度教概念——这一概念强调个体的道德行为并将其看作个人目前以及未来生活的决定因素——的一个重新解释。在这个意义上，业报在佛陀看来就是一个有助于使印度教种姓体系丧失权威的激进的、解放性的概念。但是，佛教在泰国主流习俗中一直是一个有宿命论取向、根据过去的业力接受个人现有生活遭遇的文化概念。具有讽刺意味的是，佛教在泰国文化中主要发挥着为社会等级做宗教辩护的作用，而非从等级中解放的力量。

从这种观点来看，我们就能体会到当代泰国许多改革主义僧侣的著作以及佛教入世形式的重要性。佛使比丘以及国际入世佛教协会（INEB）就是最为重要的例证。佛使比丘试图通过在一个距国家适度距离的独立领域传播佛教以此重新调整佛教与泰国文化的关系。为了使第一时期的佛教能够再次在当代生活中与佛教徒的生活更加相关,国家的调解角色需要被缩减。除此之外,在过去十年中,涌现出大量以世俗人为领导者的团体提供沉思、情绪排毒课程以及减压的方法。世俗人在泰国上座部佛教中的角色日益重要,这就对"上座部"佛教在泰国以及泰国以外地区如何转化提出了另一个主要挑战。西方文化的流入也为泰国佛教徒提出了新的论题,比如性、人权、性别、平等、善治、民主化等拒绝告退却难于与他们的生活自然融合的论题。[1] 当代环境中的泰国人似乎想要保持他们泰国佛教徒的文化身份同时也想要登上现代性与全球化这疾驰而竞争激烈的列车。

(杜　鹃译)

---

[1] 关于上一世纪泰国佛教的全面评述,参见 Phra Paisan Wisalo, *Thai Buddhism in the Future: Trends and Ways our of the Crisis*. Bangkok: Sodsri-Saritwongse Foundation, B. E. 25。

Reflections on Buddhism and Culture

Suwanna Satha-Anand[*]

Introductory Note

When we wish to explore the relationship between Buddhism and culture, we need to begin by making a distinction among at least three major moments of Buddhism.

First Moment: 'Buddhism' before the death of the Buddha Second Moment: Buddhism after the death of the Buddha until before King Asoka

Third Moment: Buddhism after King Asoka

We all realize that Buddhism as a 'trans-cultural' or 'trans-conventional' project aims at an ultimate goal which is not limited to any one culture. The phenomenon of birth, old age, sickness and death is universal. The Buddhist ultimate goal of the cessation of suffering is meant for all. However, when we wish

---

[*] Suwanna Satha-Anand was born in 1955. She received her MA and Ph. D from the University of Hawaii. She holds a position of Professor at Chulalongkorn University (Philosophy Department , Faculty of Arts). She has published about ten books on Buddhist Philosophy, Philosophy of Religion and Thai Cultural Heritage. Her numerous research articles cover the fields of women and religion, ethics in religion, and Buddhism and contemporary issues. She is the former president of the Soceity of Philosophy and Religion of Thailand and former chair of Philosophy Department of Chulalongkorn University. Her current research interests include issues in Buddhist philosophy, religion and social Change.

to move closer to the topic of Buddhism and culture, we need to be aware of the different historical moments in the long life of the Buddhist tradition.

Technically, Buddhism before the death of the Buddha does not really exist. There is only a way of life and practice proposed by Gautama Buddha. We could see Buddhism at this time as a reformist movement which offered an alternative to the prevalent Hindu system at around 500 BC.

Buddhism at the second moment was a Buddhism of the Sangha, which, at the First Council some three months after the death of the founder had collectively made a resolution not to 'change any rule laid down by the Buddha.' This conservative reaction to the death of the founder had created its own legacy within the Theravada School of Buddhism. ①

Buddhism at the third moment is a Buddhism which had been under state patronage and had become an institutionalized ideology. ② This third moment Buddhism spread to other parts of the Asian continent, becoming the Northern and the Southern Schools. The Buddhism as developed in China, Tibet, Korea, Japan and Vietnam belong to the Northern School; while the Buddhism of Thailand, Mynmar, Cambodia, Laos, belong to the Southern School. In other words, when we wish to explore the relationship between Buddhism and culture, we need to differentiate the different forms of Buddhism, namely, Buddhism as a reformist movement, Buddhism as a conservative reaction, and Buddhism as a state ideology. These three different phases and faces of Buddhism would have direct bearings on Buddhism's cultural environments. ③

In this paper, the term Buddhism is used to indicate the Buddhism of the first moment, namely, Buddhism before the death of the Buddha. The last part of this

---

① Please see a brief outline of the significance of the First Council in Edward Conze, *A Short History of Buddhism*. London and Boston: Unwin Paperbacks, 1982. See also a critical and controversial rendering of the politics of the First Council in Mettananto Bhikkhu, *Founding Events of B. E. 0001*. Bangkok: Saeng Arthit, BE. 2545.

② Please see an illuminating explanation of the shapes and forms of civilizational Buddhism in Southeast, as they evolve from that of the canonical Buddhism in Steven Collins, *Nirvana and Other Buddhist Felicities: Utopias of the Pali Imaginaire*. Cambridge: Cambridge University Press, 1998, pp. 1 – 120.

③ This paper has yet to deal with the relationship between Buddhism and culture in a reverse order of causal condition. In this latter framework, the key question then becomes, 'In what ways, Buddhism has been shaped by different local cultures, and not only the other way round?'

paper will touch on one particular form of Buddhism, namely, Thai Buddhism which has been heavily influenced by Buddhism of the second moment and the third moment.

Buddhist Reflections on Different Areas of Culture

In the Buddhist context, it seems unfeasible to use the term 'culture' as a generic term. This author understands that Buddhism proposes different attitudes toward different areas of cultural life. This paper proposes five major areas of culture and explores the different attitudes toward each area. This analysis is meant to be suggestive rather than conclusive.

Area One: Animism and Myths

This author would argue that Buddhism exercises an attitude of benign caution for pre-existing animistic and mythic beliefs and practices. Other forms of ascetic practices, tree worships, river worships, mountain worships, mythic gods, heavenly beings, celestial beings, local deities, etc. are generally tolerated in early Buddhism. The Buddha simply cautions that these worships and practices will not lead to true liberation or the cessation of sufferings. There was no open condemnation or outright rejection.[1]

Area Two: Hinduism

This author would argue that Buddhism is highly critical of various forms of Hindu beliefs and practices. The Buddha offers critical comments regarding the fact that if the water of the Ganges could wash away evils as practiced and believed by many Hindus, then all the fish and the turtles would go to heaven. He also points out that the Brahmins all had forgotten that they were born from the wombs of Brahmin mothers, not the Lord Brahma. This Hindu creation myth had been used to justify the status of the highest caste of the Brahmins as they were issued forth from the mouth of the Lord Brahma; while peoples of other castes were issued

---

[1] Please see cultural examples of Buddhist tolerance of spirit worships in Thai society in Stanley J. Tambiah, *Buddhism and the Spirit Cult in North-east Thailand*. Cambridge: Cambridge University Press, 1970.

forth from other 'lower' parts of the cosmic body of the Lord Brahma. This creation myth illustrates the theological/mythical justification of the social differentiation into different castes in ancient Hindu society.

Area Three: Language

Buddhism sees language as a tool of convention for communication purposes. The Buddha was recorded as rejecting a proposal by one of his disciples to teach in the Vedic language (a form of Sanskrit). He insisted on using the vernacular languages to spread his teachings. ① One important reading of his intention is that the Buddha wanted his teachings to 'feel natural' to different groups of peoples, and not to ascribe an element of 'sacredness' to his teachings as had been practiced by the Brahmins before him. The Buddha also coins a new first personal pronoun to address himself. He calls himself, 'Tathagata,' which indicates someone who has 'thus gone.' ② It is a personal pronoun which keeps reminding other people of a state of 'non-self,' that is, there is no permanent self behind the experiences and memory of a person. This author would argue that this innovative play of words by the Buddha indicates his attitude toward language. Language is needed for communication, but it needs to be used with caution as people can easily develop attachment to a 'self' of linguistic convention. The path to the cessation of suffering is beyond language, and language cannot fully articulate the state of enlightenment. ③

Area Four: Family

Buddhism develops an attitude of ambivalent compromise with the family. It would be difficult to evaluate the Buddhist position on the family simply by

---

① Please see a discussion of this issue in a time-honored book on Buddhist history by Sathien Bhotinantha, *Lectures on the History of Buddhism*. Bangkok: Council of Mahamakut-Rajavidyalai, B. E. 2496. Exact reference in the Buddhist canon can be found in *The Tripitaka*. Bangkok: Mahachulalongkorn-Rajavidyalai, B. E. 2539. (Vinaya Cullavagga, volume 7/No. 285 in Khuttagawattu, Khantaga)

② Please see any standard expositions of Buddhist philosophy which usually mention the term 'Tathagata' as a term the Buddha used to address himself. However, to the best of my knowledge, I have yet to come across a philosophical explanation of this use, as suggested in my paper.

③ Please see a Zen Buddhist position on the convention of language and the limit of language in 'articulating' the experience of Enlightenment in Thomas P. Kasulis, *Zen Action Zen Person*. Honolulu: University Of Hawaii Press, 1981.

analyzing the decision of Prince Siddhatta to leave his wife and child in pursuit of enlightenment. After his enlightenment, his instructions for monks to leave the household life and practice the dhamma as a monk, indicate that the family needs to be left behind. However, his initial reluctance to allow ordination for his aunt who asked and was rejected three times seems to indicate that he did not wish to encourage women to leave the household life. This maybe a necessary compromise with the secular world at that time.① And yet the first pajajika rule states clearly that sexual life and monkhood cannot be mixed. Ultimately speaking, enlightenment leads to liberation from the cycle of rebirths. This indicates a transcendence not only of the family, but also of life itself.

Area Five: Arts and Technology

Buddhism cautions against paying too much attention to the questions of arts and technology. On one occasion, the monk followers of the Buddha were hotly engaged in debates on the arts. They are asking among themselves, 'Who are truly knowledgeable about the arts? Who should study which types of arts? Which arts is the quintessential of all arts?' Some monks are saying that elephant training is the quintessential, others preferring horse training; while others naming charioteering, archer, weaponry, finger counting, mathematics, statistics, writing poetry, fantastic story telling, and practicing law. Later the debates were brought to the attention of the Buddha. He said, 'It is inappropriate for ordained monks to discuss these matters. When you get together, you should do only two things. Either discuss the dhamma or sit still as the Buddha does', He continued, 'Monks who are with little burden for livelihood, should concentrate on dedicating themselves to society. Control the six senses so as not to be reborn again. Never develop attachment to a particular place, a particular belonging, a particular hope. Get rid of ignorance, wander alone. These are activities of monks.'② This author would argue that the

---

① Please see my article on 'Women's Spiritual Life and the Family,' forthcoming in Korean to be published by Ewha Woman University, Seoul, Korea.

② Please see the canonical source and a discussion of the question of technology in Buddhism in Suwanna Satha-Anand, 'Buddhist Reflections on Technology, Reason and Human Values,' in Philip Cam, Rainier A. Ibana, Pham Van Duc Eds. *Philosophical Perspectives on Globalization*. Korea: The Korean National Commission for UNESCO and The Asia-Pacific Network for Education for Democracy, 2006. pp. 59 – 76.

Buddha is not rejecting arts and technology, but he is admonishing the monks to concentrate on other more relevant tasks as monks, namely practicing the dhamma. One might be able to say that arts and technology does not lead to the ultimate goal of Buddhism, that is, the cessation of sufferings.

From these five areas of culture, we could see that from the perspective of the ultimate goal of Buddhism, culture can be an expression of 'convention' which could be a hindrance to the path. The 'truth' and purposes of this convention needs to be constantly re-examined in light of the ultimate goal. However, if we are forced to put all the different areas of cultural life into one spectrum, we might have the following picture.

The Hindu mythic theology and sociology would be a major obstacle. This is perhaps because Hinduism offers an ultimate goal which is incongruent with Buddhism. Second, the family is a tenacious attachment. This is because the family is an institution which most powerfully tie people up with this life as defined by convention through sexual relations, marriage, property management, lineage, inheritance, social and political orders, etc. Third, arts and technology could draw attention away from the proper Buddhist goal as the mastering of these arts requires great attention and dedication in the cultivation of the different skills. Fourth/fifth, language and animism are very much part of the daily life and practice of the people which need to re-directed toward the Buddhist goal.

In sum, we might say that Buddhism proposes critical rejection, benign caution and tolerant co-existence as three possible attitudes toward pre-existing cultural practices in the various areas of human life.

Buddhism and Thai Culture

We might also need to address the question of the relationship between Buddhism and Thai culture. We should be reminded at the beginning that the shape and form of Buddhism in Thai history are those of the second and third moments of Buddhism. In other words, Buddhism as a reformist movement has never been the dominant force in Thai cultural world. Theravada Buddhism in

Thailand has been a cultural child of a conservative moment in the history of Buddhism, and basically it is a form of Buddhism which has been mediated by the state. Through a patron-client relationship with the Thai State, Buddhism has served as a cultural justification of the state and kingly rule for over 7 centuries.

According to Professor Steven Collins, Buddhism in the Three Worlds of King Ruang, has provided a cosmology for a system of social hierarchy based on the different degrees of karmic accumulation of each person. This concept of karma in the first moment Buddhism is a re-interpretation of the a pre-existing Hindu concept, which emphasizes the individual moral conduct as a determining factor of his/her present and future life. In this sense karma, according to the Buddha, was a radical and liberating concept, which helps delegitimize the Hindu caste system. However, Buddhism in mainstream Thai practices has been a cultural concept of deterministic orientation, of accepting one's present lot in life, due to past karmic force. Ironically, Buddhism in Thai culture has mostly served as religious justification for social hierarchy, rather than a liberating force from that hierarchy.

From this perspective, we could appreciate the significance of the works of many reformist monks and socially-engaged forms of Buddhism in contemporary Thailand. Buddhadasa Bhikkhu and Internal Network for Engaged Buddhists (INEB) would be most important examples. Buddhadasa was trying to re-align the relationship between Buddhism and Thai culture, by propagating Buddhism from an independent sphere within a comfortable distance from the state. The state's mediating roles need to be reduced, so that Buddhism of the first moment could again become more relevant for Buddhist life in contemporary world. Moreover, In the past decade, there has been a significant proliferation of many groups offering meditations, emotional detoxification programs, stress reduction methods, with lay people as the leaders. The increasing role of the laity in Thai Theravada Buddhism is posing another major challenge for the transformation of 'Theravada' Buddhism in Thailand and beyond. The influx of Western culture has posed new issues for Thai Buddhists, take for examples, sexuality, human rights, gender, equality, good governance, democratization, issues which refuse to go away and difficult to blend in naturally with their lives. [1] Thai people in contemporary condition seem to wish to retain their Thai Buddhist cultural identity, while also wishing to catch the rapid and fiercely competitive train of modernity and globalization.

---

[1] Please see a comprehensive critical survey of Thai Buddhism in the past century in Phra Paisan Wisalo, *Thai Buddhism in the Future: Trends and Ways our of the Crisis*. Bangkok: Sodsri-Saritwongse Foundation, B. E. 2546.

私人与公共生活之间：来自中国处境的宗教多样性的挑战

谢志斌[*]

宗教多样性的问题是中国宗教的首要特征并带来不少挑战，现代社会也挣扎于私人与公共之间的区分。如何将这两个问题——宗教多样性的问题和私人—公共之间的问题——在中国处境中联系起来，是我这篇论文的首要关切的问题。本文将考察中国人宗教生活的多样性表现及其在私人—公共生活之间表现出来的张力，并将提出两个相关的命题。

第一，宗教多样性的社会和政治上的挑战比形而上学（认识论意义）的挑战显得更为明显、重要；

第二，私人与公共之间的张力是中国宗教多样性面临挑战的主要议题。"公共"的概念对于中国学界（甚至一般民众）来说已变得越来越熟知，公共空间、公共领域、公共理性、公共价值的术语正逐渐为中国学者所关注、使用和研究，有关"公共"的思想家诸如汉娜·阿伦特、于尔根·哈贝马斯以及约翰·罗尔斯的思想和作品也得到不少引介和研究。根据我的理解，宗教信仰一直是人类精神深处、隐秘、私人的情感表达形式，同时具有明显的"公共"性，这种"公共"特征包含其外在的公开的团体的表现、宗教信徒

---

[*] 谢志斌（Xie Zhibin），男，1970年出生。2004年获得香港大学宗教哲学博士学位。上海师范大学哲学系副教授。专业领域：宗教哲学、基督教伦理等。主要著述有：《公共神学与全球化：斯塔克豪思的基督教伦理研究》（2008）、《中国的宗教多样性与公共宗教》（英文，2006）。

个人和群体对于公共生活的参与（如社会服务、社会工作以及政治生活等）、宗教与政府的关系等。

在当代中国，宗教生活一个显著特征可以说是在私人与公共之间的挣扎，而这种挣扎的一个根源在于中国社会特有的宗教多样性特征。六十年来，中国大陆经历了对宗教的怀疑、排斥以至否定并取而代之狂热的集体式信仰：曾经是宗教的空间被限制并只能隐藏在极度狭小的私人精神领地，任何公开的宗教活动被禁止，不允许有任何公共的表达和言说；20世纪70年代末以来，随着政治的改革和社会的开放，宗教场所重新开放，人们精神生活选择日益丰富多彩，他们追问生命的意义，表现出强烈的灵性渴求，各种各样的宗教信仰便是其中一种重要的表达方式。

一

作为一种事实，中国处境中的宗教多样性显然以多样的宗教（Multiplicity of Religions）为特征，而非某种特定宗教内部的多种教派。或者说，在中国，有许多具有竞争力的宗教，而不是一种单一的支配性的宗教形态；（不同）宗教的多样性要比某种宗教内部的教派差异更为基本和重要。在当代中国，宗教的类型可分为以下几种：五大主要宗教（佛教、道教、基督教、天主教、伊斯兰教）、其他传统宗教（如民间宗教、东正教、犹太教）、新兴宗教运动（如摩门教、巴哈伊教）；而且，20世纪80年代以来，所有这些类型得到某种程度的复兴，这些宗教的信仰者的数目得以明显增长。有人指出，"有超过80%的中国人可以冠之为'宗教的'，如果乡村的习俗信仰和实践也包括在内的话。"[1] 可以认为，中国本质上是个"宗教性"的国度，表现在其丰富和广泛的宗教实践、信仰和宗教生活的传统。这里我将不具体描述这些多样的宗教信仰和实践的分布情况，而是将宗教的多样性作为一个整体进而研究其社会和政治意义。

一般认为，中国人的宗教信仰大多趋向于实用。在大多数情况下，他们选择和崇拜的宗教信念基于他们实际的生活需要。一个典型的现象是很多中

---

[1] Kevin Boyle and Jwliet Sheen, eds., *Freedom of Religion and Belief: A World Report* (NY: Routledge, 1997), 177.

国人实践着混合性的宗教，比如佛教、道教和儒家的混合。最突出的中国人的宗教观念是这三种信念传统的"和谐"或"统一"。在这三种信念的共存中，他们由同样的人群混合地实践着，从而在传统的中国文化中并没有明显的宗教间的冲突，这一宗教多元化的特质完全区别于西方或中东的宗教经验，在西方或中东，排他性的宗教（如犹太教、基督教和伊斯兰教）有重要的影响。

在这种背景下，许多中国人也许并不怎么关切哪种特定的宗教在拯救上（作为宗教信仰的终极目的之一）是更为有效的，这个问题在西方不少国家关于宗教性的问题是经常被提出的。对于中国处境下的宗教多样性问题，我认为相对于形而上学的问题（哪种宗教在拯救上更为有效）而言，其社会和政治层面上（作为公共）的问题更为突出和重要。

二

第二个问题，即私人—公共的区分与中国宗教多样性的问题，我将提供以下要点：

1. 在中国，宗教事务是否真的私人化（宗教在公共生活中的有限角色）

关于宗教信仰和实践问题，中共中央在1982年颁布了19号文件，提出"宗教信仰自由政策的实质，就是要使宗教信仰问题成为公民个人自由选择的问题，成为公民个人的私事。""任何人不得利用宗教反对党的领导和社会主义制度"，"任何人不得利用宗教干预国家行政、司法、学校教育和社会公共教育，不得利用宗教进行妨碍义务教育实施的活动"。[1]

就此，德布罗阿·布朗认为"宗教作为自主的伦理力量来抵制国家政策或直接影响社会的发展，这样的想法是不现实的。"同时，"控制宗教影响的一个首要策略是使得宗教抽离出公共领域并使得宗教实践成为一种'私人的事务'。因为宗教只能在政府所允许、注册的地方实践，而且宣传有神论是被禁止的，在公共中传播宗教价值是做不到的。"[2]

---

[1] Kevin Boyle and Jwliet Sheen, (eds.), *Freedom of Religion and Belief: A World Report* (NY: Routledge, 1997), 177.

[2] Debroah A., Brown, 'The Role of Religion in Promoting Democracy in the People's Republic of China and Hong Kong,' in Beatrice Leung, (ed.), *Church and State Relations in 21st Century Asia* (Hong Kong: Center for Asia Studies, 1996), 86.

由此观之，在当今中国，宗教在中国公共领域（如政治生活、经济、教育、大众媒体等领域）的影响受到严格限制甚至禁止。中国宗教政策的一个基本点是宗教的自由仅仅是私人信仰的自由，宗教信仰仅仅是个人行为。在团体和公共中的宗教活动层面并没有得到广泛的认可。

由此看来，中国政府试图使得宗教远离"公共"尤其是"政治"生活。政府的意图是使宗教信仰成为"私人事务"，排除宗教的公共影响。这种立场与西方一些思想家主张在现代社会中宗教的私人化倾向或限制宗教在公共生活中的角色的立场不同。后者（如约翰·罗尔斯、理查德·罗蒂、罗伯特·奥迪）主张宗教在政治生活中的介入一般是为了表示对非宗教人士和团体的充分尊重，并且遵照公民的自由和平等原则；他们也认为这是保护充分的宗教自由的一个条件。

然而，在当代中国，限制和禁止宗教价值和活动在公共和政治生活中的影响，是源于政府的政治目的。这种排除宗教的公共向度并不是基于以上学者所提倡的宗教私人化或限制宗教的公共参与，而是缘于政府对于宗教的控制，包括宗教的公共表达和在政治中的影响，认为其可能对政府权力形成挑战。

但是在中国，政府限制宗教的公共影响，并竭力使宗教信仰成为私人的事，这与宗教本身和宗教实践的内涵有些距离。首先，宗教本身同时具有私人和公共的秉性，包括宗教对于公共生活的参与；其次，宗教自由的概念不仅包含私人信仰（根据良心自由的法则），而且包含宗教在团体中的表达和实践。

而在中国，政府试图管治宗教，或者为着某种政治目的利用宗教，决定了宗教的从属地位以及宗教介入国家公共事务受到的限制。从这个意义上看，宗教实践并不是纯粹私人的事，它必须面对政府的态度和管理。

2. 宗教的政治特性

可以说，"中国的宗教基本上是一种政治性或准政治性构建"。这种政治特性表现在：服务于特定的政治目的或者从事于政治上的管治。实际上，宗教信仰和实践不可能限定在私人生活，也不能与政治完全分离。这可从两个角度理解。

第一个角度是官方对于宗教的态度，其中包含两个方面。其中积极的方面是政府管理宗教的原则："宗教与社会主义相适应""宗教与和谐社会"，而消极的方面则是政府对某些宗教的敏感性，如基督教的海外联系、天主教中涉及的中梵关系、伊斯兰极端主义影响等。

这里值得注意的是政府对于不同宗教的态度，似乎某些宗教，相对于其他宗教,从官方得到更多的支持和鼓励。甚至有人认为宗教发展不平衡,提出"宗教生态论",倡导民间信仰、民间宗教等宗教形态的发展,来抗衡基督教文化的冲击(因将之视为宗教威胁)。

第二个角度是宗教人士和团体的公共诉求:即寻求更多的宗教实践空间、更广泛地参与公共生活。从这个意义上来说,我们需要注意到家庭教会等的问题。再者宗教团体要求更多空间参与公共的和政治的事务,不应仅仅局限于社会工作和服务,同时还应该涉及公民道德教育等;另外,需要有各种宗教的道德资源的公共表达如理解公共议题诸如经济生活、环境问题、政治讨论等。

三

本文主要探讨私人—公共之间的区分及其对于中国处境中的宗教多样性问题的意义。"在一些政治体制里,其政府对待宗教大都是中立的,使得宗教成为私人事务,在政府的触及之外;中国对宗教有着积极的政策。"① 一方面,中国政府各种政策的主要导向是力图使宗教信仰成为纯粹私人的事情,保留在个人精神领地,不允许超出界限而介入公共事务。另一方面恰恰相反,宗教信仰与实践已日益成为公共的不能回避的问题:政府的管治、对宗教的敏感和不同态度以及宗教团体的公共诉求等。保护私人事务、个人生活方式的选择以及公共的控制之间仍存在一定张力。在中国处境中,关于宗教的私人—公共特性及其表现形式,可理解为一种"悖论"的模式。在宗教实践和对宗教事务的管理中,私人和公共经常被混合地运作着。政府面对宗教的私人—公共性之间的张力仍有不少困难。

"西方出现的自由民主努力在一种单一的政体内容纳对于生活的多种多样的宗教立场。"② 现代社会也特别强调私人—公共的区分,同时包容各种不同的信念和价值,包括宗教信仰。然而,在中国,如何认识并充分保护这些不同的宗教信仰及其实践,尤其是它们之间的平等身份,使得它们充分享有私人的空间,也以一种平衡的方式使得它们进入公共生活,无论是给出限制或给予鼓励:这确实是一个真正的挑战。

---

① Richard Madsen, 'Back to the Future: Pre-modern Religious Policy in Post-Secular China,' http://www.fpri.org/enotes/201003.madsen.postsecularchina.html.
② Miroslav Volf, "A Voice of One's Own: Public Faith in a Pluralistic World," in Thomas Banchoff, (ed.), *Democracy and the New Religious Pluralism* (Oxford University Press, 2007), 273.

Between Private and Public Life: The Challenge of Religious Diversity in the Chinese Context

Xie Zhibin[*]

The problem of religious diversity characterizes religions in China and raises several issues. Modern society also struggles between the distinction between the private and the public. How to relate to these two problems, i. e., the problem of religious diversity, and the problem of the private and the public, becomes my primary concern in this paper. My paper will examine the presentation and tension of religious diversity between private and public life among Chinese and will propose two relevant theses:

(1) The social and political challenges from the problem of religious diversity shows more significance than the metaphysical challenge from within;

(2) The tension between the private and the public is the main change for the problem of religious diversity in China.

The concept of 'the public', relevant terms (such as public square, public sphere, and public reason), and the figures (such as Hannah Arendt, Jurgen Habermas and John Rawls who are concerned with the 'public' problem) have

---

[*] Xie Zhibin was born in China in 1970. He received his Ph D from the University of Hong Kong in 2004. He holds a position of associate professor at the Department of Philosophy of Shanghai Normal University. His publications include *Public Theology and Globalization: A Study in Max Stackhouse's Christian Ethics* (in Chinese, 2008), *Religious Diversity and Public Religion in China* (in English, 2006). His current research interests focus on philosophy of religion, Christian social ethics.

become more and more familiar with the Chinese academia even among many ordinary Chinese. In my understanding, the term of 'public', with reference to religion, means the communal quality of religious belief and practice, religious persons and groups' involvement in public life, religion's relationship with state and with political issues. Essentially religious beliefs are the private and inner experience of human being, yet they are subject to external, publicized, and communal forms.

In contemporary China, one characteristic of religious life may be defined as the struggle between the private and the pubic, and this struggle derives from its specific religious diversity in the Chinese context. During these six decades, the attitudes to religious belief and practice have been doubt, exclusion, even denial, and today more tolerance. The space of religious practice was strictly restrained within very narrow private spiritual domain, thus any public religious activities were forbidden until the end of 1970s. Since 1980s, together with the social and political reform including the change of state's religious policy, many Chinese have more and more options in spiritual life, including diverse religious beliefs.

I

As a matter of fact, religious diversity in the Chinese context is obviously characterized by a multiplicity of religions, rather than variety within one certain religion. In other words, in China, they are many competing religions, rather than a single dominant religion, and diversity among religions is more basic and important than denominational diversity within a particular religion. In contemporary China, the types of religion may be categories as follows: five major religions (i. e., Buddhism, Daoism, Christianity, Catholicism, Islam), folk religions, traditional religions (Orthodoxy Christianity, Judaism), new religious movement (such as Mormonism, Ba'hai,). In addition, all these types of religion have received certain revival and the number of various religious believers has increased rapidly since 1980s. According to a recent survey from Beijing, only 15% of the population is atheists in China. It has been pointed out that 'as much as 80 percent of China's population may be termed "religious" if customary beliefs and practices in the countryside are included. '① In my view, China is a religious country essentially by virtue of its rich and widespread traditions of religious practice (when and where allowed), beliefs, and religious life, especially in the rural areas and among ethnic minorities throughout the country. We may have a picture that the wide population in China practices their rich and quite diverse religious beliefs. Here I will not go to the detailed distribution of various religious beliefs and practice in this country, yet I will take the diversity of religions as a whole and study its social and political implications.

It is said that many Chinese religious beliefs are tend to be pragmatic. In most circumstances, they choose and follow religious beliefs based on their practical life needs. One typical phenomenon is that many Chinese practice mixed religion such as the mixture of Buddhism, Taoism, and Confucianism. The most typical Chinese religious ideal is 'harmony' or 'unity' of these three traditions of belief. In the coexistence of these three beliefs, their mixed practice by the same people, and the general absence of tension between religions in traditional Chinese culture, this characteristic religious pluralism is different from the religious experience of the West, or the Middle East where the exclusivist religions (such as Judaism, Christianity, and Islam) have dominant influence. Under this condition, many Chinese might not care too much which confined religion is more effective for salvation, as the problem of religious diversity raise in many Western counties, where Christianity has dominant influence. As for the problem of religious diversity in China, I would say that it raises more social and political (public) issues than metaphysical issue.

II

For the second thesis, that is, the issue of private/public distinction and the problem of religious diversity in China, I will offer the following two issues:

(1) The first issue : are religious affairs really private in China? (The limited

---

① Kevin Boyle and Jwliet Sheen, (eds.), *Freedom of Religion and Belief: A World Report* (NY: Routledge), p. 177.

role of religion in the public life)

In 1982, the Central Committee of Chinese Communist Party (CCP) issued Document 19, which laid out its basic viewpoints and policy on the problem of religion under communism in China. The document states, 'religion will not be permitted to meddle in the administrative or the juridical affairs of states, nor to intervene in the schools or public education.'① Article 36 of the Constitution also emphasizes that the religious are not allowed to disrupt public order or impair the health of citizens.

It is evident that religion's influence on the public sphere, such as political life, the areas of economics, education, science, and the mass media, is strictly restricted and even prohibited in present-day China. The religious voice is muted there. Deborah A. Brown writes that in China 'the idea of religion as autonomous ethical force that can resist state policy or directly influence the development of society is anathema.' He continues, 'A principal strategy for controlling religious influence is to force religion from the public sphere and to make religious practice a "private matter." Because religion officially can be practiced only at state-approved, registered sites, and because the propagation of theism is forbidden, the spread of religious values in the public sector is frustrated.'② Here Brown's points help to understand how the Chinese government interprets the issue of religious practice. As Document 19 states, 'the crux of policy of freedom of religious belief is to make the question of religious belief a private matter, one of individual free choice for citizens.'③ General speaking, one basic point in Chinese religious policy is that freedom of religion is simply the freedom of private belief and religious belief is only an individual act. The level of freedom of religious activity in the community as well as in the public, particularly that of spontaneous communal religious worship has not been widely

---

① See the English version of Document 19 in Donald E. MacInnis, *Religion in China: Policy and Practice* (Maryknoll, NY: Orbis Books, 1989), 15.

② Debroah A., Brown, 'The Role of Religion in Promoting Democracy in the People's Republic of China and Hong Kong', in Beatrice Leung, (ed.), *Church and State Relations in 21ˢᵗ Century Asia* (Hong Kong: Center for Asia Studies, 1996), 86.

③ Donald E. MacInnis, *Religion in China: Policy and Practice*, 15.

acknowledged by the government. 'They distinguish between personal worship and participation in organized religious activities. It is the latter that they go to great lengths to control, not the former.'[1]

Therefore, the Chinese government simply aims to keep religion away from the public especially 'political' issues, and thus 'any monastic political activities are viewed as subversive.'[2] The government's intention to transform religious belief into 'private matter' and to preclude religious public influence should be distinguished from the liberal privatization of religion or restraint on religion in public life in a modern liberal democracy. Some liberal scholars (like Richard Rorty) are concerned with the fact of the conflict and conversation difficulty between the religious and the non-religious in the public sphere. Its purpose is to protect religious liberty and to preserve a democratic political community.[3] Others (like John Rawls and Robert Audi)'s liberal restraints on religion in politics also show adequate respect to the nonreligious people and community and follow the principle of freedom and equality of citizens. They also take it as a condition for guaranteeing full religious liberty.[4]

By way of contrast, in contemporary China, restraint on and prohibition of religious values and activities in the public and political real, for the sake of the state's political purposes, weakens the freedom of religious belief and practice This sort of exclusion is not motivated by privatization or restraint as some liberal scholars propose, but by the state's control of religion, including religion's public expression and influence in politics, given its potential to challenge to state power. The government tends to 'fear both an active involvement by religious believers in

---

[1] Human Right Watch/Asia, *China: State Control of Religion* (New York: Human Rights Watch, 1997), 2.

[2] David C. Yu, complied, *Religion in Postwar China: a Critical Analysis and Annotated Bibliography* (Westport, CT: Greenwood Press, 1994), 6.

[3] See Richard Rorty, 'Religion as Conversation-Stopper', *Common Knowledge* 3/1 (1994): 1–6 and 'Religion in the Public Square: A Reconsideration', *Journal of Religious Ethics* 31/1 (2003): 141–149.

[4] See John Rawls, *Political Liberalism*, paperback edition (New York: Columbia University Press, 1996) and 'The Idea of Public Reason Revisited', University of Chicago Law Review 64 (1997): 765–807; Robert Audi and Nicholas Wolterstorff, *Religion in the Public Square: The Place of Religious Convictions in Political Debate* (Lanham, MD: Rowman and Littlefield, 1997).

politics, and a longer term ideological threat to Marxism.'①

The state's restraint on religion's public influence in China, and its attempt to reduce religious belief to a private matter, does not fulfill the meaning of religion and religious practice in the following senses. First, religion has both private and public qualities, which includes its inevitable involvement in public life, including political matters. Second, the conception of religious freedom contains not only private belief in terms of freedom of conscience but also religious expression and practice in community.② The government's attempt to supervise religion, or to use religion for political purposes, confirmed both the historically subordinate role of religion in China and the restriction of religious involvement in public affairs of the state. In this sense, religious practice is not fully a private matter and has to confront with governmental attitudes and management.

(2) The second issue: the political nature of religion in China

We have seen the political nature of religions in China, either for political purpose or subject to political control. Religious beliefs and practice will not be confined within private life nor separated from politics. These can be further understood from two angles. ③One angle is official attitude to religions, which contains two sides. The positive side is the governing principle of religious affairs, namely, 'accommodation of religion to socialist society', and most currently, 'religious service to harmonious society'. The negative side is the fact that Chinese government is always sensitive to some religions: such as Protestantism with its foreign connection, the problem of Sino—Vatican relationship in the case of Catholicism, and the influence of extremism in Islam. These three religions have been political issues.

Here it is important to note that it seems that Chinese government shows different attitudes to religions. Some types of religions receive more encouraged than others do. It has been said that the numbers of certain religion (such as

---

① Alan Hunter and Kim-Kwong Chan, *Protestantism in Contemporary China* (Cambridge: Cambridge University Press, 1993), 57.
② See Human Right Watch/Asia, *China: State Control of Religion*, 2 – 3.
③ Richard Madsen, 'Back to the Future: Pre-modern Religious Policy in Post-Secular China', http://www.fpri.org/enotes/201003.madsen.postsecularchina.html

Christianity)'s followers has increased rapidly (or over development), which is seen as a shock to society, comparing to other religions. Accordingly, recently there is an orientation to encourage Chinese folk religions, Buddhism, Taoism to counterweight Christian influence or so called 'religious threat'. This position is named 'religious ecology' to deal with the problem of 'the unbalance of religious development.' Of course, this orientation and policy remains questionable. Is it acceptable for the state to give special support to any specific religious group (s)?

The other angle is the public appeal from the side of religious communities in terms of full rights to religious practice and to involvement in public affairs. At this point, we may recognize the fact of some unofficial or unregistered religious groups (such as Protestant house churches, underground Catholic churches). Various religious groups also call for more space to get involved in some public and political issues. Besides social services and social work they perform which seem to be promoted by the government, religious people and groups also desire for expressing views on some political issues based on their religious convictions. Still, there are diverse religious moral resources which may contribute to public good, either civil moral education or the moral understanding of some public issues such as economic life, environmental issues, and finally public political debate.

III

In this paper I have explored the issue of private-public distinction and its implications for the problem of religious diversity in the Chinese context. As Richard Madsen claims, 'Unlike liberal democratic governments, which for the most part purport to be neutral towards religion, making religion a private matter beyond the reach of the state, the Chinese government has an active policy toward religion.' On the one hand, Chinese authority intends to make religious belief private affairs solely without getting involved in the public domain; on the other, in practice it never exists as purely private, becoming 'public' issue in terms of governmental management of, sensitivity to and different attitudes to religions, on the one hand, and public appeal from various religious groups on the other. Most of these private matters are serve public scrutiny and control, which seems to be indifferent to the principle that the private matter and individual choices/practice of perspectives of life should be fully protected. In the Chinese context, it could be understood as a sort of paradoxical pattern with regard to religion's private-public character. In the area of religious practice and management of religious affairs, the private and public is often mixed. The state is still struggling for the private and public qualities of religion itself.

As Miroslav Volf says, 'Liberal democracy emerged in the West was an attempt to accommodate diverse religious perspectives on life within a single polity.'[1] Modern society is characterized by the private-public distinction as well as by its diverse beliefs and values,[2] including religious beliefs. Yet it is really a challenge in China to recognize and then protect these religious beliefs, particularly freedom and equality among them, making them fully private and having them in public, either restraint or encouragement, in a balanced way.

---

[1] Miroslav Volf, 'A Voice of One's Own: Public Faith in a Pluralistic World', in Thomas Banchoff, (ed.), *Democracy and the New Religious Pluralism* (Oxford University Press, 2007), 273.

[2] Miroslav Volf, 'A Voice of One's Own: Public Faith in a Pluralistic World', in Thomas Banchoff, (ed.), *Democracy and the New Religious Pluralism* (Oxford University Press, 2007), 273.

狂野的东方
——抑或体制变革后的生活

霍尔腾西娅·霍苏[*]

匈牙利及其他东欧中欧国家的体制变革走过20年之后正在接近尾声。一种新的社会结构需要以一种新精英与社会之间的全新关系来强化。在国家社会主义之后，新的生活方式和行为模式已经出现。

然而，在民主政治和新资本主义的市场体制下，新的社会结构蒙受了巨大的不平等之苦，而这种不平等正在传给下几代人。这种现象的根源在于缺乏有指导的和社会控制的转型战略。资本主义在匈牙利的强化发生处于一种国际背景下，而这种国际背景在集体主义时代之后必然在社会行动者之间造成若干新的紧张关系。由于经济权力的集中和全球化的加剧，在重新分配机会方面展开了一场尖锐的社会斗争。这场斗争较以往任何时候都更加残酷、更加粗野，并且预计会进一步加剧，因为相当数量的社会群体的生活前景已经恶化。

然而，匈牙利精英拒绝承认这种现象。本文重点将对于实行民主制第一个十年中的新社会结构、社会价值取向和心态以及精英们的责任做一简略描述和诊断。

---

[*] 霍尔腾西娅·霍苏（Hortenzia Hosszu，中文名字郝淡雅），女，1974年出生。2008年获匈牙利米什科尔茨大学文学博士。匈牙利科学院政治学所研究人员。主要研究领域：政治学、治理研究。主要著述有：《印度政治史》（2009）、"匈牙利治理转型"（2009）、"匈牙利全球化与社会保险的某些问题"（2007）等。

新精英

20世纪90年代体制变革之后,老的共产党精英转换其政治权力的机会微乎其微。因为在20世纪80年代末,共产党精英不再作为一个步调一致的社会群体而存在,此时政治体制领域已经由年轻的技术专家官员所占据。

然而,当今匈牙利精英的核心是从社会主义时期的内部、从以下提及的三个精英群体产生的。

改革派精英的历史起始于对马克思主义本质的反思。在20世纪60年代,马克思主义是禁果,但是这一学说的批判精神和激进主义促使青年知识分子去面对国家社会主义的理想与现实。在这个时期,大部分青年知识分子都相信社会主义,认为它可以由党的领导人发起的改革来改变。第一次决定性的改变开始于60年代的反改革过程。从这个时刻起,党的上层领导就不再可能相信他们适合发动改革。

这种思想的第一个征兆是"七七宪章"行动,以及随之而来的关于他们对马克思主义的态度的讨论。[①] 从70年代中期起,新知识分子精英越发膨胀的政治野心导致了与马克思主义的决裂。

然而,从80年代初开始,国家党内部成长起了新的一代,他们的特点是坚决实行市场改革,但与老精英有着很硬的关系。这个称为"后期卡达尔主义技术专家官员"[②]的青年技术专家官员群体虽然是社会主义官僚制的产物,但却以主张保守—自由的价值观体系为其特征。正是由于这个原因,这个群体在政治决策制度中获得了越来越强的讨价还价地位。

在政治体制变革中起决定作用的却不是青年技术专家官员,而是两个精英群体:民主反对派和新改革派知识分子。新改革派知识分子大多数都是在国家科研机构任职从事社会问题研究的人员。这个群体有两个分支,一个以民主反对派为中心,另一个是民粹派作家群体。民主反对派仍然将自己置于制度权力之外,因为自从70年代他们被解职以来,他们一直就处在警察的严密监视之下。

[①] 捷尔吉·本采和基什·亚诺什的出版物"A Soviet type of society seen through the eyes of Marxist"中第一次出现这一观点,即马克思主义在这些社会中并没有真实的社会住址。

[②] 卡达尔·亚诺什从1956年至1988年是匈牙利共产党领袖。

这三个群体的主要目的就是要大幅度削减老的国家党和体制的权力,以及最后社会主义制度的合法性。但在同时这些群体之间的关系却是不明确和不平衡的,因为这些反对派精英的合作建立在这样一种信念上,即后期卡达尔主义专家治国派会在民主反对派和新知识分子中发现自己的意识形态理论家。当时,最强大的精英群体无疑是后期卡达尔主义技术专家官员,其意图是要掌握正式权力地位。

精英群体的价值观体系在某些方面是相似的。正如我们所提到的,他们处在社会主义体制内部,所以他们信守左派思想并且从内部批判体制。唯一的例外是民粹派作家群体。另一个共同特点是所有的精英群体都相信体制行将被改变。

最近,这三个群体之间的脆弱结盟解体了,但是令人感到意外的是,他们之间的冲突没有任何意识形态性质,因为所有群体都致力于和平的、民主的、以市场为基础的过渡。在圆桌会谈期间,① 他们显然一致认为,必须在很短的时间内按照发达(西欧)民主国家的模式对匈牙利经济和社会进行转型。但是他们的计算中忽略了经济改革对于社会的影响。

在体制变革之后,后期卡达尔主义技术专家官员瞄准了商业部门,主要是银行的位置。这个群体的第二级和第三级成员在国家官僚机构占据着中层位置。民主反对派成立了一个新的政党,② 但是它并没有放弃其政治势力的意思,而是转向其正式角色。这个新政党继续着知识分子的批判传统,但只是在反对执政联盟的意义上。

新改革派知识分子是最为多样化的,因为他们中间一些领导成员成为了政治家,另一些人转向了公共管理部门或经济企业。综上所述,精英结构的变化呈现为以下几种形式:政治家、商人、官僚以及政党知识分子。

精英与社会:狂野的东方

虽然匈牙利的经济指标在 20 世纪 80 年代中期和 90 年代逐步上升,但是社会发展却是不平衡的,人的生活质量大幅度恶化。无论如何,快速扩大

---

① 匈牙利圆桌会谈是 1989 年国家政党代表和新形成的民主政治力量在匈牙利布达佩斯进行的一系列形式化的、极为条文主义的讨论,最终的结局是建立新的多党政治体制。
② SZDSZ:自由民主主义者联盟。

市场的代价是动摇了制度化了的社会保障体系，实质上在社会行动者之间造成新的紧张关系。这种现象在文学中被称为"狂野的东方"。在这个狂野的东方，旧的社会网络、关系被打破了，人人都竭力在新形成的社会中找到其新的社会地位。这里暂且不提这种现象的学术背景以及人的关系和情绪的关联性，只是简略地概述一下关于匈牙利社会的情绪状态的调查，这种情绪状态会清楚地告诉我们"狂野的东方"是什么意思。

社会的情绪状态过去而且现在仍然非常糟糕。但是由于社会行动者之间的情感关系很难评价，所以只列举几个关于这一问题的硬数据。[1] 根据调查结果，早在1983~1988年期间，神经质抑郁综合征的发病频率和严重程度急剧上升。1983年抑郁者的比率是24.3%，1988年受访者中有34%抱怨具有抑郁症候，1995年这个数字是30.5%。[2]

根据另一项调查，[3] 社会资本的作用在20世纪90年代大幅上升，为了成功地获得利益，人们需要具有更多的关系。然而，在1986~1993年之间，18~24岁年龄组的人有精神朋友的人数[4]从65%降至23.4%，25~34岁年龄组从39%降至17.9%，35~44岁成年人组从28%降至14.2%，1984年自杀率达到了高峰，当年的自杀率是十万分之四十六。[5]

尤利娅·索洛伊和阿格奈什·沃伊道对这种日趋更甚的不信任所做的一项说明指出，在国家社会主义时期，对大多数人来说做运营商的机遇是有限的，所以大部分情感精力都指向了私人领域，尤其是家庭。因此，在体制变革时期，私人领域承载着在本质上是不能满足的期望。这产生了一种永久的紧张关系，表现为酗酒、家庭破裂等。[6]

在社会主义时代，当第二经济（即正式工作时间之后的兼职工作）渠道开放时，给予人们一个从来不知的自我提升机会，同时也带来了削弱情感关系的副作用。机遇的差别化进一步削弱了以前的情感共同体，并且经常造

---

[1] 例如，玛丽娅·科普的调查；Rudolf Andorka, 1994 (Merre tart a magyar társadalom?, Antológia Kiadó, Lakitelek); László Laki, 1996 ("Töredékes helyzetkép a perifériáról" in Társadalmi Szemle, November 1996, pp. 46 - 61.)。

[2] Kopp, Mária-Skrabski, Árpád-Löke, János-Szendrák, Sándor: "Magyar lelkiállapot az átalakuló társadalomban", in Századvég, Fall 1996. pp. 87 - 102.

[3] Utasi, ágnes: *Hungarian Peculiarities in the Choice of Friends*, conference paper, 1996.

[4] 乌塔希将那些与他们分担情绪的问题和感受的人称为精神朋友。

[5] Központi Statisztikai Hivatal.

[6] Szalai, Júlia-Vajda, Ágnes, A 'szociális' és az ' egészségügyi' ellátás határán, in Szociálpolitikai Értesítő, 1988/1.

成家庭关系紧张。有时，生活在朝不保夕状态中或已经丢失了工作的家庭成员，明显显得沉默寡言，甚至在家庭内公然实施攻击行为。不仅家庭关系如此，职场的情况同样如此。在失业的冲击下，雇员之间出现了激烈的竞争，彼此关系紧张。与此同时，新的企业主千方百计地阻止公司内形成任何建立在团结上、有利于雇员权益的关系。然而，体制变革的获胜者日子也同样不好过。突然间的多次飞黄腾达伴随的是朋友和同事的嫉妒乃至攻击，有时是来自家庭成员。在这样的社会环境中，个人可能发现自己处在一种情感真空之中。

此外，担负着代表社会这一角色的精英沿循同样的模式来获得新的社会地位。匈牙利精英所获得的地位并不是技能出色的结果，而主要是其符号资本的利益回报所得。除了不明确的精英权势集团，社会或市场中没有任何人能控制精英的前进。

但是，对社会的大多数人而言，有更多选择的新价值观产生的却是极大的失望，因为他们的现实机遇快速减少而非增加。这种糟糕的情绪状态的后果之一是，宗教热和各种教派的作用呈上升势头，暴力和攻击行为有增无减。这是上面所提到的抑郁症增多、自杀率上升的主要原因。这个进程在政治体制变革之后加快了。

精英的变形

正如上文已经提到的，卡达尔主义专家治国派与民主反对派在 20 世纪 80 年代的暗地结盟的基础是技术专家官员在民主反对派中看到了其自己的意识形态理论家。民主反对派以及与他们联在一起的新改革派知识分子的唯一现实的社会基础是卡达尔主义精英。在成功地实施了政治体制变革之后，这个联盟解体了。

与成功实施的体制变革并行的是知识分子分崩离析和社会主义的垮台，之后，他们的活动也随之市场化。三条不同的道路开始形成。第一条道路是"媒体人物"界。他们具有在媒体上侃侃而谈的技能：详细地分析问题并且经验地（或准经验地）证实他们的思想，因为媒体并不关注理论探究。

第二条道路是高等教育界。大多数知识分子除了他们在大学就职外还充当政治经济精英的顾问。这个人群小心翼翼地捍卫对其特定知识资本的垄断，并且极力避免综合全面地探讨社会问题。

第三条道路显然是政界。1994年，后期卡达尔主义精英（在击败了其主要对手基督教—保守派政治力量之后）掌握了权力，所以新精英可以稳固其权力地位。1994年大选之后，获得顶级政治权力的专家治国派得以将其经济资本和重新获得的政治资本转换为文化资本，然后又将这种文化资本转换回经济和政治资本。后期卡达尔主义的专家治国派只关注意识形态上的"最小国家"，直到他们动摇和征服这个国家。

在1990~1994年这个时期，不仅选票的分布"转向左派"，而且参加投票的公众对于经济政策的态度也转向左派，他们变得更加反对市场经济。在所考察的各个领域，1994年大选获胜者来自左翼群体的支持率的上升幅度大大超过来自右翼群体的支持。但社会党在1994~1998年期间的情况则恰好相反。虽然其来自右翼群体的选票比例有所增长，但是却丢掉了左翼群体的选票。为了组成政府，社会党在1998年变得非常右倾，但是对于经济政策的态度却没有相似的改变。此外，1998年大选获胜者来自反对而非赞成市场经济的选票比例有所增长。

匈牙利社会党和自由民主主义者联盟的执政联盟在1998年大选中被右翼青年民主主义者联盟所击败，后者与小农党和保守的匈牙利民主论坛成立了联合政府。新政权领导人的社会化不同于后卡达尔主义精英。在20世纪80年代国家社会主义已经在走向崩溃，借助意识形态中的缺口对于个人利益的承认成为可能。这些条件使注重个人成功的强硬人格社会化。由于他们当时的年龄所限，他们并不具有一个经济委托人或能够表达他们的意识形态的文化精英。因此，1998年议会选举之后，执政党青年民主主义者联盟开始建造其经济和文化地位。该党在最近的2006年大选获胜之后，其领导人披露说，体制变革以"摧毁社会党"而告结束，更重要的是，以稳固了党的新精英而告结束。

精英的责任

正如我们所看到的，在政治和经济变革期间，由于精英们与社会越来越（自我）分离，所以他们非常欠缺解决社会问题的社会关系和社会经验。这就是为什么精英们把社会看作只是他们活动的一个对象的原因所在。然而，他们不时体验的是一种微弱的悔恨感和一种他们需要展示团结的期望。精英们并未（因为他们不能）把这种期望转变为一种情感规范。精英们薄弱的社会关系的另一个后果不是情感态度的责任。主要的问题是缺乏批判传统。不懂得过去,不讨论过去共同的痛苦经验,是无法保持批判传统的。但是知识界缄默不语。

如今,知识分子的批判角色仍然需要恢复。一方面,它可以起到防止经济精英日趋更甚的过度统治的作用。另一方面,对于以敌视的态度来理解社会中正在发生的事情,越来越需要扩大其约束范围。最后,信息革命也是一个崭新的挑战,它将从根本上重塑知识分子与社会之间的关联。除了这种困境以及变化的经济政治形势之外,我在最后希望精英与社会将再一次同舟共济。

(萧俊明 译)

参考文献

Andorka, Rudolf (1994), Merre tart a magyar társadalom?, Antológia Kiadó, Lakitelek.

Kopp, Mária-Skrabski, Árpád-Löke, János-Szendrák, Sándor (1996), 'Magyar lelkiállapot az átalakuló társadalomban', in Századvég, Fall 1996. pp. 87 – 102.

Kopp, Mária-Skrabski Árpád (1986), 'Magyar lelkiállapot az ezredforduló után', in Távlatok, 1986. szám. pp. 1 – 15.

Laki, László (1996), 'Töredékes helyzetkép a perifériáról', in Társadalmi Szemle, November 1996, pp. 46 – 61.

Szalai, Erzsébet (1994), 'The Power Structure in Hungary After the Political Transition', in Bryant, Christopher G. A.-Mourzycki, Edmund (eds.): *The New Great Transformation. Change and Continuity in East Central Europe*, Routledge, London, 1994, pp. 120 – 143.

Szalai, Júlia-Vajda, Ágnes (1988), 'A ' szociális' és az ' egészségügyi' ellátás határán', in Szociálpolitikai Értesítő, 1988/1.

Szelényi, Iván (1990), 'The Prospect and Limits of the East European New Class Project: An Autocritical Reflection on the Intellectuals on the Road to Class Power', in *Új osztály, állam, politika.* Európa Könyvkiadó, Budapest, pp. 7 – 50.

Utasi, Ágnes (1996), 'Hungarian Peculiarities in the Choice of Friends', conference paper.

Wild East-Or the Life after System-change

Hortenzia Hosszú[*]

After 20 years system-change in Hungary and the other Eastern Central European countries is coming to end. A new social structure has to be consolidated with a new relationship between new elites and society. After the age of state socialism new lifestyles and behavior patterns have emerged.

However, under the democratic political and the neo-capitalist market systems, the new social structure suffers from significant inequalities, which are becoming hereditary over the generations. The root of this phenomenon is the lack of guided and socially controlled strategy of transformation. The consolidation of capitalism in Hungary takes place in an international context which goes to a several new tensions among the social actor after the age of collectivism. As the result of power concentration in the economy and the intensive globalization a sharp social struggle was opened on the field on re-distribution of opportunities. This fight is grimmer

---

[*] Hortenzia Hosszu was born in Balassagyarmat (Hungary) in1974. She was awarded his doctoral degree in literary science in 2008 at University of Miskolc, (Miskolc, Hungary). She is now a research fellow of the Institute for Political Science (IPS) of Hungarian Academy of Sciences (HAS). She has published a book in political history of India (*India politikai t? rténete.* 2009), several book chapters and numerous research articles both in Hungarian and English, including 'Transformation of Governance in Hungary' (2009), 'Some Question of Globalization and Social Security in case of Hungary' (2207). Her current research interests include issues in comparative politics, governmental and political Systems, governmental reforms, governance (efficiency, capacity).

and tougher than ever, and is expected to intensify further because the life perspectives of significant social groups have worsened.

However, the Hungarian elite refuse to admit this phenomenon. My focus is the following: giving a brief description and diagnosis about the new social structure, and value-orientation and mentality of the society with the responsibility of elites in the first decade of democracy.

New Elite

After the regime-change in the '90s the old, communist elite had a very limited opportunity to convert its political power, because the communist elite no longer existed as a uniform social group at the end of eighties, and by that time the political system was occupied by young technocrats.

However, the core of the current Hungarian elite developed from the internal opposition during socialism, from the three lately mentioned groups of elite.

The history of the reformist elite started with the reflection on the substance of Marxism. In the 1960s it was a forbidden fruit, but the critical spirit and radicalism of the doctrine prompted young intelligentsia to confront the ideals and realities of state socialism. At that time the majority of them believed in the human face of socialism which could be changed by reforms by party leaders. The first decisive change began in the counter reform process in the 1960s. From that point in time, it was no longer possible that the upper levels of the party leadership convinced of their suitability in bringing about reforms. First sign of this thinking was the Charter 77 action and the following debate about their attitude towards Marxism. [1] From the middle of 1970's the new intellectual elite strengthened their political ambitions leading to break from Marxism.

However, from the beginning of the 1980's a new generation grew up within the state party, which was characterized by a commitment towards market reform,

---

[1] György Bence and Kis János in their publication 'A Soviet type of society seen through the eyes of Marxist' the idea first appeared that the Marxism has no real social address in these societies.

but with the strong relationship with the old elite. This young technocrat group, which was called 'late-Kádárist technocrats'[①], was described by a conservative-liberal system of values, although they were the products of socialist bureaucracy. For that very reason this group gained an increasingly strong bargaining position within the political decision-making system.

Instead of young technocrats two groups of elite had played decisive roles in the change of political system: democratic opposition and new reformist intellectuals. The new reformist intellectuals were for the most part employed in state research institutes dealing with the social issues. This group of elite had two subgroups, one segment gathering around democratic opposition, and another was the group of populist writers. The democratic opposition continued to place themselves apart from the institutional powers, because since 1970s they dismissed from their jobs, placed under tight police supervision.

The main purpose of these three groups was to considerably reduce the powers of the old state party, institutions and finally the legitimation of the socialist system. Nevertheless, at the same time the relationship among the groups was ambivalent, and unbalanced, because the collaboration of counter elite was built on that believe that the late-Kádárist technocracy would discover their own ideologists in the democratic opposition and the new intellectuals. That time unquestionably the strongest elite group was late-Kádárist technocrats, which were intent on seizing formal power positions.

The value system of the elite groups in some respect was similar. As we mentioned they were inside the socialist system, so they were committed to leftist ideas and criticized the regime from inside. Only exception was the group of populist writers. Another common trait was that all the elite groups believed that the system would to be changed.

Lately the fragile alliance between these three groups dissolved, but surprisingly the original conflict had no ideological nature because all groups committed themselves with peaceful, democratic, market-based transition. During the

---

① Kádár János was Hungarian communist leader from 1956 to 1988.

roundtable talks[①] there was obvious that they agreed that the Hungarian economy and society must be transformed on the model of developed (Western-European) democratic countries within a very short of time. But the elite omitted from the calculation the impacts of the economical change on the society.

After regime-change, the late-Kádárist technocrats oriented themselves towards the business sector, mainly in bank-positions. The third-and second-rank members of this group occupied the middle level positions in state bureaucracy. The democratic opposition formulated a new party[②], but it did not mean that it gave up its political influence, rather that it turned to its formal role. The new party continued the critical intellectual tradition but only in the sense of being opposed to the ruling coalition.

The new reformist intelligentsia was the most diversified, because some of their leading members became politicians, others gravitated the public administration or towards economic enterprise. Summarizing above, the changes in structure of the elites had assumed the following forms: politicians, businessman, bureaucrats, and party intelligentsia.

Elites and the Society: Wild East

Although the economic indicators of Hungary step by step were improving during the mid 1980s and 1990s, but the social development was unbalanced, and the human quality of the life had significantly deteriorated. The price of having rapidly expanding market shake the institutionalized social security system and by nature opened new tensions among social actors. This phenomenon in the literature is called 'Wild East', where the old social networks, connections broken up and everybody tried to find his/her new social status in the newly formed society. Not mentioning here the scholarly background of this phenomena and its connection nature of human relations and emotions I briefly sum up surveys about emotional

---

① Hungarian Roundtable Talks were a series of formalized, highly legalistic discussion among the state-party representatives and newly formed democratic political forces in 1989 held in Budapest, Hungary ended with the creation of the new, multi-party political system.
② SZDSZ: Alliance of Liberal Democrats.

status the Hungarian society, which clearly shows what Wild East means.

The emotional state of the Hungarian society was (and still is) very poor. But since the emotional relations among the social actors are difficult to assess, there are just a few hard data about the issue.[①] According the findings there were significant increase in the frequency and gravity of the neurotic depressive syndrome as early as between 1983 – 1988. In 1983 the rate of depressed was 24.3 per cent in 1988 with 34 per cent of the interviewed complained of such symptoms, and in 1995 this number was 30.5 per cent.[②]

As another survey[③] shows the role of social capital has significantly increased in the '90s, for their interest to be promoted successfully, people needed to have more relations. However, between 1986 and 1993 the number of those who had spiritual friends[④] decreased from 65 to 23.4 percent among the 18 – 24 years-old cohorts, from 39 to 17.9 per cent among the 25 – 34 year-olds, and from 28 to 14.2 among the 35 – 44 years-olds adults. Suicide rate reached its peak in 1984, when 46 out of 100 000 people killed themselves.[⑤] One of the explanations for the growing distrust among people was given by Júlia Szalai and ágnes Vajda whose pointed out that in the state socialism when carrier opportunities were limited for most of the people, the majority of emotional energies were directed toward the private sphere, in particular the family. As a result, during the system-change the private sphere was loaded with expectations that are by nature family unable to meet. This yielded and still yields a permanent tension which manifests in the high rate of alcoholism, family break-ups, etc…[⑥]

During the socialist age when the channel of second economy (namely part-time job after the official working hours) opened up was given an unknown opportunity

---

[①] For example, Mária Kopp surveys; Rudolf Andorka, 1994 (Merre tart a magyar társadalom?, Antológia Kiadó, Lakitelek); László Laki, 1996 ('Töredékes helyzetkép a perifériáról' in Társadalmi Szemle, November 1996, pp. 46 – 61.).

[②] Kopp, Mária-Skrabski, Árpád-Löke, János-Szendrák, Sándor: 'Magyar lelkiállapot az átalakuló társadalomban', in Századvég, Fall 1996. pp. 87 – 102.

[③] Utasi, Ágnes, *Hungarian Peculiarities in the Choice of Friends*, conference paper, 1996.

[④] Utasi calls spiritual friends those with whom they can share their emotional problems, feelings.

[⑤] Központi Statisztikai Hivatal.

[⑥] Szalai, Júlia-Vajda, Ágnes, A'szociális' és az 'egészségügyi' ellátás határán, in Szociálpolitikai Értesítő, 1988/1.

for self-promotion arose with the side effect of weakening the emotional relationships. The differentiation of opportunities weakened further the former emotional communities and often ended with family tensions. Sometimes, those family members, whose lived in existential uncertainty or lost their jobs, felt overt which manifested itself in uncommunicative or overtly aggressive behavior even within their family. Besides the family tensions, in the workplaces the situation was the same: under the threat of unemployment emerged a sharp competition and tension among the employees. At the same time, the new owners did their best to prevent the firm any of solidarity-based relations, which could help the rights of the employees. But the winners of the regime-change also suffered. Sudden rises in the social status several times accompanied with jealousy and finally aggression of friends and colleagues, and sometimes even among family members. In such social circumstances people easily found themselves in an emotional vacuum.

Moreover, the elite whose role was standing for society followed the same pattern of having new social status. Since the position which the Hungarian elite had achieved was not resulted by outstanding skills but mainly by the interest returns its symbolic capital. Besides the unclear establishment of the elite none of the society, or the market had had control over the advance of the elite.

However, for the majority of the society the new values increased in their choices yielded a great frustration, because their real opportunities displayed a rapid decline rather than growth. As one of the results of the poor emotional status of the society increased religiosity and started growing the influence of various sects, but in the same time appeared the expansion of violence and overt aggression. This was the primary reason for the above-mentioned growth of depression, the increase in suicide rates. This process accelerated after the political system change.

Metamorphosis of the Elite

As already mentioned, the basis for the latent alliance of the Kádárist technocracy and democratic opposition in the 1980s was that conception that the technocrats saw their own ideologist in the opposition. The only real social base for the democratic opposition and the new reformer intellectuals who linked up with them was the

Kádárist elite. After the successfully executed political change alliance broke up.

After successfully implemented regime change which went hand in hand with the disintegration of intellectuals and the fall of socialism was followed by a marketization of their activities. Three separated paths were taking shape. One of them was the sphere of 'media personalities' who had the skills appearing in the media: analyzing social and political problems in details and confirmed their thoughts empirically (or quasi-empirically) because the media not interested theoretical approaches.

Second trait was the sphere of higher education. However, most of them besides their jobs at universities worked as consultant to the political and economic elites. This group of people defended jealously the monopoly of their specific knowledge capital, and restrain from approaching social problems comprehensively.

The third trait was obviously the politics. In 1994 late-Kádárist elite came into power (after the victory over their main rival, Christian-conservative political force), so the new elite could stabilize its position of power. Following the 1994 elections, the acquisition of top level and political power made it possible for the technocracy to convert its economic and it's regained political capital into cultural capital and then converted this capital back into economic and political capitals. The late-Kádárist technocracy was only interested in the ideology 'minimal state' until it had shaken and conquered this state.

In the 1990 −1994 period not only did the distribution of the votes 'take a turn to the left', the attitude of the voting public towards economic policy also moved to the left, it became more opposed to the market, and in all categories examined, the winner of the 1994 elections increased its support much more among groups of left wing persuasions than among those on the right. The exact opposite of this happened to the socialist party between 1994 and 1998. While it increased its proportion of votes in the right wing groups, it lost votes on the left. To make up of the government became much more right wing in 1998 without a similar change in the attitudes towards economic policy. Moreover, the winner of 1998 increased its proportion of votes in groups that were against the market rather than for it.

The coalition of the Hungarian Socialist Party (MSZP) and the Liberal Democrats (SZDSZ) was defeated in 1998 by the right wing Association of Young

Democrats (FIDESZ) ? established a coalition government with the Small-holders Party and the conservative Forum of the Hungarian Democrats (MDF). The socialization of the leadership of the new political power was different than the late-Kádárist elite. In the 1980s the state socialism was already disintegrating and through the gaps in the ideology there were possibilities for recognition of individual interest. These conditions socialize hard personalities focused on individual success. Due to their age at that time they did not have an economic clientele, or cultural elite capable of articulating their ideology. Therefore after the parliamentary election in 1998 the ruling party, FIDESZ started building up economic and cultural positions and after the party latest victory in the 2006 the party leader reveled that the system-change is come to end with the 'destroy of socialist party' and more importantly the stabilizing of the new elite of the party.

Responsibility of Elites

As we can see, during the political and economical changes the elite' social relations and experiences about the social issues were quite poor, because of their increasing (self) segregation from the society. This is reason why the elite considered society a mere subject of their activities. What they experienced at times, however, was a faint sense of remorse and an expectation that they needed show solidarity. The elite did not (because it could not) turn this expectation into an emotional norm. Another consequence of the weak social relation of the elite was exempt from the emotional attitudes. The main problem was the lack of the critical tradition. Critical tradition could not be maintained without understanding the past and discussing about its painful experiences in common, but the intelligentsia was in silence.

Nowadays the critical intellectual's role still needs to be renewed. On the one hand, it is to serve as a protection against the increasing over-dominance of the economic elites. On the other, there is a growing need for expanding the limits of the holistic approach understanding what happening in the society. Finally, the information revolution is also a brand-new challenge, which will fundamentally reshape the connection between intelligentsia and society. Besides the dilemmas and the changed economic, political situation I hope at the end the elite and the society will be again on the same side.

References

Andorka, Rudolf (1994), Merre tart a magyar társadalom?, Antológia Kiadó, Lakitelek.

Kopp, Mária-Skrabski, Árpád-Löke, János-Szendrák, Sándor (1996), 'Magyar lelkiállapot az átalakuló társadalomban', in Századvég, Fall 1996. pp. 87 -102.

Kopp, Mária-Skrabski Árpád (1986), 'Magyar lelkiállapot az ezredforduló után', in Távlatok, 1986. szám. pp. 1 -15.

Laki, László (1996), 'Töredékes helyzetkép a perifériáról', in Társadalmi Szemle, November 1996, pp. 46 -61.

Szalai, Erzsébet (1994), 'The Power Structure in Hungary After the Political Transition', in Bryant, Christopher G. A. -Mourzycki, Edmund (eds.): *The New Great Transformation. Change and Continuity in East Central Europe*, Routledge, London, 1994, pp. 120 -143.

Szalai, Júlia-Vajda, Ágnes (1988), 'A'szociális' és az 'egészségügyi' ellátás határán', in Szociálpolitikai Értesítő, 1988/1.

Szelényi, Iván (1990), 'The Prospect and Limits of the East European New Class Project: An Autocritical Reflection on the Intellectuals on the Road to Class Power', in *Új osztály, állam, politika*. Európa Könyvkiadó, Budapest, pp. 7 -50.

Utasi, Ágnes (1996), 'Hungarian Peculiarities in the Choice of Friends', conference paper.

韩流的文化启示

——兼论韩流对现代社会生活方式的影响及其文化根源探析

朴光海[*]

一 引言

　　自 20 世纪 90 年代末开始，以韩剧为代表的韩国电影、歌舞、音乐、服饰、游戏、整容、料理以及其他韩国商品等汇聚成一股"韩流"，在中国兴起一股流行热潮。这股流行热潮以中国为震源地，逐渐向中国大陆周边的国家和地区扩展和蔓延，并在短短几年间就席卷了亚洲大部分地区，甚至还扩展到了中东、中亚和俄罗斯等地。在这些国家和地区，韩流的影响力已经超越了一般意义上的文化流行现象层面，而开始逐渐影响到人们的衣食住行等生活习惯。在中国，韩流的到来打破和改变了一部分人群的生活习惯和生活方式，进而成为现代生活方式的一种载体。韩流是一种创新文化，它以东亚传统文化为本源，融合西方现代文化要素而形成，即它的基因来自于东亚传统文化，而形式则是借用西方现代文化。所以可以说，韩流是东西方文化、传统与现代文化相结合、相融合的产物。从韩流这一文化形式可以看出，传统性与现代性没有必然的对立，如果将二者的

---

[*] 朴光海（Piao Guanghai），男，1972 年出生。2009 年获中国社会科学院哲学博士学位。中国社会科学院文献信息中心副研究员。专业领域：韩国哲学、韩国文化、中韩文化交流等。主要著述有："韩国学界研究花潭哲学的现状及特点"（2009）、"中韩关系发展中的'韩流'与'汉风'"（2008）、《日本韩国国家形象的塑造与形成（韩国篇）》（2007）等。

长处和优势因素挖掘出来并加以融合和改进,即优势互补、相互交融,就会创造出更具价值的东西。韩流的经验告诉我们,发展现代化,要立足本民族传统文化,在继承、发展和创新传统文化的基础上,努力实现现代化。

二 韩流成为现代生活方式的一种载体

西方早期的社会学家凡勃伦(Thorstein Veblen)说:"生活方式可以概括地把它说成是一种流行的精神态度或生活理论"[①]。在不同历史时期、不同社会发展阶段,不同阶层、不同年龄、不同性别、不同职业的人,都各自有着自己的生活形态和生活方式。尤其是在注重个性完美的现代社会,人们更加重视自己的生活意愿,并按照自己的审美取向和价值取向自由地选择自己的生活方式。所以,选择什么样的生活方式,完全取决于个人。

韩流在中国盛行已有十多年的时间了,韩流对一部分人的生活方式产生了很大的影响,尤其是对人们的闲暇生活方式和消费生活方式产生了较大影响。例如,闲暇时打开电视看韩剧已经成为许多中国家庭闲暇生活的一种习惯。韩剧对于中国观众来说可谓老少皆宜。据新浪网调查,在接受调查的网民中有83.12%的人表示喜欢"韩剧",在问到你最喜欢哪个国家或地区的影视时,有54.55%选择了"韩剧"。[②]年轻人看韩剧则更为灵活和方便,他们通过互联网或干脆买来影碟一口气看完,而有关韩剧的话题更是人们茶余饭后津津乐道的谈资。韩剧对于中国人认识和了解韩国和韩国文化起到了重要的媒介作用,韩剧中干净整洁、充满现代化气息的城市风貌和美丽的自然风光吸引着人们对韩国旅游的向往。据韩国文化体育观光部统计,从2000年开始,每年有几十万中国游客涌向韩国,2009年中国访韩游客数为134.2万人,占整个访韩外国游客的19%。[③]着迷于韩国歌舞明星和韩国时尚的青少年,不仅模仿明星的舞姿和演唱,就连打扮也仿效那些明星,将头发染成其他颜色,穿肥大的裤子和高高的松糕鞋,更有甚者,直接拿着自己喜欢的明星的照片到美容店整容,"哈韩一族"在中国的大街小巷悄然出现;韩国

[①] 凡勃伦:《有闲阶级论》,蔡受百译,商务印书馆,1982,第16页。
[②] "特别关注:'韩剧'热与中国青少年的成长",http://theory.people.com.cn/GB/40555/4154221.html。
[③] 韩国文化体育观光部:http://www.mcst.go.kr/main.jsp。

餐厅、韩国美容店经常顾客盈门，许多人乐此不疲地光顾韩国店体验别样的韩国风情；韩国化妆品、时装、服饰、手机、家电、汽车等成为人们喜爱的商品；大批中国学生到韩国留学深造，截至2009年，在韩留学的中国学生数达到5.7万人，占韩国外国留学生总数的60%以上，如此等等都说明韩流已经成为一部分人生活方式的载体，而且在他们的生活中占据着重要地位。

韩流作为一种流行文化，能在短短的时间内风靡中国，并且能被中国人欣赏和接受，凸显了韩流的独到之处。那么，中国人为什么会喜欢韩流，并将其作为一种生活方式呢？

首先，中国人在接受韩流方面没有任何障碍，而且容易产生情感共鸣和文化认同。这一点非常重要。从文化传播的角度来看，一种文化要传播到另外一个文化圈并产生一定的影响，就要具备一定的优越性和可相互交流沟通的基础——即所谓的文化认同。韩流就具备了这样的要素。中韩两国都同属东亚文化圈，两国的文化十分相近，具有同质感。韩国文化和中国文化有着密切的关联，与其他外来文化相比，韩国文化具有无法比拟的优势，在中国更容易得到认同和接受。另外，中韩两国在感情表达、价值观念和思维方式等方面也都很相近。因此，两国在跨国文化的传播中存在文化趋同性。可以说，两国文化上的相通性为韩流在中国的流行提供了首要基础和条件。而且，两国人的身材、长相都很相近，具有相似的生活习惯和习俗。韩国文化与欧美文化相比较，显得优雅而恬淡，和中国人传统的价值观念、审美情趣、道德评判比较相近，所以容易产生心理认同，中国人就比较容易接受。韩剧可谓是韩流的代表，它在中国受众面最广，影响面也最大。中国观众能够接受和喜欢韩剧的主要原因还是在于韩剧所表现和宣扬的审美趋向、价值观念、道德评判和传统文化等因素能够被中国人所接受和认同。人们会对韩剧里呈现的家庭氛围感到亲切和产生共鸣；对人物之间似曾相识的言谈对话、举止行为，发出会心微笑。从韩剧的内容上来看，几乎每部韩剧都涉及重视家庭、孝敬老人、长幼有序、兄弟友爱等传统伦理美德，并渗透着诸多儒家传统文化的因子。这些都是中国人熟悉而喜爱，但却又正在缺失的东西。所以，中国观众自然乐于接受以韩剧为代表的韩国文化。另外，韩剧生活气息浓厚、场景时尚、画面清雅、演员的表演朴实自然，这些也都是人们喜欢韩剧的原因。

其次，韩流中蕴涵的新颖、时尚、现代、前卫元素深深吸引了人们，尤其是年轻人。韩剧中演员们的服饰和佩戴的饰品都经过精心设计与搭配，色彩艳丽、个性张扬、夸张大胆，随意而另类，充满时尚感，深深影响着观众们的审美观，并使人们不自觉地去模仿和追崇。韩国歌舞现代而充满时尚动感，韩流明星的衣着打扮更是前卫、流行，这些无不深深吸引着中国的年轻一代。

最后，韩流作为时尚流行文化满足了人们追求时尚、彰显个性的需求，从而成为人们生活方式选择的一种载体。随着生活水平的提高，很多人在日常生活和消费中更加注重展现个性和宣扬自我，他们追求时尚、流行和个性的文化，以充分显示主体的个性、品位和气质。而以韩剧为主，以韩国电影、歌舞、服饰、餐饮、旅游、整容、韩国商品为代表的韩流正是综合了传统因素和现代元素形成的时尚流行文化，其形式的时尚化、流行化和内容的传统化满足了人们对新文化的需求，尤其是满足了青少年渴望新鲜、个性化文化的需求。以韩流为代表的韩国现代文化，是以包括中国传统文化底蕴作为根源的东方文化为基础，接受并发展了欧美和世界的现代文化而形成的，所以对中国青年既有新鲜感，又有相当的亲和力，容易被接受。

三 韩流形成的文化根源

综观韩国的历史，可以说韩国文化是在本民族传统文化的基础上融合其他外来文化要素而形成的一种复合型文化，它具有鲜明的多元化、融合性特征。韩流作为韩国的大众文化，显然也具有这样的特征。

首先，以儒家文化为代表的东亚传统文化无疑是其源头文化之一。在韩流文化中，特别是韩流的代表——影视作品中处处体现出东亚传统文化中倡导的重视家庭、重视教育、孝敬老人、长幼有序、兄弟友爱等传统伦理美德，并渗透着诸多传统儒家文化的因子。虽然作品中的叙事手法、表现方式等都非常西化，而且场景也非常现代，但其骨子里的东西仍然是传统的，体现了东方式的伦理观念和社会道德规范。中韩两国地理上临近，两国的文化交流源远流长。早在三国时期随着汉字的传入，中国的儒家文化也自然而然传播到了朝鲜半岛，并且与当时社会的规范制度相折中、相融合，逐渐成为统治阶级的思想主体，整个民族的文化渊源。韩国受儒教文化影响至深，历代王朝对中国儒家文化进行了大量的吸收和借鉴，并加以本土化改造，构成了以儒教文化为内核的韩国传统文化，许多中华优秀的文化传统在韩国保存下来并得以发扬。这里值得一提的是，在保护和保存传统方面，韩国似乎比中国做了更多的努力,尽管日本帝国主义长达三十六年的殖民统治,使得其民族文化传统和资源被破坏殆尽;尽管长达三年的朝鲜战争又使整个半岛饱受战争的摧残和洗礼;尽管目前韩国的现代化程度虽然已很高,但是,与儒家的发源地中国相比,韩国似乎更多地保存和保留了儒家文化的传统并加以发扬。比如韩国每年都要举行祭孔活动,并严格按照中国古代礼制进行,这种祭孔活动在韩国已经延续了1600多年。而在中国,这种祭祀活动已经消失,中国举行祭孔大典要参照和借鉴韩国祭孔活动的程序。又如,韩国的传统节日氛围非常浓厚,每到传统节日,韩国人就要全家聚在一起吃团圆饭,或者去祭拜先祖,或者举行跪拜仪式。总之,韩国的传统节日感觉更具有传统性,与之相反,中国的传统节日氛围似乎感觉越来越淡薄,而且趋于简单化。

此外,儒家文化中的选贤文化、注重教育以及忠君孝道思想在韩国受到了极高的重视,并且已经深深融入韩国的民族文化之中。[1]例如,在儒家思想中提倡对父母尽孝,对国家尽忠。在韩国,这种以忠孝为支柱的儒教秩序、倡导大家庭和等级制度、长幼有序的礼节服从精神,经过长期的体验和教化已经建立起一套以社会风俗和价值观念为基础的自律性道德规范。我们在一些韩国影视作品中也能看到的周末团圆、遇事全家商讨、按照古礼举行各种仪式等民俗习惯在现代韩国还一贯地保持着。在大多数韩国家庭中,男子和父亲仍然居于家庭中心地位,家长处于家庭的绝对主导地位,"父权制"家庭依然是韩国现代社会普遍存在的、而且是得到社会认可的一种家庭形式。媳妇要恪守妇道,侍奉公婆,相夫教子。家庭是韩国消费、收入、分配以及社会福利的基本单位,现代韩国人的价值观、思想方式和行为方式仍以家庭生活为主。家庭的需要先于个人的需要,这是韩国家庭制度,特别是韩国传统大家庭制度的本质所在。[2] 如今,儒家文化已经深深根植于韩国社会,在政治体制、经济模式以及社会生活等各个方面都产生了一些积极的影响。可以说,儒家文化是现代韩国文化的传统根基,是推动韩国自身文化向前发展和进步的内驱动力之一。

其次,日本殖民文化的影响。日本在对朝鲜半岛实施三十六年的殖民统

---

[1] 李明伟:《韩国:传统与现代结合的新模式》,《新视野》2003年第2期,第79页。
[2] 张东霞:《反思儒家文化对韩国现代化的积极影响》,http://www.sne.snnu.edu.cn/xsjt/jsjy/jxhd/lunwen/se02/0211.htm。

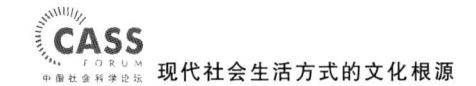

治过程中，主要从以下三个方面对韩国现代社会的形成及韩国现当代文化的构建产生了影响。第一，在向朝鲜强制推行和实施殖民地政策的过程中，将日本现代化的运作模式和现代化的事物也强加给了朝鲜人民，这在客观上缩短了朝鲜的现代化进程。现代法律制度、税收制度、城市商业化，乃至兴修水利、推广优良品种等，都在这个时期以强迫命令的方式推行。这种殖民统治打破了朝鲜社会旧的封建体制，造成了经济的快速发展和社会的重大变化。[①] 第二，日本的殖民统治虽然严重地破坏了朝鲜的经济发展、掠走了大批资源，给朝鲜人民带来了极大的痛苦与灾难，但是从客观上对朝鲜旧的社会体制、政治传统以及传统文化进行了改造，铲除了弊端。朝鲜王朝（1392～1910年）末期，由于政府的腐败和堕落，官场上任人唯亲、官员欺压百姓的现象颇为严重，百姓们怨声载道，再加上保守的知识分子只专注于繁琐无用的空理空谈和道德说教，整个社会毫无生机，陷入严重的败落境地。而日本帝国主义带有军事色彩的高效政府管理模式的殖民统治，客观上铲除了朝鲜旧体制、旧民族文化中的弊端，加速了朝鲜经济与社会的变化。正是由于朝鲜封建旧制度的解体，本民族的传统文化才得到了改造与更新的机会。[②] 第三，日本对朝鲜半岛实施的侵略和殖民地化，使得朝鲜人民蒙受了巨大的灾难和痛苦。不得使用本民族语言和姓名、全部要改用日本语言和日本姓氏，这些极端的民族文化扼杀政策和"皇民化"政策，唤醒了朝鲜人民的民族精神和反抗精神，并形成了极其强烈的民族自尊心和危机意识。这种强烈的民族意识和危机意识已经渗透到了韩国人的血液之中，而且一直延续到现在。韩国自1945年8月15日摆脱日本帝国主义殖民统治迎来光复，便开始对日本文化采取全面和严格的封杀政策，"五十年来没有上映过一部日本电影或电视剧，日本歌曲也在'禁唱''禁播'之列"[③]。虽然在文化上对日本予以阻止和封杀，但是从民族利益出发学习它的先进科学技术、先进管理模式，借鉴它的有益经验，并与之积极发展经济贸易，这种既排斥对方、又要从对方身上获得实利的民族精神着实让人叹服。正是这种民族精神和民族意识促使他们不断地发奋图强、自力更生，创造出让世人瞩目的"汉江奇迹"，并迈进世界新兴工业国的行列。另外，朴正熙执政时期为

---

① 李明伟：《韩国：传统与现代结合的新模式》，《新视野》2003年第2期，第79页。
② 李明伟：《韩国：传统与现代结合的新模式》，《新视野》2003年第2期，第79页。
③ 冯玉忠：《我看韩国》，中国友谊出版公司，1996，第19页。

推动韩国经济快速发展和建构新的文化价值导向所采取的一系列政策和措施，都是借鉴和仿效了日本的模式，这种做法使得韩国很快摆脱了效率低下的传统官僚政治的影响，经济得到了恢复并飞速发展，新的制度、新的文化理念也得以建构和发展。

总之，不论是现代化理念的引领，还是民族精神的激发，亦不论是经济的主观往来，还是文化的客观改造，日本文化始终都徘徊在韩国文化的边缘和外围。① 尽管如此，随着时间的流逝和推移，日本的文化价值观念在一定程度上已经渗透到了韩国文化之中，这是毫无争议的客观事实，并且或多或少地影响着韩国政治、经济、社会和文化的发展。

最后，西方现代文化可以说是韩流文化的另外一个源头。韩国的影视作品除了体现出东方传统文化因子之外，也体现出可贵的平民思想和关注普通人命运的现代观念以及西方文化提倡的国家民主、自由，鼓励个性张扬，强调并肯定个人对自由、自主、成功的渴望和追求等，这正是韩国文化对西方文化的吸收和借鉴。而且，韩国影视剧的叙事铺陈手法、表现方式其实也非常西化；韩国电影采用的是好莱坞式的运作模式，从制作到拍摄，再到包装、后期的宣传、推介和销售，都是一套完整的亚洲版好莱坞模式。另外，韩国影视作品、韩流明星、歌舞作品、韩国服饰等韩流产品都表现出了韩国人充满现代感的生活方式和追求流行时尚、彰显个性的精神风貌，这些要素其实都来自西方现代文化。众所周知，由于历史的原因，韩国同样受到以美国文化为首的西方现代文化的影响。以基督教为代表的西方现代文化给韩国带来了先进的科学文化和教育，它作为西方宗教为韩国人接受人本主义、自由民主主义等西方思想意识起到了重要的启蒙作用。② 韩国作家李光洙认为，基督教对朝鲜所做的贡献可以分为八项：第一，引进了西方文明；第二，重新规范了日益衰落的道德标准；第三，促进和普及了教育；第四，提高了妇女的社会地位；第五，修改了早期的婚姻制度；第六，普及了朝鲜字母和朝鲜文字；第七，使传统的价值观念和伦理观现代化；第八，刺激了个性的发展。③ 可以说，基督教文化对现代韩国社会的发展以及韩国文化的形

---

① 孙雪岩：《"韩流"探源——解读韩国的融合文化》，《聊城大学学报》2009年第1期，第81页。
② 李正奎：《韩国近代社会的变迁与基督教》，《延边大学学报》2001年第2期，第95页。
③ 〔韩〕宋丙洛：《韩国经济的崛起》，张胜纪等译，商务印书馆，1994，第57页。

成发挥了至关重要的作用。①

除上述几种文化源头之外，韩国的本土文化，诸如传统巫俗文化、萨满文化、花郎文化、习俗文化、器皿文化以及各种祭祀文化等也都是韩流文化形成的重要来源。

由此可见，韩流文化是由以儒家文化为代表的东亚传统文化和以基督教文化为代表的西方现代文化构成的，其基础是东亚传统文化，同时吸收、融合了西方现代文化。所以可以说，韩流是东方传统文化与西方现代文化相融合的产物。在现代社会的发展中，韩国保持了儒教的传统，但并没有被儒教束缚手脚，在弘扬东方儒家文化优良传统的同时，学习吸收了包括基督教文化和罗马文化圈等在内的西方文化及世界上其他先进文化。韩国文化的各个部分融合转化，最终形成了以儒家伦理为主、西方基督教伦理为辅的新儒家伦理②，以及以东方儒教文化为基础、以西方基督教文化为主导的独特的韩国文化。③

四　韩流的经验与文化启示

韩流可以说是在民族传统文化的基础上融合西方文化要素创新的一种新文化，既体现了民族性又展现了现代性。韩流对传统文化进行了创新，这种创新就是吸收了西方文化的精髓，并将其和东亚传统文化进行了创造性的融合，从而创造出今天的韩流文化。因此可以说，韩流文化是东方文化与西方文化、传统文化与现代文化相结合、相融合的产物。韩流的流行与发展得益于民族文化传统与现代文明精神、东方文化与西方文化的有机结合，创造了韩国现代文化的超强优势。正如韩国文化体育观光部副部长裴钟信所说的那样，"实际上，韩国也是在充分吸收了西方文化优秀部分的基础上重新将其本土化。比如韩剧，也是在吸收和消化西方文化的长处后，加上韩国特有的意蕴才形成的。兼容并蓄、突出自我，这是韩国流行文化的成功之道。"

从韩流的事例我们可以看出，在发展现代文化的过程中，我们应该重视对传统文化的传承和发展，而且应该以传统文化为本。传统文化是一个国家

---

① 孙西辉：《韩国现代化进程中的文化动因探析》，《理论学刊》2007年第1期，第111页。
② 罗峰：《韩国文化与现代政治转型》，《东北亚研究》1998年第3期，第26页。
③ 李明伟：《韩国：传统与现代结合的新模式》，《新视野》2003年第2期，第80页。

或一个民族在长期的社会实践和发展中积淀下来的物质文明和精神文明的文化遗产，它具有特殊性和民族性，体现了一个民族最本质、最具特色的东西。可以说，传统文化是一个国家实现民族振兴，走向现代化的重要精神支柱和精神动力。传承和利用好了这些传统文化，现代化进程或许会更加顺畅。

在重视对传统文化的传承和发展的同时，我们也要吸收和融合现代性。现代性作为一种文明形态产生于欧洲，它包藏着人类的共性，是人类生存和进步的表现，在一定的历史时期和一定的意义上，代表了人类发展的方向，所以能够被东方接受，且已横扫全球。① 现代性作为一种文明形态是外来的，韩国在走上现代化的过程中，不仅没有与原本的儒家文化发生根本性的冲突，而且受到儒家文化的包容与促进。② 韩流的成功经验表明，传统性与现代性不是必然对立的关系，现代性既然是一种进步，就必定能够和本民族好的文化结合。其实，任何现代化只能从现实传统文化出发，否则便成为无源之水、无本之木，而且脱离传统的现代化也不可能赢得人们的普遍认同和支持。陈寅恪先生说过："其真能于思想上自成系统有所创获者，必须一方面吸收输入外来之学说，一方面不忘本来民族之地位。"③

另外，韩流之所以能够取得成功与其对自身好的传统文化的坚持和对西方文化有选择地吸收和创新有着密切的关系。实际上，传统文化也好，西方文化也罢，各自都有着自己的长处和短处，所以在传承发展传统，吸收西方现代文化，促进传统性与现代性融合的过程中，对于传统文化与西方文化，我们不应该一概否定，也不能全部继承和吸收，应取其精华，去其糟粕，正确发挥其作用。那种毫无批判的、不考虑时代发展情况而全盘继承的做法和完全否定民族传统文化，鼓吹全部要西化的做法都是不科学的，也是不可取的。

总之，韩流的经验告诉我们，在发展现代化的过程中，既要重视对传统文化的传承和发展，以其为本，同时也要吸收、融合和借鉴现代文化，但要注意汲取精华，清除糟粕，促进传统性与现代性融合，从而创造出更加先进、更加符合人类社会发展需求和潮流的文化。

---

① 刘长林：《儒家思想、中国的韩流和现代性反思》，《东洋社会思想》第15辑，2007，第116页。

② 刘长林：《儒家思想、中国的韩流和现代性反思》，《新视野》2003年第2期，第113页。

③ http://wenda.tianya.cn/wenda/thread?tid=4f00c99455bff46b.

参考文献

〔韩〕白元淡：《东亚的文化选择：韩流》，韩国，五角星出版社，2005。
〔韩〕崔凤永：《韩国文化的性格》，韩国，四季节出版社，1998。
方心清、王毅杰：《现代生活方式前沿报告》，社会科学文献出版社，2006。
〔韩〕韩国历史研究会编《韩国历史》，历史批评社，1992。
〔韩〕韩国哲学会编《韩国哲学史》（下卷），东明社，1987。
〔韩〕韩右劲、李成茂：《韩国文化史》（朝鲜后期篇），韩国：一志社，2004。
〔韩〕黄秉泰：《儒学与现代化》，社会科学文献出版社，1995。
金健人主编《"韩流"冲击波现象考察与文化研究》，国际文化出版公司，2008。
〔韩〕李丙焘：《韩国儒学史》，亚细亚文化社，1987。
李明伟：《韩国：传统与现代结合的新模式》，《新视野》2003年第2期。
李胜利、范小青：《中韩电视剧比较研究》，中国广播电视台出版社，2006。
李正奎：《韩国近代社会的变迁与基督教》，《延边大学学报》2001年第2期。
刘长林：《儒家思想、中国的韩流和现代性反思》，《东洋社会思想》第15辑，2007。
〔韩〕刘尚哲等著《韩流的秘密》，韩国，思想之树出版社，2004。
罗峰：《韩国文化与现代政治转型》，《东北亚研究》1998年第3期。
〔韩〕宋丙洛：《韩国经济的崛起》，张胜纪等译，商务印书馆，1994。
〔韩〕宋荣培：《东西方哲学的交汇与思维方式的差异》，河北人民出版社，2006。
孙西辉：《韩国现代化进程中的文化动因探析》，《理论学刊》2007年第1期。
孙雪岩：《'韩流'探源——解读韩国的融合文化》，《聊城大学学报》2009年第1期。
徐远和：《中韩传统思想与现代化》，《当代韩国》2001年冬季号。
张东霞：《反思儒家文化对韩国现代化的积极影响》，http：//www.sne.snnu.edu.cn/xsjt/jsjy/jxhd/lunwen/se02/0211.htm。
张立文等主编《传统文化与现代化》，中国人民大学出版社，1987。

The Cultural Implications of the Korean Wave: Its Cultural Origin and Impacts on Chinese Lifestyle in Modern Society

Piao Guanghai[*]

Introduction

From the late 1990s, *Hallyu*, or the Korean Wave, which is represented by a potpourri of Korean TV dramas, songs and dances, games, food, plastic surgeries, and so on, set off a big boom in China. The wave then spread from China to its neighboring countries and regions, and within a few years, swept over much of Asia and some of the Middle East and Russia. The impact of the Korean Wave in these countries and regions has extended far beyond the general sense of cultural popularity to many areas of everyday life, such as food, clothing and people's behavior. In the Chinese case, the Korean Wave has transformed the living habits and lifestyles of some Chinese people, and has come to be regarded as a symbol of modern social lifestyle. Essentially, the Korean Wave is a kind of creative culture

---

[*] Piao Guanghai was born in China in 1972. He received his PhD in Chinese philosophy from the Institute of Philosophy of the Chinese Academy of Social Sciences in 2009. He is now associate professor at the Center for Documentation and Information of CASS. His publications include 'The Status Quo and Characteristics of Hwadam Philosophy Studies in Korean Academia' (2009), ' "Korean Wave" and "Chinese Wind" in the Development of Sino-Korean Relationship' (2008), *The Shaping and Formation of Japanese and Korean National Image* (co-author, 2007). His research interests focus on Korean philosophy, Korean culture and cultural exchanges between China and Korea.

that takes traditional east-Asian culture as its base, mingled with some modern western cultural elements. That is to say, it is traditional in essence and modernized in form. The Korean Wave can thus be viewed as a blending of eastern and western cultures, or of traditional and modern cultures. The Korean Wave itself demonstrates that there is no necessary opposition between traditions and modernity, and that the advantages of two cultures can be exploited and combined to supplement and reinforce each other. The Korean Wave experience tells us that modernization can be achieved only when it is based on the inheritance, development and innovation of traditional cultures of a people.

The Korean Wave as a Carrier of Modern Lifestyle

In his *The Theory of the Leisure Class*, the American sociologist Thorsten Veblen characterized lifestyle broadly as 'a prevalent spiritual attitude or a prevalent theory of life.'[①] Different people of different genders, at different ages, in different occupations, from different classes, or in different periods of time have different living conditions and lifestyles. In the modern society focusing on individuality, people tend to follow their own will and choose lifestyles consistent with their own aesthetics and values. Therefore, the lifestyle issue can be really individualistic.

In the past decade, the Korean Wave has dramatically influenced the lifestyle of some Chinese people, especially their leisure and consumption. For instance, many Chinese families have grown accustomed to watching Korean TV dramas in their spare time. Korean TV dramas have a wide appeal to the Chinese audience, young and old. A recent survey conducted by SINA reveals that 83.12% of the Internet users liked 'Korean TV dramas'; when asked about the preferred movies of different countries or regions, 54.55% of them chose 'Korean movies.' Young people seem to have easier and readier access to Korean TV dramas. They simply go on the Internet or buy VCDs/DVDs to watch Korean TV dramas, often without a break. Topics of Korean TV dramas are popular among people at their

---

① Thorsten Veblen, *The Theory of the Leisure Class*, trans. by Cai Shoubai, The Commercial Press, 1982, p. 16.

leisure. Korean TV dramas also play an important role in helping the Chinese people understand Korea and its culture, in that both the modern and neatly-manicured cities and beautiful natural landscapes hold a strong allure to the Chinese. According to the statistics of the Korean Ministry of Culture, Sport and Tourism, from 2000 on, hundreds of thousands of Chinese tourists have been traveling to Korea every year. In 2009 particularly, Korea received over 1.34 million tourists from China, or 19% of all inbound tourists. [1] Chinese teenagers mimic the singing and dancing of Korean stars, and make themselves up in the same fashion by dying their hair and wearing baggy trousers and platform shoes. Some of them even take the pictures of their favorite stars to plastic surgeons; Korean restaurants and beauty salons are often packed with Chinese customers, who are eager to have a Korean experience; Korean cosmetics, costumes, apparel, cell-phones, cars and electronic household appliances all tickle their fancy. Every year, a large number of Chinese students go to Korea to study; and as of 2009, there had been 57000 Chinese students in Korea, making up 60% of all overseas students in Korea. All these show that the Korean Wave has become a carrier of lifestyle for some Chinese, and has assumed an important position in their lives.

The Korean Wave, as a pop culture, is highly distinctive in that it should have won the hearts of many Chinese within a short period of time. Why, then, do Chinese people prefer the Korean Wave instead of others, and take it as one of their lifestyles?

Firstly, the Chinese people are more apt to accept the Korean Wave, which tends to evoke emotional affinity and cultural identity in them. This is very important because from the perspective of cultural communication, a culture must possess some advantages for mutual exchanges, i.e. the so-called cultural identity, if it is to be transmitted to another culture and influence it. Obviously, the Korean Wave possesses such an advantage. Both Korea and China are part of the east-Asian cultural sphere, and share a high degree of homogeneity. The Koreans and the Chinese have much in common in emotional expressions, values and thinking patterns, and tend toward each other in cross-cultural communication. This cultural affinity lays a foundation for the prevalence of the Korean Wave in China.

---

[1] http://www.mest.go.kr/main.jsp.

Moreover, the Koreans and the Chinese are similar in height and looks, and have identical living habits and customs. In contrast to the European and American cultures, the Korean culture appears more elegant and genteel to the Chinese, which is congruent with traditional Chinese values, aesthetics and ethics. Here, Korean TV dramas can be taken as a representative of the Korean Wave, since they have the largest audience and are the most influential in China. In terms of content, almost all Korean TV dramas display traditional virtues and ethics such as commitment to family, filial piety, order of seniority, brotherhood, and many other elements of traditional Confucianism. All these are what the Chinese used to cherish, but are missing now. In Korean TV dramas, they find intimacy with that they see, and give an understanding smile at the used-to-be-familiar conversations among the characters. Still, the smart settings, enchanting scenes and natural performance of Korean characters all underlie the reason why Korean TV dramas take to the Chinese so much.

Secondly, the new, modern, fashionable and avant-garde elements contained in the Korean Wave have a great appeal to the Chinese people, especially young people. The clothing and decorations of the characters in Korean TV dramas are properly designed and matched, characterized by brightness, boldness and high individuality. These have produced a profound influence on the aesthetics of the Chinese audience, and tempted them to follow up in an unconscious way. Korean stars look popular and avant-garde in their make-up and dress-up, and their songs and dances are full of vigor and look modern. All these elements are highly appealing to the Chinese youngsters.

Finally, as a fashionable pop culture, the Korean Wave concurs with people's demand for fashion and individuality, and thus becomes a carrier of people's lifestyles. With the improvement of living conditions, many people begin to put more emphasis on individuality in their daily life and consumption. Thus, they try to express their personality and tastes through the pursuit of a fashionable, popular and individualized culture. In this sense, the Korean Wave chiefly represented by Korean TV dramas successfully combines traditional and modern elements into a fashionable pop culture, which echoes the demand of the people for a new culture, and the particular demand of the youngsters for a new and individualized culture.

The Cultural Origins of the Korean Wave

An overview of the Korean history reveals that Korean culture is a hybrid one which combines traditional Korean cultures and foreign cultural elements. By character, it is distinctively diversified and integrative.

First of all, the Korean culture owes its source to traditional east-Asian culture represented by Confucianism. Traditional virtues such as commitment to family and education, filial piety, order of seniority and brotherhood are pervasive in the Korean Wave, especially in Korean films and TV dramas. Although these works are westernized in narration and representation, and modern in settings, they remain essentially traditional, centering on eastern ethics and social norms. Situated in close proximity to each other, China and Korea boast of an ancient history of cultural exchanges. With the introduction of the Chinese language during the Three Kingdoms period, Chinese Confucianism was spread over to the Korean peninsula, and after some compromise and intermingling with Korean social norms, eventually became the ideological mainstay of the ruling class and a source for Korean culture. The influence of Confucianism on Korea is enormous, as can be seen from the fact that all Koran dynasties drew largely on Chinese Confucianism and tried to domesticate it. As such, many of the Chinese cultures and traditions are preserved and upheld in Korea. Indeed, although Japan had exercised an imperialist rule in Korea for 36 years, which all but destroyed Korean traditions and resources, although the 3-year Korean War had severely devastated the Korean peninsula, and although Korea has now achieved a higher degree of modernization, Korea seems to have preserved more Confucianist cultures than China, the source country of Confucianism. For instance, *Confucius* memorial ceremonies are held every year in strict accord with ancient Chinese rituals, which have lasted in Korea for over 1600 years. In China, however, such activities have largely disappeared. Korea is also well known for its strong atmosphere of traditional festivals. On each festival, Korean families will come together for reunion meals, pay tribute to their ancestors or hold worshipping ceremonies. So Korean festivals are generally acclaimed for their strong traditional atmosphere, whereas Chinese festivals tend to be simplified, and are widely criticized for a lack of atmosphere.

In addition, the official selection culture and ideas of loyalty, filial piety and commitment to education in Confucianism, are also highly valued in Korea. For instance, Confucianism embraces the idea that people show filial piety to their parents and loyalty to the nation. This Confucianist system characterized by loyalty, filial piety, big families and order of seniority has been established in Korea as a set of self-disciplinary ethics based on social customs and values, after a long time of experience and education. As can be seen from Korean films and TV dramas, many folk customs and traditions such as weekend reunions, consultations among family members and various ceremonies held in accord with ancient rituals are still well preserved in modern Korea. In much of Korea, the male still dominates the family, whereas a patriarch assumes an absolute position in his family. 'Patriarchal' families are still the most prevalent and widely recognized ones in modern Korean society. Wives are expected to abide scrupulously by chastity, wait upon their parents-in-law, and support their husbands and raise children. The family is the basic unit of consumption, income, distribution and social welfare, and modern Koreans still think, behave and view things in terms of family life. The demand of a family precedes that of an individual, which is the essence of the Korean family system, specifically of the Korean traditional system of big families. Today, the deeply-entrenched Confucianism is playing a positive part in the political system, economic model and social life of Korea. It can thus be said that Confucianism lies at the traditional foundation of modern Korean culture, and motivates the progress and development of the Korean culture.

The second reason has to do with the impacts of the Japanese colonization. During its colonial rule in the Korean peninsula for 36 years, Japan had influenced the formation of modern Korean society and construction of modern Korean culture in the following three aspects. First, in the compulsive implementation of its colonial policies, Japan imposed its modernized models of operation and other modern things on Korea, which has objectively shortened the Korean course of modernization. Besides, the modern sense of legal system, tax system and even water conservancy projects were also carried out in the form of orders and commands. Japan's colonization demolished the old feudalism of the Korean society, resulting in rapid economic development and dramatic social changes in Korea. Second, the Japanese colonization actually transformed the old Korean social system, political traditions and traditional cultures by uprooting the disadvantages, although it severely destroyed the Korean economy, plundered many resources, and caused great misery to the Korean people. Toward the end of the Korean kingdom (1392 −1910), there was widespread corruption, nepotism and persecution of people in the Korean government; intellectuals were generally conservative, focusing solely on idle theoretical talk and moral preaching. The whole society was thrown into decadence and despair. The Japanese military-style and efficient model of governance actually wiped out the existing weaknesses in the old Korean institution and traditional cultures, hereby speeding up the economic and social transformation of Korea. In other words, it was just the demolishment of Korean feudalism that enabled the transformation and renewal of traditional Korean cultures. Third, the Japanese invasion and colonization was a total disaster and trauma to the Korean people. Japan's extremist policies, including replacing the Korean language with Japanese, and replacing Korean names with Japanese ones, fuelled violent Korean nationalism among the Korean people, which later developed into a strong sense of national pride and crisis. The strong sense of national pride and crisis has found its way deep into the Koreans and has persisted till this day. Therefore, as soon as it threw off the yoke of Japanese colonization on August 15, 1945, Korea began to enforce *a complete and strict ban* on Japanese culture, such that 'for as long as 50 years, no Japanese films or TV dramas were ever released in Korea. More than that, Japanese songs were also on the blacklist banned from singing or playing.' The cultural ban adopted by the Korean government, mingled with its endeavor to develop economic and trade relations with Japan to learn its advanced technologies and management ideas, is astonishingly paradoxical. The national spirit and consciousness has enabled Korea to create the world-famous 'Han Kang Miracle', establishing Korea as one of the emerging industrialized powers in the world. In order to promote economic development and construct new cultural values, former President Park Chung-hee adopted a series of policies and measures in his reign, drawing greatly on the

Japanese practices. Thanks to the implementation of these policies and measures, Korea soon overcame the inefficiency of traditional bureaucracy; its economy was soon recovered and began to develop rapidly; and new institutions and cultural ideas also began to be established or improved.

In general, the Japanese culture has largely remained outside the Korean culture, whether in terms of the leadership of modern ideas, inspiration of nationalism, subjective economic exchanges or actual cultural transformation. This notwithstanding, the Japanese cultural values have, undeniably, insinuated into the Korean culture, and are influencing the Korean politics, economy, society and culture in a more or less degree.

Third, modern western culture can be viewed as another important source of the Korean Wave. The Korean films and TV dramas not only highlight traditional oriental cultures, but highlight those modern ideas that are characteristic of modern western cultures, such as civility, stress on the fate of common people, as well as those ideas advocated by western culture, such as democracy, liberty and individuality. These are the elements that stem from the western culture.[①] Moreover, the narration and representation of Korean TV dramas are actually westernized; Korean films follow closely the Hollywood model, from screenwriting to shooting, and from packaging to promotion and sales. Other Korean elements, including Korean stars, songs and dances, clothing and apparel, also display the modernized lifestyle and pursuit of fashion and individuality. These elements can also be traced to modern western culture. It is known to all that for historical reasons, Korea was once under the influence of modern western culture represented by the American culture. The modern western culture, as represented by Christianity, has brought along advanced science, culture and education to Korea, and has played an important role in the Koreans' reception of western ideas like humanism and liberal nationalism. Lee Kwang-su, a Korean writer, believed that Christianity has contributed to the Korean society in the following 8 aspects: 1. Introduction of Western civilization; 2. Rearmament of a decaying morality; 3. Promotion and popularization of education; 4. Enhancemt of the social status

---

① http://ks.cn.yahoo.com/question/1407040603598.html.

of women; 5. Rectification of the early marriage system; 6. Popularization of the Korean alphabet and vernacular literature; 7. Modernization of traditional values and philosophy; and 8. Stimulation of individuality.[1] In this sense, the Christian culture has played a critical role in the development of modern Korean society and formation of the Korean culture.

In addition to the above-mentioned cultural sources, the domestic Korean culture, such as the traditional witchcraft, shamanism, hwarang culture and sacrificing culture, are also important sources of the Korean Wave.

It becomes apparent that the Korean Wave is a combination of traditional oriental culture (as represented by Confucianism) and modern western culture (as represented by Christianity). It is basically a traditional oriental culture, mingled by modern western culture. In its course of modernization, Korea managed to preserve good Confucianist traditions, but was not confined to them. Rather, it transcended them and assimilated other cultures (typically the western culture, including Christianity) to its advantage. Hence the formation of a unique Korean culture, with Confucianism as its base and western Christianity as its form.

The Korean Wave Experience and Its Cultural Implications

In the above, we have pointed out that the Korean Wave is a new hybrid culture that combines traditional Korean culture with modern western culture, highlighting both traditions and modernity. It draws on some good elements from western culture, and integrates them with the traditional Korean culture in a rather creative way. The integration has resulted in a competitive advantage of modern Korean culture. As noted by Bae Jhong-shin, Vice Minister of the Korean Ministry of Culture, Sport and Tourism, 'The success of the Korean Wave lies in that it takes advantage of other cultures while highlighting its own

---

[1] Song Byung-Nak, *The Rise of Korean Economy*, trans. by Zhang Sheng Ji et al., 1994, The Commercial Press.

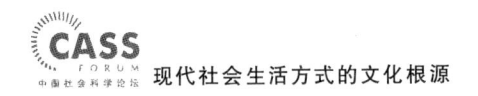

distinctiveness.'①

The Korean Wave experience shows that in the process of developing a modern culture, we should attach importance to the inheritance and development of traditional cultures. The traditional cultures of a nation are those cultural heritages of material and spiritual civilizations that have been accumulated in its long history of social practices and development. They are national and peculiar, reflecting the most essential and distinctive things of that nation. In other words, they are a mental pillar and an important source of a country's national revival and modernization. If we can make good use of these traditional cultures, we will carry modernization on more smoothly.

Meanwhile, we should also lay stress on the introduction and integration of modernity. As a form of civilization originating in Europe, modernity embodies the universal attributes of human beings, marking the existence and progress of man. In a sense, it represents the direction of human development in a particular period of time. That is why it has been accepted by the east and the whole world. In the course of modernization, Korea was not caught up in the conflict between traditional Confucianism and foreign modernity. Instead, modernity was tolerated and reinforced by Confucianism. The Korean experience demonstrates that traditions and modernity are not necessarily opposed to each other. Since modernity marks the progress of man, it can be culturally combined with those good elements in traditional cultures. Actually, any modernization must base itself on traditional cultures, otherwise it would be as groundless as water without a source and a tree without root. As put it aptly by Chen Yinge, 'A real innovative and self-contained system must introduce foreign doctrines while maintaining its own national status.'②

Finally, the Korean Wave also owes its success to Korea's insistence on good traditional cultures and its critical selection and innovation of western culture. Actually, all cultures, be it eastern or western, have their own advantages and disadvantages. Therefore, we should not totally repudiate eastern or western

---

① http://culture.people.com.cn/GB/27296/3851923.html.
② http://wenda.tianya.cn/wenda/thread?tid=4fooc99455bff46b.

culture, nor should we copy indiscriminately the experience of one or the other. Rather, we should incorporate the advantages while eliminating the disadvantages of both cultures. It is thus unscientific and unadvisable to deny national traditional cultures without critical analysis and follow mechanically the practices of foreign cultures, regardless of the advance of the times.

In conclusion, the Korean Wave experience tells us that in the course of modernization, we should lay as much stress on the inheritance and development of traditional cultures as on the introduction of modern foreign cultures, so as to create a more advanced culture that concurs with the advance of times and the progress of human society.

(Translated from the Chinese by Wang Wen'e)

References

Choi Bong-Young (1998), *The Character of Korean Culture*, Korea: Seasons Press.

Fang Xinqing and Wang Yijie (2006), *A Presentation about the Study of Modern Life Styles*, Social Sciences Academic Press.

Hwang Byung-Tae (1995), *Confucianism and Modernization*, Social Sciences Academic Press.

Jin Jianren (2008), (ed.), *Review of the Impact of 'Korean Wave' and Cultural Studies*, International Culture Publishing Corporation.

Korean History Research Association (1992), (ed.), *Korean History*, History Criticism Press.

Korean Philosophy Association (1987), (ed.), *The History of Korean History* (II), Dongmyung Press.

Lee Byung Do (1987), *The History of Korean Confucianism*, Asian Press.

Li Mingwei (2003), "Korea: A New Mode of Combining Tradition and Modernity", *Expanding Horizons*, Vol. 2.

Li Shengli and Fan Xiaoqing (2006), *A Comparison Study of TV Series in China and Korea*, China Radio & Television Publishing House.

Li Zhengkui (2001), "The Evolution of Korean Modern Society and Christianity", *Journal of Yanbian University*, Vol. 2.

Liu Changlin (2007), "Reflections on Confucianism, Korean Wave in China and Modernity", *Journal of East Asian Social Thoughts*, Vol. 15.

Luo Feng (1998), "Korean Culture and the Transformation of Modern Politics", *Journal of Northeast Asian Studies*, Vol. 3.

Paik Won-dam (2005), *The Cultural Choice of East Asia: Korean Wave*, Korea: Pentagon Press.

Song Byung-Nak (1994), *The Rise of Korean Economy*, trans. by Zhang Sheng Ji et al., The Commercial Press.

Song Yeong-Bae (2006), *Philosophical Cohesion and Thinking Mode Differences: East and West*, HeBei People's Publishing Press.

Sun Xihui (2007), "An Analysis of the Culture Drive in the Course of Korea's Modernization", *Theory Journal*, Vol. 1.

Sun Xueyan (2009), *The Origins of Korean Wave: on the Cohesion Culture of Korea*, Journal of Liaocheng University, Vol. 1.

Xu Yuanhe (2001), "Traditional Thoughts and Modernization of China and Korea", *Contemporary Korea*, Winter. Yoo Sang-chul et al. (2004), *The Secrets of Korean Wave*, Korea: The Tree of Thoughts Press.

Zhang Dongxia, "Some Reflections on the Positive Effect of Confucian Culture on Korea's Modernization", http://www.sne.snnu.edu.cn/xsjt/jsjy/jxhd/lunwen/se02/0211.htm.

Zhang Liwen et al. (1987), (eds), *Traditional Culture and Modernization*, Beijing: China Renmin University Press.

现代韩国人的生活方式与巫俗文化的关系

黄棕源[*]

一 巫俗在韩国文化中的定位

在当今社会,东方人的生活方式与西方人基本相同。我们平时不穿戴传统服饰,一般都穿西式的服装;不在传统住宅里生活,一般都在西式的房屋中居住;除了一些传统节日以外,几乎不玩传统游戏,在大部分时间里,我们都享受从西方传来的各种娱乐休闲文化。

现在有些人强调文化的特殊性或相对性,主张东西方文化是两种不同类型的文化。当然,这有一定的道理。无论是宗教信仰、思维方式、世界观、人生观等精神方面,还是经济体制、社会政治制度、文化遗产等物质方面,东西方文化均呈现出截然不同的特征。然而,在认同这种文化特殊性的同时,我们也绝不能忽视文化的普遍性。尽管长期以来东方人和西方人分别在各自的自然环境、历史条件以及思想传统的作用下形成并发展了自己独特的文化,但人类毕竟是有共性的,也有共同的价值追求,因此我们不仅能够了解外国文化,必要时还可以接纳外来文化。举例来说,古代中国和印度的文

---

[*] 黄棕源(Hwang Jongwon,韩国),男,1969年出生。北京大学哲学系博士。北京大学朝鲜语言文化系(朝鲜文化研究所)副教授。专业领域:中国哲学、韩国哲学、韩国文化。主要著述有:《中国的实学争论和对尹拯实学的新探》(2009)《试论程颢"生理"》、《"生意"与"仁"的生命论意义》(2007)《李敦化'新人哲学'述评》(2006)等。

化是两种不同类型的文化，而中国却从印度积极接受了佛教文化。究其原因，正是因为中国人需要佛教，所以才接受了佛教。尽管中国有儒教、道教等土生土长的宗教文化，对于所谓的终极问题，人们却不能从中得到满意的答案，而佛教却对这一问题给予了充分的解答，从宗教学的角度看，这就是中国人接纳佛教文化的根本理由。又比如说，近代以来东方人大量接受了西方文化。同样，这也正是基于东方人的需要。尽管东方各民族有着各自固有的传统生活方式，但是在接触和了解西方的各种生活方式以后，却在生活的方方面面做出了改变。为什么韩国人脱掉了"韩服"而穿上了西装呢？因为韩国的传统服饰穿起来不方便。为什么中国人离开了四合院住进了高楼呢？因为公寓住起来更加舒适。无论是多么热爱传统文化的人，也很难否定来自西方的现代服饰以及居住文化比传统的东西更为方便舒适这一事实。

我在这里之所以强调文化的普遍性，是因为不少人过分地强调了文化的特殊性，并不是为了否定文化的特殊性。恰恰相反，我也认为任何文化都有特殊性，也很重视文化的特殊性，正如韩国学者朴异汶所言，"任何文化都要追求普遍的价值，同时也不能丧失各自的相对性。"[①] 从这一方面来看，东方人的生活方式有其特殊的一面，与西方人不尽相同，而这一特殊性主要是源自东方人的文化传统。中国人常说，儒、释、道是中国的三大文化传统，细想这话，意思是自古至今，儒、释、道三教的文化影响绵延不绝，并且在现代中国文化中也没有完全丧失其生命力。那么，在韩国文化史上影响很大且至今仍有生命力的文化传统是什么呢？过去，不少人认为韩国的文化传统与中国一样，也是儒、释、道，但是后来有些学者发现，韩国的文化传统与中国相比有其独特的一面。具体言之，韩国人自古信仰巫俗，虽然后来自中国传入的儒教与佛教产生了巨大的影响，而且到了朝鲜王朝时期，巫俗还不断遭到打压，但它始终没有丧失其生命力，致使道教没有在韩国扎根。韩国学者崔俊植据此作出了判断，韩国的文化传统不是儒、释、道，而是巫、儒、佛，并提出了如下的有力证据。他指出："如果道教像佛教那样在韩国扎根的话，韩国的版图上应该有很多道教寺庙亦即道观，不过，韩国几乎没有道观。为什么会这样呢？原因很简单，韩国有巫教，它扮演了道教在中国承担的角色，所以韩国没必要接受道教；韩国的巫师做了中国道士所做的事，所以韩国人没必要接受道教。这一点还同样适用于老庄思想。很多学

---

① 〔韩〕朴异汶：《文明的未来与生态世界观》，当代出版社，1997，第220页。

者说，老庄似乎是韩国的传统，但过去的韩国宗教界几乎没研究过老庄，这种倾向在朝鲜王朝尤为突出。我们很难找到老庄思想在朝鲜文化中的影响。"①道家或道教在韩国文化中的影响真的这么微不足道吗？这尚待进一步研究，但有一点是可以肯定的，那就是巫俗对于韩国文化的影响确实很大，至少比道家或道教大得多。据此，我也基本上认同巫、儒、佛是韩国的三大文化传统。

佛教在朝鲜的兴盛长达千年以上，然而自朝鲜王朝政府推出"崇儒抑佛"政策以后，佛教就开始走向没落。它不仅在朝鲜王朝五百年间一直遭受迫害，在日本殖民统治时期也为帝国主义所利用。尽管近几十年来佛教在韩国呈现出复苏之势，但由于长期处于低迷状态，从对整个韩国文化的影响层面上来看，它就远远不如巫俗或儒教。佛教对现代韩国文化的影响主要局限于文化遗产以及宗教信仰方面，佛教文化遗产在韩国政府指定和保护的国宝、宝物中占有相当大的比重；目前韩国的佛教信徒超过一千万。佛教与基督教、天主教鼎足而立，成为支撑韩国宗教文化的三大力量之一。尽管如此，在当今韩国文化的其他领域，例如衣食住行等日常生活乃至社会人际关系中，我们很难找出佛教文化的痕迹。

相形之下，巫俗与儒教的很多思想观念以及行为习惯对于当今韩国社会文化仍有很深的影响，在相当程度上仍然支配着韩国人的日常生活。例如：韩国人喜欢喝酒、唱歌、跳舞，玩的时候十分注重集体精神，喜欢粗放的、快速的风格，这一切都源于巫俗；又如：韩国人重视孝道、祖先祭祀，社会上存在比较严重的男女不平等现象，也有着十分严格的等级秩序，而这一切都来自儒教。在韩国的这两大文化传统中，对中国人来说，比较熟悉的是儒教，比较陌生的则是巫俗。从某种程度上来说，对于巫俗的了解乃是中国人能否更加全面了解韩国文化的关键。基于这种认识，笔者将在本文中主要介绍现代韩国生活文化中的一些独特现象，并着重分析这些现象与巫俗的关系，以此论证现代韩国生活文化中的一些特殊面貌实则源于巫俗文化传统。

二 韩国人喜欢喝酒：巫祭的重演

现代人的生活可以分为工作时间与休息时间：在一天的工作生活中，白

---

① 〔韩〕崔俊植：《从文化的视角解读韩国的宗教》，四季出版社，1998，第9~10页。

天是工作时间，晚上以后则是休息时间；在一周的生活中，周一至周五是工作时间，周末则是休息时间。人为什么要休息？因为只有休息，才能补充能量，获取继续工作的动力。因而人们常说，休息是为身体充电的时间，休息的目的就在于以更加良好的状态返回工作岗位。休息的方法又可分为两种，一种是吃饭、睡觉等纯粹增加身体能量的活动；另一种是游戏、体育、旅游、庆典活动等，虽然这需要消耗能量，却能有效地缓解和释放各种压力，人们经常把它称作休闲娱乐活动。

韩国人类学者李基重运用伊利亚德（Mircea Eliade）的神圣与世俗概念解释工作时间与休息时间的象征意义。他说："简单讲，白天是从事劳动的时间，是在公司上班的时间，夜晚则是离开公司的休闲时间，是业余时间。也就是说，白天是日常生活的时间，夜晚则是摆脱日常生活的时间。伊利亚德把日常生活的时间称做世俗的时间，把摆脱日常生活的时间称作神圣的时间。依据他的这个图式，白天是世俗的时间，夜晚则是神圣的时间。"[①] 通过他的阐释，我们不难发现人们为摆脱日常生活所进行的娱乐休闲活动与神圣的宗教活动有着某种关联。

韩国人所进行的各种娱乐休闲活动也与韩国的宗教文化传统尤其是韩国最古老的巫俗传统有着密不可分的关系。韩国人在闲暇时间里最频繁、最普遍的娱乐休闲活动就是喝酒、唱歌、跳舞。而这与巫俗传统有着极为密切的关联。

韩国人喜欢喝酒，也经常喝酒。更准确地说，这句话的意思是韩国人普遍能喝酒，喝酒的频率较高，而并不是指韩国人都是海量。[②] 韩国人跟亲朋好友相聚，一般都会喝酒。从大学生的新生迎新会、开讲派对、停课派对、五月大同节，到上班族的公司聚餐、大学和高中同学会，再到各种大大小小的聚会，只要是韩国人聚集的地方，就肯定有酒。为什么韩国人这么喜欢喝酒呢？有人说，现在工作压力太大了，一下班就得喝酒，释放一些压力。然

---

① 国际韩国学会：《韩国文化与韩国人》，四季出版社，1998，第85页。
② 过去很多人说，韩国人均酒精消耗量仅次于俄罗斯，排名世界第二（请参阅〔韩〕崔俊植《让韩国人跳起舞来吧》，四季出版社，2007，第33页），但对这个问题，最近人们似乎有不同的认识：《E-Daily》在2010年4月10日的报道中说，最近经合组织公布的统计数据"Health Data 2009"显示2007年度韩国人均酒精消耗量在16个调查对象国中排名第十一，表明韩国人的酒量并不高；《Herald Economy》则在2010年8月9日的报道中说，韩国男性人均酒类产品消耗量排名世界第三。尽管目前有关这方面的统计数据以及调查分析各不相同，但从整个韩国社会的氛围来看，韩国人确实喜欢喝酒，经常喝酒，这似乎是不争的事实。

现代韩国人的生活方式与巫俗文化的关系

而无论是在哪个国家，凡是现代人都有工作压力，难道只有韩国人才有工作压力吗？还有人做出另外一种解释，韩国社会的等级秩序非常严格，白天工作时，下级必须无条件服从上级的命令，一般都不敢提出异议，所以晚上经常在一起喝酒，以此来缓和上下级之间的矛盾。这话有一定的道理，但也不能充分说明为什么韩国人经常以喝酒的方式来解决上下级之间的矛盾。释放压力的办法很多，解决矛盾的办法也不少，为什么韩国人不选择其他的办法，而只是试图通过喝酒来解决这些问题呢？理由很简单，韩国人觉得这个办法最有意思，最有成效。韩国宗教学者赵兴胤在对韩中日三国的休闲娱乐、庆典文化进行比较时说："韩国的娱乐文化非常薄弱，虽然有许多庆典活动，但社会体育的基础尚未奠定，因此，至今也没有健康的休闲文化。"[①] 意思是说，与中国或日本文化相比，韩国的休闲娱乐文化非常单调，除了喝酒、唱歌、跳舞以外，几乎没有别的。这话没错，韩国确实没有丰富多彩的休闲娱乐文化，但在这里还有一个问题需要弄清楚：是因为娱乐休闲文化薄弱，韩国人才经常喝酒呢？还是因为韩国人非常喜欢喝酒，娱乐休闲文化才相对薄弱呢？笔者认为，后者更接近真实情况。很多韩国人可能觉得喝酒、唱歌、跳舞比任何其他形式的活动都更精彩、更有趣。

韩国人的这种意识正是来自于巫俗传统。巫俗是什么？比如说，有人面临一个比较严重的问题，但通过常规方法不能解决，这时他就会找巫师，凭借巫师的神秘力量，祈求神灵的帮助，从而达到解决问题的目的，这就是巫俗。巫俗与佛教或基督教不同，没有系统的教义，也没有什么经典，因此在巫俗仪式中最重要的就是巫师与神灵沟通的环节，也就是巫祭。举行巫祭时，巫婆摆设各种酒食，以唱歌和跳舞来消灾祈福或安慰死者的魂灵。虽然巫婆举行巫祭时不喝酒，但她在整个过程中不断进入一种无我之境，也就是说，巫婆在巫祭的每个阶段召请并接待不同的神灵，包括天神、山神、七星神等自然神以及祖先神、将军神等人神，在这一过程中，还要不断传达神意。而此时，巫婆是根本没有自我意识的，她不知道自己在说些什么，做些什么。巫婆认为，这实际上是一种神灵附体，也就是神灵借巫婆之口传达自己的意思。这样，巫婆随时能够进入一种神人合一的状态，追求一种没有他我之分的、无序的世界。与此相类似，韩国人喝酒，追求的也是无

---

① 〔韩〕赵兴胤：《东亚的传统生活文化》，《世界民族》2001年第5期，第77页。

序、混沌。由于受到儒家文化的影响，在刚开始饮酒时，韩国人十分注重饮酒礼节。比如说，不能给自己倒酒，在对方将杯中酒饮尽后，要为对方倒酒。与长辈同饮时，在得到长辈允许之前必须扭过头来喝酒，等等。但酒过三巡之后，气氛就发生了变化。为了转换氛围，韩国人常常会换地方接着喝，去喝"第二茬"、"第三茬"甚至"第四茬"，直到喝醉为止。喝醉了，就达到什么样的状态呢？达到没有自我意识的状态，也就是忘我之境。

刚才我提到韩国人换地方喝酒，这也是一个很独特的现象。韩国人开始喝酒，一般在餐馆里喝，边吃饭边喝烧酒。如果你觉得差不多了，就说"去喝第二茬"，再找个酒吧喝啤酒，或者找个歌厅边喝边唱。如果你觉得还不够，那么还可以再喝"第三茬""第四茬"。为什么这样喝？很多人只是认为这是为了转换环境和氛围，却不清楚这种饮酒习惯形成的文化根源。我个人认为，韩国人饮酒习惯的形成也在一定程度上受到了巫俗的影响。巫祭一般是由十几个步骤组成的，尽管巫祭程序会因人或地区而异，但"请神"、"娱神"和"送神"都是不可或缺的重要组成部分。在"请神"阶段，巫婆召请自己侍奉的神灵以及祭主的祖先神；在"娱神"阶段，巫婆以歌舞、酒食来接待各种不同的神灵；到了"送神"阶段，巫婆重新召请所有的神灵，包括召请神之外的牛鬼蛇神，让大家一起游戏娱乐，达到神界与人界的大和谐。这样，如同巫祭中各个步骤会产生不同的气氛，韩国人以换地方喝酒的方式来营造不同的氛围；又如同巫祭到了结尾部分实现神与人、神与神之间的合一，韩国人喝醉了，就达到忘我之境，实现彼此之间的合一。

三 韩国人喜欢唱歌跳舞：巫婆能歌善舞

韩国人在酒酣之际，经常会载歌载舞，这时练歌房是他们的首选。在练歌房唱歌时，他们很少坐着唱，大都站着唱。几首歌之后，气氛变得热烈起来，大家就开始合唱，最后变成所有人勾肩搭背大声合唱乱舞乱跳的混乱场面。由于韩国人特别喜欢到练歌房去唱歌，因而尽管它是日本人的发明，却在韩国更受欢迎。可以说，无论是韩国国内，还是世界各地，只要是韩国人生活的地方，就有练歌房。

当然，韩国人并不是在酒后才会唱歌跳舞，而是随时随地都会唱歌跳

现代韩国人的生活方式与巫俗文化的关系

舞。崔俊植在介绍韩国人不择场所唱歌跳舞的现象时说:"由于韩国人太喜欢唱歌和跳舞,甚至在公路上行驶的观光巴士里也唱歌和(站着)跳舞。当广播电台的无限练歌房节目通过电波传送伴奏音乐时,听众会将话筒当作麦克风随之演唱,在全世界很难找到与此相类似的民族。电视台也不例外,没有一天会停止播放歌曲或类似于唱歌的娱乐节目,星期日早晨播放的类似于 TV 练歌房的节目,不仅享有很高的人气,而且还获得过官方颁奖。"① 诚如他所言,韩国人喜欢在观光巴士里唱歌跳舞,敢于在收音机前唱歌。值得注意的是,他们这么喜欢唱歌不是一天两天的事。这里有一个典型的例子。星期天中午韩国 KBS 电视台播出全国演唱比赛,在这个节目里上台唱歌的不是专业歌手,而是普通的老百姓。虽然他们在全国观众面前唱歌,但却丝毫没有胆怯,很多人像在练歌房里与亲朋好友唱歌时那样高唱乱跳,经常令人爆笑。这个节目已经播出了 30 多年,人气依然很旺。

　　那么,为什么韩国人这么喜欢唱歌跳舞呢?这也与巫俗有很紧密的联系。如前所述,巫祭不可缺少歌舞,巫婆必须具备能歌善舞的能力。韩国巫俗研究者一致认为,韩国的巫婆除了作为祭司长和预言家之外,还是一个综合艺人。巫婆作为祭司长主持巫祭,作为预言家传达神灵的预言,作为综合艺人传承传统民俗歌舞。此外,在巫婆的功能问题上还有一点需要补充说明。这就是韩国的巫婆按其种类往往会侧重于上述三个功能中的某一两个功能。韩国的巫婆以汉江为界分为汉江以北的降神巫和汉江以南的世袭巫:降神巫是指通过神灵附体与诸多神灵相沟通的巫婆。她们主持巫祭,经常传达神意,也唱歌跳舞,发挥上述的三个功能,但正如"降神巫"这一名称所显示的那样,她们更侧重于预言家功能,唱歌跳舞的水平远远不如世袭巫。世袭巫是指在世代继承巫业的家庭中成长的巫婆。由于世袭巫从小专门学习巫祭所需的歌舞,对于巫歌和巫舞,她们都很精通,但通常没有与神灵沟通的能力,因此,在举行巫祭时,她们与占卜师做一些分工,世袭巫在家人乐师的伴奏下唱歌跳舞,主持巫祭,需要召请神灵时,占卜师上来与她进行配合。如此看来,就与诸多神灵沟通的能力讲,降神巫具有神秘的宗教力量,但从文化艺术方面的影响力来看,世袭巫在传统民间艺术的传承中发挥了不容忽视的作用。比如说,韩国最有代表性的民俗音乐盘瑟俚、Sinawi、散调

---

① 崔俊植:《从韩国宗教的现实及其透视镜观察到的韩国文化》,《当代韩国》2006 年秋季号,第 71～72 页。

189

等都起源于世袭巫的巫歌和巫乐,韩国最有代表性的舞蹈驱邪舞也源自于巫舞。

再查阅更早期的相关历史记载,我们就会发现韩国人喜欢喝酒、唱歌、跳舞的倾向还可以追溯到部族国家时期。根据历史记载,夫余、高句丽、濊、三韩等位于现在的中国东北地区以及韩半岛的部族国家都举行祭天仪式,而这些国家举行这一宗教仪式的方式极为相似。《三国志·魏志》中与夫余祭天仪式相关的记载如下:"以殷正月祭天,国中大会,连日饮食歌舞,名曰迎鼓";与濊相关的记载如下:"十月节祭天,昼夜饮酒歌舞,名之为舞天";与三韩相关的记载如下:"五月下种讫,祭鬼神。群聚歌舞饮酒,昼夜无休。其舞数十人俱起,相随踏地,低昂手足,相应节奏,有似铎舞。十月农功毕,亦复如之。"① 尽管这些国家祭天的时间或名称各不相同,但人们参与这些活动、庆祝节日的方式却大同小异,都是连续数日间饮酒、唱歌、跳舞。很多学者认为,部族国家时期的神祇信仰以及祭天仪式就是后来民间巫俗信仰以及巫祭的原型。据此我们还可以说,韩国人特别喜欢喝酒、唱歌、跳舞的文化现象近则源于民间巫俗信仰,远则源于上古时期的上帝神祇。

四 韩国人喜欢大家一起行动:洞祭中的集体精神

俄罗斯出生的韩国学者朴露子在回忆他赴韩留学期间的韩国大学生时说:"对他们来说,组成自由的主要因素即个人空间和个人时间似乎不太重要。我们理所当然地认为,为在日常生活中确保自由可以做一些行为,比如说,当人家劝酒、劝唱歌、邀请参加聚餐时,根据个人的兴趣或情况可以行使拒绝权,而在他们看来,这只不过是一种自私自利的行为。'大家一起做'的原则还适用于喝醉后说些淫语、爆笑或唱歌的场合。在他们的社会中,我们几乎看不到有人在这些场合上说些不同的话,做些不同的行为。"② 尽管这位学者以批判的眼光看待韩国人在日常生活中的一些比较独特的行为方式,但我们从中可以获取一条很重要的信息,这就是韩国人在业余时间里很重视集体行动。

---

① 《三国志·魏志》卷三十《乌丸鲜卑东夷》。
② 〔韩〕朴露子:《你们的大韩民国1》,HanGyeoRae 出版社,2001,第20页。

现代韩国人的生活方式与巫俗文化的关系

在日常生活中,或者休闲娱乐的时候,韩国人特别喜欢大家一起行动,而这种倾向在饮食、服饰、休闲娱乐文化中都有所体现。在饮食文化中的典型例子是韩国人喝汤的方式。韩国的汤分为两种,一种是多放水的,另一种是少放水的。喝多放水的汤时,把它分到每个人的小碗里,但喝少放水的汤时,根本不用小碗,而是把汤锅放在餐桌上,大家一起喝一锅汤。西方人认为这很不卫生,韩国人却不以为然。另外,韩国人很不喜欢一个人吃饭,觉得一个人用餐很孤独,没胃口,常说大家一起吃更好吃。正因为如此,我们在韩国很难看到一个人在餐厅里吃饭的情况。集体精神还体现在韩国的现代服饰文化里。韩国人特别讲究穿着、打扮,因而在购买化妆品和衣服上也不惜重金。不过,韩国人在穿着上有一个共同特点,尽管他们大都赶时髦,但衣服的款式、风格却都差不多,今年流行什么,大家就穿什么,没有个性。不仅如此,韩国社会到处都强调服装的统一,上班时间,白领必须穿正装,工人必须穿工作服,学生必须穿校服,因此,在韩国一些大城市的上下班时间里,我们看到的就是穿着千篇一律的人群。

韩国人的集体精神在休闲娱乐文化中表现得淋漓尽致。例如:在现代体育项目中,韩国人最爱看足球和棒球比赛。而观看重要的国际足球或棒球赛事时,成千上万的人就会云集于街头,穿着统一的红色T恤,按照统一的口令呐喊助威,有学者干脆将之称为一场"巫祭"。再比如说,大多数韩国人会加入多样的小团体,以此度过自己的业余时光。这里所说的小团体大都是以血缘、地缘或"学缘"为主的,主要有宗亲会、同乡会、各级学校的同学会等。除此之外,小团体还包括单位的聚餐以及名目繁多的爱好者协会等。当然,这些小团体中有个人自愿加入的,也有半强制性加入的,有儒家文化影响很浓厚的,也有充满现代文化气息的,但不管怎样,这些小团体大都十分注重内部成员的情感沟通、集体行动、团结一致,因此,往往忽视内部成员个人的兴趣爱好或特殊情况。

那么,韩国人的这种很强烈的集体精神或共同体意识是从何而来的呢?我认为,这也同样是源于巫祭尤其是"洞祭"所追求的合作团结精神。巫祭按其目的可分为"荐新祭"、"死灵祭"和"洞祭"。"荐新祭"以防止厄运、祈求个人或家庭的安宁与幸福为目的;"死灵祭"则以安慰死者的魂灵、祈求其往生极乐为目的,有人夭亡或非正常死亡的情况下就常常举行这一祭祀;"洞祭"是指为了祈求丰收或村落的安宁在农村或渔村定期或不定期举行的祭祀。朝鲜王朝普及儒教祭礼,当时巫俗"洞祭"也被儒教"洞祭"所代替，结果目前最普遍的部落祭也是由村落祭官主持的祭祀，祭祀程序及氛围与一般的祖先祭祀十分相近，但也有巫、儒混合型"洞祭"以及纯粹的巫俗"洞祭"。例如："别神祭""都堂祭"等就相当于后者。"都堂祭"是指在都城里举行的"洞祭"，巫婆主持祭祀、百姓参与祭祀的全过程，祈求都城的安宁与繁荣；"别神祭"在韩国的湖南地区举行，由世袭巫和祭官共同主持，但世袭巫还是起主导作用，祈求市场繁荣或渔民满载而归。值得注意的是，如果留心观察这些巫俗"洞祭"，便会发现它十分注重所有参与者的合作团结。比如说，自"别神祭"的筹备阶段起，几乎所有的村民都参与到这一活动中来，一起制作或购买所需的祭品。准备就绪后，在正式开始祭祀之前，所有村民聚在一起，一边喝酒，一边在乐师的伴奏下集体疯狂地跳舞，痛快地玩一次。这样做，不仅能够缓解疲劳，也可以实现村民们的情感沟通以及团结一致。由此可见，在日常生活中，或者游戏的时候，韩国人喜欢大家一起行动的倾向在很大程度上来自举行"洞祭"时重视合作团结的集体记忆。

五 韩国人喜欢快速的、粗放的风格：来自巫歌与巫舞

无论是哪个地区或国家，凡是实现现代化的社会，生活节奏都很快。有趣的是，韩国似乎比任何国家都更能适应这种快节奏的现代生活方式。众所周知，韩国是信息技术强国。目前，韩国的宽带网速在全世界上最快，手机信号覆盖率也最高，信息技术基础设施特别发达。当然，这首先是韩国政府加强基础设施建设、大力推动全民信息化的结果，但也与韩国人的民族气质有一定的关系。韩国人性急，做事很快，如果办事很慢，他们就忍不住，容易发火。

这种急躁的性格当然是有缺欠的，但从积极的层面上来理解，也可以说是一种活泼开朗的性格。我们在首尔东大门服装市场的成功案例中就可以清楚地看到韩国人所具有的这一普遍性格。根据崔俊植的介绍，这一市场的最大特色就是快捷。崔俊植在书中介绍道："从款式设计到剪裁、从装饰辅料到商标制作等，做一件衣服所需的一切材料都可以在市场内解决。据说无论什么样的品种，只要订单一下，从设计到最终成品出来，一天足矣。即使来自日本的订单，只需三天就可以把新衣服挂在日本当地商场里，可见其速度

之快。也许有些人不太相信，东大门市场里的新款式服装，每天少的时候有2000多种，多的时候达到4000多种。"①

疾风骤雨般的办事方式往往容易导致做得不够精致。过分强调快速与类似于军事作战的经济发展战略相结合，韩国取得了20世纪70年代经济飞速发展的辉煌成绩，也饱受了90年代的各种磨难。百货商店、大桥坍塌，金融危机爆发等就是很好的例子。然而不够精致也未必全坏，这也可以理解为韩国人喜欢粗放、简单、朴素的倾向。先看看韩国菜中拌饭和生鱼片的用餐方式。拌饭刚上来时，碗中各种材料排放得整整齐齐，色调搭配也赏心悦目，但用餐时却要将这些材料搅拌在一起，原来整齐好看的材料也瞬间就变得杂乱无章了。生鱼片原本是日本菜，后来由于韩国长期处于日本的殖民统治下，韩国人也慢慢喜欢上了它。日式与韩式生鱼片并不完全一样，前者非常精致，看起来也很好看；后者不够精致，看起来也不怎么样，但韩国人还是更喜欢吃韩式生鱼片。究其原因，就是因为它的分量更多，看起来更朴素，吃起来更简单方便。

韩国人喜欢粗放、简单、朴素的倾向也是由来已久的。我们透过朝鲜后期的各种艺术形式就可见一斑。最典型的例子就是前文已提到的盘瑟俚。中国有京剧，韩国则有盘瑟俚，二者在两国传统音乐中的地位很相似，但是，两者间又存在很多不同点。盘瑟俚舞台十分简约朴素，一个演唱者和一个鼓手就是全部的演出阵容。演唱者采用说唱结合的方式进行表演，有时也会借助手中的道具——折扇来做一些简单的动作。鼓手则坐在演唱者的旁边，一会儿击鼓伴奏，一会儿发出感叹，与歌声相呼应。至于唱法，盘瑟俚的歌声非常粗犷，无论是演唱者还是听众，都认为声音越粗放越好。由此可见，盘瑟俚的特征就是朴素和粗放，与华丽而讲究的京剧形成鲜明的对比。此外，我们通过朝鲜的一些建筑也可以看到韩国人崇尚简约、朴素的特点。例如：朝鲜的很多建筑设计重视不对称，认为如果上下左右对称，人工的味道就太浓，而自然界本身就是不对称的。基于这种想法，朝鲜的建筑师往往把整个建筑设计成不对称的结构。朝鲜四大王宫中的"昌德宫"是最为典型的例子。再比如说，朝鲜的很多建筑直接使用未加工的建筑材料，即使经过加工，也是非常简单的粗加工。参观"禅云寺""青龙寺"等一些佛教寺庙，就会发现很多建筑的确使用了未加工或粗加工的

---

① 〔韩〕崔俊植：《对韩国文化的根本理解》，《当代韩国》2006年夏季号，第64页。

木材。

现代韩国人也好，朝鲜时期的艺术家也好，为什么韩国人喜欢或崇尚粗放、简单、朴素呢？从根本上讲，这正是源于巫祭。巫婆的舞蹈动作很简单，只是蹦蹦跳跳；而巫婆的歌声也正如盘瑟俚一样，非常粗犷。由此可见，巫歌和巫舞粗犷、简单、朴素的特点不仅体现于朝鲜的各种艺术形式中，还蕴藏在现代韩国人的心灵深处，并时时表现出来。

The Lifestyle of Contemporary Koreans and Its Relationship to Shamanist Culture

Hwang Jongwon[*]

I Position of Shamanism in Korean Culture

In the contemporary society, people in the East share similar lifestyles with those in the West. Instead of traditional costumes, we wear Western-style clothes. Generally, we live in Western-style houses instead of traditional ones. We seldom play traditional games except at traditional festivals. And mostly we enjoy entertainment and leisure activities that derive from the West.

Nowadays, cultural particularity or relativity is emphasized by those who claim that Eastern culture and Western culture are of different types. This is true in some degree. Eastern culture and Western culture have totally different characteristics in terms of religion, thinking mode, world view, philosophy, economic system, socio-political system and cultural heritage. However, recognizing cultural peculiarity does not mean we should ignore cultural universality. Under respective

---

[*] Hwang Jongwon was born in Korea in 1969. he received his Ph. D in Chinese Philosophy from Peking University. He holds a position of associate professor at the Institute of Korean Culture of Peking University. He is specialized in Chinese philosophy, Korean philosophy and Korean culture. His publications include *China's Debates on Actual Learning and Their New Exploration of Yuan Jeong's Actual Learning* (2009), *A Probe into the Biotic Implication of Cheng Hao's 'Shengli', 'Shengyi' and 'Benevolence'* (2007) and *A Review on Lee Don Hwa's New Philosophy of Humanity* (2006).

natural and historical conditions as well as ideological tradition, the Easterners and Westerners have developed peculiar cultures of their own. However, human beings do share some beliefs and values. Therefore we are able to understand and accept, if necessary, foreign cultures. For example, despite the differences between ancient Chinese culture and Indian culture, China readily accepted Buddhism, simply because the Chinese needed it. Compared with Chinese folk religions (such as Taoism and Confucianism), Buddhism did a better work in providing the Chinese with satisfactory answers to the ultimate questions. Similarly, the Easterners have accepted Western culture for their needs. Despite their own traditional life styles, the Easterners have seen some changes taking place in many aspects of their life during their contact with the West. Nowadays, the Koreans wear business suits instead of Hanbok which is inconvenient to wear. The Chinese live in apartment buildings instead of central courtyards because the apartments are more comfortable. No one can deny the convenience and comfort brought about by Western cultures, not even one who is enthusiastic about traditions.

The reason why I put such an emphasis here on cultural universality is that cultural particularity is over emphasized by many people. I do not deny the peculiarity of cultures, and I believe each culture has its own peculiar characteristics. Just as a Korean scholar Park I-mun puts it, 'any culture will pursue universal values while retaining their own relativity'.[1] The special aspects in Eastern life styles which are quite distinct from Western life styles are derived from Eastern cultural traditions. It is often said that Confucianism, Buddhism and Taoism are three cultural traditions of China, which have great influence and still play a vital role in modern Chinese culture. What are the cultural traditions of Korea that are important and influential to the Korean life? It was widely believed that Korea shared with China similar cultural traditions: Confucianism, Buddhism and Taoism. But later some scholars have come to realize the peculiarity of the Korean culture, namely Shamanism. As an ancient belief in Korea, Shamanism has survived the great impact of Confucianism and Buddhism from China and the

---

[1] Park I-mun, *The Future of Civilization and the Ecological World View*, Contemporary Press, 1997, p. 220.

continuing suppression during the Korean Dynasty and still remain vital, preventing Taoism from being deeply rooted in Korea. Korean scholar Choi Joon Sik argued that the cultural traditions of Korea were not Confucianism, Buddhism and Taoism, but Shamanism, Confucianism and Buddhism. To support his view, he pointed out that 'If Taoism had been deeply rooted in Korea as Buddhism did, there should have been many Taoist temples in Korea. On the contrary, there is hardly any Taoist temple in Korea. The reason for this is that Korean Shamanism plays a similar role in Korea as Taoism in China, so the Koreans find it unnecessary to accept Taoism. This also applies to the philosophies of Laozi and Zhuangzi, which are believed by many scholars as the tradition of Korea, but were hardly studied by Korean religious scholars in the past, especially in the Korean Dynasty. The influence of Laozi's and Zhuangzi's philosophies on Korean culture can hardly be found'.[1] Further study is needed to see whether Taoism had such a tiny influence in Korean culture. But to be sure, Shamanism does have great impacts on Korean culture, at least greater than Taoism. Therefore I agree with the point that Shamanism, Confucianism and Buddhism are three cultural traditions in Korea.

Buddhism had been flourishing for over a thousand years before the policy of 'encouraging Confucianism and oppressing Buddhism' put forth by the government of Korean Dynasty, from then Buddhism started to decline. Buddhism was oppressed during the 500 years of Korean Dynasty and was employed by imperialist invaders during the Japanese colonial period. Despite the revitalization of Buddhism in recent decades, its influence on Korean culture as a whole is much less than that of Shamanism or Confucianism, due to its long-term downturn. The influence of Buddhism on modern Korean culture is mainly limited to the aspects of cultural heritage and religious belief: the Buddhist cultural heritage accounts for a big proportion of the government protected national treasures; and there are over 10 million Buddhists in Korea. Buddhism, Christianity and Catholicism are three major strengths supporting the religious culture in Korea. However, Buddhist

---

[1] Choi Joon Sik, *On the Religions in Korea: A Cultural Perspective*, Korea: Seasons Press, 1998, pp. 9–10.

culture can hardly be found in such aspects of Korean culture as clothing, food, shelter, transportation and even daily life and social relations.

On the contrary, Shamanism and Confucianism have deep influences on the contemporary Korean social culture in the aspects of ideas and behavioral habits, dominating the daily lives of the Koreans to a certain degree. For example, the Koreans like drinking, singing and dancing, and they like to have fun in a collective, straightforward and fast way, which is originated from Shamanism. The emphasis on filial piety and ancestor worshipping, severe gender inequality and strict social hierarchy in Korean society also have their origins from Confucianism. Since Shamanism is not as familiar as Confucianism to the Chinese, understanding Shamanism is the key to the understanding of Korean culture. I will mainly discuss some special aspects in Korean culture and discuss their relationship with Shamanism, demonstrating that some special phenomena in Korean culture are derived from Shamanist cultural tradition.

II Drinking: Representation of Shamanistic Rites

Modern life can be divided into two parts: work and leisure. Usually people work at daytime and rest at night; they work through Monday to Friday and have rest on Saturday and Sunday. People rest to recharge and go back work in a better condition. There are two ways of having rest: one is to have meals and sleep to refresh oneself, the other is to play games, have sports and travel to relieve pressure from work. The latter is called leisure and entertainment activities.

Korean anthropologist Lee Kijung interpreted the symbolic meaning of working time and leisure time in terms of Mircea Eliade's concept of the sacred and the profane. He said, 'In brief, people go to work at day time and have rest at night. That is to say, day time, which is called by Eliade the profane, is for daily life; while night, which is called by Eliade the sacred, is for shaking off the daily life. According to him, day time is the profane time and night is the sacred time.'[1] It is not difficult to see some connections between the leisure activities aiming at

---

[1] International Korean Association, *Korean Culture and the Koreans*, Seasons Press, 1998, p. 85.

The Lifestyle of Contemporary Koreans and Its Relationship to Shamanist Culture

shaking off daily life and the sacred religious activities.

The various kinds of entertainments taken by the Koreans are closely related to Korean religious cultural tradition, especially the ancient Shamanist tradition. The most popular leisure activities in Korea are drinking, singing and dancing, which are closely related to the Shamanist tradition.

The Koreans like drinking, and they often drink. That does not mean every Korean can handle much liquor. ① The Koreans drink on many occasions, from welcome party for the freshmen, celebration party for the new school year, celebration party for the school closing, university student May festival to company party, classmate reunion party and all kinds of parties. Why do the Koreans like drinking so much? Some believe the Koreans drink to release the pressure from work. However, people in other countries also have the problem of work pressure. Another explanation is the strict hierarchy of Korean society, according to which the subordinates must obey the superiors and should raise no objections. They go to drink together after work to ease the tension. This point, while reasonable, can not fully explain why the Koreans choose to release pressure and ease tension by drinking, which is not the only way of solving problems. The reason is that the Koreans believe drinking is the most interesting and effective way. Korean religious scholar Cho Hungyoun compared the leisure, entertainment and celebration cultures of Korea, China and Japan, 'the entertainment culture in Korea is very weak, although there are many celebration activities, the foundation of social sports has not been laid, and there is no healthy leisure culture.' ② He meant that the leisure and entertainment culture of Korea was very dull compared to those of China or Japan, only composed of drinking, singing and dancing. This

---

① It was said by many in the past that the Koreans' liquor consumption was only next to the Russians' and ranked second in the world (see Choi Joon Sik, *Let the Koreans Dance*, Seasons Press, 2007, p. 33.). However, recently there has been different views. *E-Daily* reported in April 10th. 2010 that according to *Health Data 2009* of OECD, the liquor consumption of the Koreans ranked 11th. in the 16 surveyed countries; in the report of *Herald Economy* in August 9th. 2010, the average liquor consumption of Korean males ranked third in the world. Despite the difference of the related data and analysis, it seems for sure that the Koreans like drinking and often drink.

② Cho Hung Youn, 'Traditional Life Culture in East Asia', *World Ethno-National Studies*, Vol. 5, 2001, p. 77.

is true that there is no colorful leisure culture in Korea. However, is that the dull leisure culture has led to the Koreans' interest in drinking or vice versa? I believe the latter that drinking, singing and dancing are more interesting to the Koreans than other leisure activities.

This idea of the Koreans is from the Shamanist tradition. What is Shamanism? For example, a man who faced with a problem which can not be resolved in common ways will go to a Shaman, who is believed to possess mysterious power to communicate with the spirits. In this way the man can get help from the spirits through the Shaman. Distinct from Buddhism or Christianity, Shamanism has neither systemized doctrines nor classics, therefore the most important part in Shamanistic rite is the communication with the spirits by Shamans, namely the *gut*. During the *gut*, the Shaman serves various kinds of food and drink, sings and dances to prevent misfortune and gain good fortune, or comfort the spirit of a deceased person. Although the Shaman does not drink while holding a *gut*, she constantly moves into trance states, being possessed by different spirits including god generals and mountain spirits, and conveys the will of the gods. During this process, the shaman has no self-awareness and does not know what she is saying or doing. It is believed by the shaman that she is possessed by some spirits who are expressing their wills through the shaman. The shaman can become one with the spirits at any moment, pursuing a state of self-loss and disorder, which is also pursued by the Koreans who are drinking. Influenced by the Confucian culture, the Koreans pay attention to the formalities at the beginning of drinking. For example, a person can not pour alcohol for himself but pour for another who has finished his drinking. When you drink alcohol in front of your elders, you are supposed to turn away while drinking, unless with permission. However, when the alcohol has been round three times, the Koreans will go to the second, the third and even the forth places to continue drinking until they get drunk. The state of being drunk is the state of self-loss.

It is a special phenomenon that the Koreans change places to drink. Generally, the Koreans start drinking at a restaurant while having a meal. Then they go to a second place, a bar to have beer or a KTV to sing while drinking. If they are still not satisfied, they can go to the third or forth places to continue drinking. What is the cultural root of this drinking habit? Personally I think it is partly influenced by Shamanism. The Shamanistic rite is composed of some ten steps, although the whole process varies according to different people or regions: 'the evocation of gods', 'the ritual of playing with gods' and 'the ritual of seeing-off gods' are indispensable parts of the Shamanistic rite. At the stage of 'the evocation of gods', the Shaman will evoke the gods she is serving; in 'the ritual of playing with gods', the Shaman will treat various gods by singing, dancing, drinks and food; when it is time to see off the gods, the Shaman will evoke all the gods and play with them, achieving harmony between the spirits and human beings. Just like the different step of the Shamanistic rite will have different atmosphere, the Koreans manage to produce different atmosphere by changing places to drink. And like 'becoming one with the the spirits' at the end of a Shamanistic rite, the Koreans will enter trance after getting drunk, becoming one with each other.

III The Koreans Like Singing and Dancing: Shamans Are Good at Singing and Dancing

Drinking to their hearts' content, the Koreans often dance and sing, and KTV is their first choice. In a KTV, the Koreans stand there singing, and after several songs warming up the atmosphere, they start to sing and dance together. The Japanese invented KTV is much more welcomed in Korea. We can say that around the world as well as in Korea, where there are Koreans, there is KTV.

The Koreans will dance and sing anytime and anywhere, not just after drinking. Choi Joonsik interpreted this phenomenon, 'The Koreans like singing and dancing so much that they will sing and dance in a bus. They will sing to the music accompaniment delivered by a radio program, which can hardly be seen in any other country in the world. And there are many music TV programs which are very hot and have received official awards.'[1] Just like what he has said, the Koreans like to sing in a bus and before a radio. It is noteworthy that there has

---

[1] Choi Joon Sik, 'Korean Culture: A Perspective of the Reality of Korean Religions', *Contemporary Korea*, Autumn, 2006, pp. 71–72.

been a long tradition that the Koreans like singing so much. For example, in the KBS National Singing Competitions, the participants were not professional singers. Instead of being timid in front of all the audiences, these participants showed excellent performance. This TV program has been hot for more than 30 years in Korea.

Why do the Koreans like singing and dancing so much? This has much to do with Shamanism. The shamans must be good at singing and dancing, which are necessary parts of Shamanistic rites. It is maintained by Korean scholars of Shamanism that the shamans in Korea act as all-round artists besides chief priests and prophets. A shaman performs Shamanistic rite as chief priest, delivers prediction of gods as a prophet, and inherits traditional folk singing and dancing as an all-round artist. Korean shamans are mainly involved in one or two of the above mentioned functions. Korean shamans in the area north of the Han River are Kangshinmu and in the area south of the Han River are Seseummu. Kanshinmu communicates with gods or spirits by being possessed by them. They hold Shamanistic rites by singing, dancing and conveying god's will. Their functions are focused on making prediction and their singing and dancing is not as good as Seseummu. Seseummu have their status as shamans pass down through family bloodlines. Seseummu starts to learn singing and dancing of the Shamanistic rites when they are children. Although they are very good at singing and dancing, they can not communicate with god or spirits. Seseummu holds a Shamaniscit rite by singing and dancing to the accompaniment of a family musician, and when a god or spirit is needed, a Kangshinmu will come up to do her part. Kangshinmu possesses a kind of mysterious religious power while Seseummu plays an important role in inheriting the traditional folk arts. For example, the most representative folk music like Pansaoli, Sinawi and Sanjo were originated from the songs and music of Seseummu, and the most representative dance, namely the exorcism dance, was also originated from Shamanistic dance.

Earlier historical records show that the Koreans' tendency toward drinking, singing and dancing can be traced back to the tribal country period. According to historical records, all the tribal countries located in the Northeastern area of China and the Korean Peninsula like Pu'yo (Korean Buyeo), Goguryeo, Yae, Samhan

(Proto-Three Kingdoms Period) held sacrifice-offering ceremony for Heaven, and they had very similar styles of holding the religious ceremony. It is recorded in *Three Kingdoms: Records of Wei* that in first month of the lunar calendar, people will worship the gods by having foods and drinks, singing and dancing for several days. The record related to Yae shows that in worshiping the gods in October, people will drink, sing and dance day and night. The record related to Samhan shows after seeding down in May, people will offer sacrifice to the spirits and gods, drink, sing and dance day and night, and this will be repeated in October after harvesting. [1] Despite the different time or names of these ceremonies, the styles were similar including drinking, singing and dancing for several days. Many scholars maintained that the religious belief and sacrifice-offering ceremonies in tribal country period served as the prototype of the later folk Shamanistic belief and Shamanistic rites. Therefore we can say that the Korean cultural phenomenon of drinking, singing and dancing is originated from Shamanism and the belief in gods in ancient times.

IV The Koreans Like to Do Things Together: the Collective Spirit of Maeul-gut

Korean scholar Park Noja who was born in Russia recalled his time in Korea when he was studying there and the Korean university students: 'For them, private space and private time as major factors of freedom does not seem very important. We take it for granted that we can refuse to do something such as drinking, singing and going to a party to ensure our personal freedom. However, the Koreans take it as being selfish. The principle of "doing things together" also applies to mumbling drunk words, laughing or singing. We can hardly see any difference in such kind of situation in Korea.' [2] Although this scholar sees the unique behavior style of the Koreans in a critical perspective, we can get an important message from it that the Koreans treasure collective activities in their

---

[1] Three Kingdoms: Record of Wei, Vol. 30.
[2] Park No-Ja, *Your Republic of Korea*, I, HanGyeoRae Press, 2001, p. 20.

spare time.

The tendency of 'doing things together' can be found in many aspects in the daily life of the Koreans, such as catering, clothing and leisure. The way of having soup is a typical case in Korean catering culture. There are two types of soup in Korea: watery and waterless. The Koreans distribute watery soup into different porringer of each person; but when they have waterless soup, they take the soup from the same boiler put on the table, which is considered by the Westerners as unhealthy. And the Koreans do not like to have meals alone, but prefer doing it together with many others. They always say that taking food together makes the food more delicious to them. Therefore we can hardly find a Korean eating alone in a restaurant. This collective spirit can also be seen in the modern culture of clothing and making-up in Korea. The Koreans pay much attention to and spend a lot on their clothing and making-up. However, the Koreans always try to go with the latest trends and in most cases their style of clothing are similar. In addition, the unity of clothes is emphasized everywhere in Korea: white collar workers are required to wear formal suits at work, workers must wear work uniforms, and students must wear school uniforms. In big cities of Korea, we can always see people dressing in similar fashion.

The collective spirit of the Koreans is fully demonstrated in the leisure and entertainment culture in Korea. For example, the Koreans love to watch football and baseball games. While watching important international football and baseball games, thousands of Koreans get together on the street in the same red T-shirts, screaming for cheer, which is called by some scholars as 'Shamanistic rite'. And most Koreans will join various small groups to spend their spare time. Mostly these small groups are formed by blood-ties, geographical ties or 'classmate ties', namely Family Association, Association of Fellow Provincials and Alumni Association. In addition, there are other kinds of small groups like various fans associations. The Koreans volunteer or are partly forced to join these small groups, which are deeply influenced by Confucianism or filled with modern culture. Anyway, communication, collective activities and unity are emphasized in these small groups, while personal interests or peculiarities of members are neglected.

Where did the strong collective spirit or community awareness come from? I think it is also derived from the collaborative spirit pursued by the Shamanistic rite, especially Maeul-gut. According to the aims, the Shamanistic rites can be divided into Chaesu-gut, Jinoggi-gut and Maeul-gut. The aims of Chaesu-gut is to prevent misfortune and pray for the peace and happiness for individuals and families; Jinoggi-gut is to comfort the spirits of the deceased persons and pray for the deceased persons to regain life in a bliss, this gut is usually held when someone died a tragic death; Maeul-gut is held occasionally in villages for harvest or peace. The Korean Dynasty promoted Confucian rites, by which the Shamanistic Maeul-gut was replaced. Therefore, the most popular tribal rites are held by the village rite officials, and the process and atmosphere are very similar to that of ancestor enshrining. But there are also Shamanism-Confucianism Maeul-gut and pure Shamanistic Maeul-gut, for example, Byeolsin-gut and Dodang-gut. Dodang-gut is held in the capital by Shamans and participated by common people, to pray for the peace and prosperity of the capital; Byeolsin-gut is held in Honam Region of Korea by Seseummu and rite official with the Seseummu dominating the whole process, to pray for market prosperity and harvest of fishermen. If you observe these Shamanistic Maeul-gut closely, you will find that the cooperation of all participants are emphasized. For example, since preparing a Byeolsin-gut, almost all the villagers will participate in this activity, making or purchasing necessary offerings. Before the rite begins, the villagers will drink and dance together to relax and communicate with each other. We can see that in daily lives or when playing games, Koreans' tendency of doing things together are originated from the collective memory of emphasizing cooperation and solidarity in Maeul-gut.

V The Style of Being Fast and Straightforward: Shamanistic Singing and Dancing

The pace of life is very fast in every modern society of the world. It is interesting that compared to other countries, Korea better adapts to the modern life style of fast pace. With the fastest broadband, the widest wireless coverage and advanced IT infrastructure, it is well known that Korea is a country with strong IT competency. This is due to the government promotion of infrastructure and informationization, and also has to do with the national character of the Koreans. The Koreans are hot-tempered and tardiness makes them get angry.

This hot temper has negative aspects as well as positive ones, namely an active and open character. The success of the Dongdaemun market in Seoul demonstrates the general disposition of the Koreans. According to Choi Joonsik, dispatch is the major feature of this market. In his book, Choi Joonsik pointed out that 'From design to tailoring, from decoration to brand-making, the whole process of making clothes can be finished inside the market. It is said that right after an order was placed, from design to the end product it only took one day. And it only took three days to finish an order from Japan and place the new product in the local markets in Japan. Maybe for someone it is hard to believe that there are 2000 to 4000 kinds of new-styled clothes in Dongdaemun market every day.'[1]

Efficiency usually results in coarseness. The rapid economic growth in 1970s and the sufferings in 1990s of Korea were attributable to the combination of the emphasis on efficiency and the military-like economic strategies. The collapse of department store and bridge and the eruption of financial crisis serve as vivid examples. This kind of efficiency can be explained as the Korean tendency of being straightforward, simple and plain, which can be exemplified in Bibimbap and Shashimi. At first, the ingredients of a pot of Bibimbap are placed beautifully, which are to be mixed round before eating. During the long-term Japanese colonial rule, the Koreans started to be fond of the famous Japanese food Shashimi. Japanese Shashimi is not completely the same as Korean Shashimi, the former looks delicate and pretty, while the latter does not look as good as the former. However, the Koreans like Korean Shashimi, which looks more and is easier to eat.

The Korean tendency of being straightforward, simple and plain has a long tradition, which can be seen in the various art forms in the later period of Korea.

The most typical example is the above mentioned Pansaoli. The position of Pansaoli in Korean traditional music is similar to that of Peking Opera in Chinese

---

[1] Choi Joon Sik, 'A Fundamental Understanding of Korean Culture', *Contemporary Korea*, Summer, 2006, p. 64.

traditional music. However, there are many differences between the two. Pansaoli stage is simply decorated, and the performers are a singer and a drummer. The singer will combine singing and narrating to do the performance, and sometimes he/she will use properties, such as a folding fan, to do some simple action. The drummer will sit beside the singer, drumming for the singer or sighing with emotion in cooperation with the singer. Pansaoli singers sing in a very straightforward way. Simplicity and wildness are the characteristics of Pansaoli, a bright contrast to the gorgeous and exquisite Peking Opera. In addition, Korean architecture also presents the characteristics of simplicity. For example, asymmetry is emphasized in Korean architecture because it is believed in Korea that the nature is not symmetric, and it will be too artificial to make the architecture symmetric. Therefore the architectures in Korea are designed to be asymmetric. The most typical example is the Changdeokgung Palace. In addition, most of the building materials are raw materials or just simply processed. If you go to some Buddhist temples like Seonunsa Temple and Black Dragon Temple, you will see raw wood or simply processed wood on the temple buildings.

Why do the Koreans like being straightforward, simple and plain? This tendency is originated from Shamanism. The dance movement of a Shaman is simple and the singing of a Shaman is as wild as that of Pansaoli. The characteristics of Shamanistic singing and dancing of being straightforward, simple and plain is demonstrated in various types of Korean arts and deeply rooted in the heart of the Koreans.

(Translated from the Chinese by Chen Yuan)

文化多样性的假想与宗教的永恒性

西尔维娅·曼奇尼[*]

国内和国际的现实不断促使公众跟从一系列离奇的千篇一律的事件、话语和评论。这些事件、话语和评论无不强调"宗教的永恒性",引证公共当局对待基督教遗产和教会的新感情,陈述从吕克·费里到克利福德·格尔茨等知识分子——总之是世俗人士——的言论。在这些人士看来,建立在信仰和超验性之上的意义境域乃是被看作现代人避免丧失文化认同、摆脱存在危机和相对主义威胁的绕不过的护栏。在这样的背景下,在法国重新燃起关于世俗性争论的尼古拉·萨科齐最近的言论,看来同样呼唤我们进行若干反思;罗马学界拒绝接待教皇本笃十六世为罗马大学新学年开学典礼致辞,许多知识分子的激烈反应被媒体广泛炒作,闹得沸沸扬扬;大量文章和著作出现,声称重新发现了基督教的启示及其"深刻意义"(瓦拉迪耶,2007;《时代》,2007;勒努瓦,2007)。我们不禁要问这些话语的基础是什么,怎样解释这些话语,如何把它们与我们的现代性的构建方向协调起来。

问题所在

在诸如此类被认为是将人们今天看重的合法化和创建作用归还神圣的言

---

[*] 西尔维娅·曼奇尼(Silvia Mancini),洛桑大学宗教比较史教授。著有《E. 德马蒂诺〈魔法世界〉后记》(巴黎,2004);《模仿与宗教仪式——为教皇庇护现象学哭丧》(《宗教史评论》,2006);《心理主义的产生——处于人文科学与生命科学交汇点的宗教仪式活动》(巴黎,2006)。

文化多样性的假想与宗教的永恒性

论中，引人注意的第一个现象乃是它们与死灰复燃的民族主义思潮合流，宗教往往被描述为与政治领域和认同价值密切相关的重要的民族标志。事实上，每当必须确立欧洲整合其他文化的界限，以及必须采取制度性措施来应对要求有更大的公众可见度的来势汹涌的宗教认同之时，宗教问题往往卷土重来。在以中东的长期冲突、恐怖主义威胁、原教旨主义激增为主导的这种形势下，种种事态表明欧洲仿佛正在经历很难从法律的视角来理解的民族和文化差异的难题，而我们沉浸其间的多元文化体系使之更为凸显。显而易见，在这样的框架内，政治负责人以及知识分子和媒体无不面临着这样的难题：即促使人们乃至自己清醒地认识到，当今一种特殊的人类学模式界定着和突出着西方文化，并描述着它与其他文明相比较的特点。当涉及识别个人和群体的身份时，这个模式主要是以表达为一种法律地位的包容的公民身份的平等准则为基础，而不是以主要显示民族、教派、种族或者社会性别（gender）等属性的宗教正统准则为基础。

然而，如果说这些难题正在出现，那么这并不是由于制度的层面，而是由于符号本身的层面缺乏一个真正能适应包容和权利普遍平等的公民模式的意义域，来专门界定我们的文化。这是由于没有醒悟到，一方面，只有一个属于我们的与"公民的"——不是宗教的——模式相合拍的符号意义，才能够驱散时时出现在关于"回归神圣"和被理解为强大的社会向量的"宗教认同"的现实争论中的文化偏见；另一方面，这些偏见乃是被理解为宗教基础的一元神论的直接遗产：一切一元神论因其排他主义的本质，无不将自己的教义设想为绝对的和普世的，其权威性植根于一种元历史和元社会的超验性之中（阿斯曼，2007；奥热，1982）。事实上，恰恰是这一点与作为我们全部现代文化制度和实践基础的契约论公民观迥然相对立。我们面对的一方面是一个以契约和自主性（指这个词积极的意义）为基础的平等和包容的社会政治模式；另一方面则是在西方被视为超验的、普世的和必然的基础的一个价值域，其中包括今天关于大举回归宗教认同及各种宗教认同彼此相容的主流话语，而诸如"现代性宏大叙事（马克思主义、科学主义、历史哲学、世俗性……）的终结""后世俗和后现代阶段的降临""上帝的报复""回归关于生命和价值意义的基本疑问"等词句，则是它们反复使用的表述。

然而，问题正在于，人类学和宗教比较史所发展起来的反思是否能够达到与来自公民和政治社会的最保守阶层的这些陈词滥调相对立的另一种诊断，须知"回归宗教"论的最虔诚的代言人确实就是新自由主义模式和新世界秩序的鼓吹者。那么，他们的话语的真实含义是什么？这个问题预先提出了另一个问题。一方面是建立在包容和权利普遍平等基础上的模式，另一方面是从法的视角来理解多民族社会显露的各种价值差异和世界观差异的困难，上面已经提到的这个遍及欧洲而使它左右为难的矛盾来自哪里？

一个事实是，显见的世俗化完全是针对公民社会的某些阶层实施的。另一个事实是，在西方构建世界观的意义域的符号世俗化看来已经失败。这一失败的标志主要表现为将"意义权力"、依然十分强大的创建功能和语义超载力归属宗教，还表现在西方坚持从宗教的视角来思考其他文明及其符号的和社会的等级（加斯巴罗，2006、2007；萨巴图奇，2002；盖拉尼，2003、2005、2006）。有待我们去做的是追溯这一矛盾的历史原因并解析其中的各种因素。

多样文化主义——思考政治与宗教之间关系的一种方式

在瑞士及其他欧洲国家，教会的代表们坚决主张从各种宗教之间关系的视角来思考不同文明之间的关系。由此产生了旨在建立被认为能平息冲突的跨宗教对话的主要倡议。产生自一元神论传统的各派教会主张从神学差异的视角——更普遍地说，从不同的世界观——来思考不同文明之间的关系，这是完全可以理解的。因此，必须鼓励相互宽容，而这种宽容的制度上的升华则是多样文化主义和社团间共居的联邦模式。作为宗教社团的联邦主义理念基础的观点认为，人们之间的关系由一个超乎政治和法律的公认文化价值特别是伦理价值体系所主导。

然而，并非只有教会从各种宗教的差异性视角提出文明的差异性问题。公民社会的许多代言人也开始这样转变。譬如说，我们看到诸多政治家、知识分子、媒体等面对全球化孕育的符号视角的多样性，步尘教会之后，从各种"世界观""价值体系""生活理念"之间差异的视角，来提出文化之间的差异性和相容性——也就是说，促使它们没有过多的冲突而共处——问题。至于这些教会本身，则或明或暗地完全尊奉一种差异主义——亦称"多样文化主义"——的人类学模式。这个模式强调民族之间的差异、文化的"差异价值",并认为诸如此类的差异比各种文明之间交流所形成的历史过程以及与这个过程联结在一起的社会文化的复合性更为重要。根据这样的观点,文化之间的差异依照某种道德和符号的平等准则部分地趋于消失,这种道德和符号的平等是作为"生活形态",亦即作为应对和解决人类生存条件的基本问题的不同模态赋予文化的。

经历了20世纪60年代和70年代人类学中以确立跨文化类型的进路的尝试(列维-斯特劳斯,1949、1958、1962、1964～1971;戈德利耶,1984、1996;德科拉,2005)为重要标志的衰落阶段之后,多样文化或曰"差异主义"模式今天在社会科学内部重新受到青睐。在这个模式的支持者看来,各种文化——被认为是自在的和自为的——并列地生存着,各自表达着其符号倾向、原创的"天赋",以及特殊的社会潜在力量。那么,这个人类学模式来自何方?它植根于浪漫主义前期的历史特殊论,特别是约翰·戈特弗里德·赫尔德及其弟子的理论。美国文化人类学的奠基者弗朗兹·博厄斯将它从德国移植到美国。在美国,这一学说经过文化科学的修正和改头换面(斯托金,1968;曼奇尼,1999、2000、2007)。这个差异主义模式建立在将一个民族的环境、语言、制度、习惯、艺术和宗教重新联结起来的一种有机关联性观念基础上。正是这样的关联性给民族精神打上了独特的烙印。然而,即使撇开与这种观念的保守主义的乃至种族主义的偏向相关的风险不谈,还是有两个特征值得强调。

首先第一个特征是,断言"文化精神"是各种文明所固有的,这种观念适与自由主义观念相匹配。各种符号结构事实上只不过是对于人的本性需要的最适当的回应。因此,在一个多样文化社会中,每个社会群体各自的符号结构之间关系的管理和调节,落在价值和"生活观"市场的肩上。既然由人性引导并赋予其正当性的精神并不受社会规则制约,那么实际上只能放任这种精神自由地表达并尝试开发其特殊的内涵。在一个多样文化社会中,多种"生活形态"相互接近,而非重新结合;为了避免它们彼此之间的冲突,一种承认政策——宽容的现代形象——成为制度上的补救之法,而正确的政治策略则是其官方的保障(加斯巴罗,2006、2007)。无论如何,如果用个人主义来处理个人之间和群体之间的冲突(这是多样文化主义的主张,它将文化与个性进行类比),那么宽容和正确的政治策略对于保障在场的文化群体的制度和社会的公正很少有效,这些群体的差异身份压倒了平等的公民原则(迪蒙,1983;296～298;1991;269)。

必须强调的第二个特征是，旨在用包罗万象的系统方式理解现代性的所有一般理论，从差异主义的视角来看无不被指责为源自启蒙运动的理性主义幻想，具体地说也就是一种必须解构的幻想，以有利于回归自然的普遍主义与文化特殊论之间的基本关系。诸如今天流行的文化新相对主义的根源即在于此，而其在伦理方面的正当性得到从自然和自然规律引出的无可改变的论据证明。在各种文化之间关系的博弈中，自然是普遍适用的，而每一种文化是自为的。最优者将压倒一切，而且它的胜利将成为命运、精神优越性的征象，而经济、政治和军事上所取得的成就即是这种精神优越性的证明。因此，多样文化主义模式产生并基本上传播于美洲的自由主义新教文化国家，随后从 20 世纪 80 年代开始侵入欧洲，这绝非偶然。

多元文化主义——思考政治与宗教之间关系的另一种方式

"多元文化主义"模式的灵感并非源于确立了文化精神与自然之间固有连续性的前期浪漫主义或者浪漫主义本身的历史特殊论。它是源于 16 世纪末开始形成的欧洲现代性的公民传统或曰契约论传统的最有代表性的产物。这个模式之所以说是多元文化的，其含义在于它并不将文化理解为具有某种认同本质的特殊精神的具体化身，而是理解为不同社会之间不断互动所形成的、历史地决定的人造物。这说明为什么每一种文化在其作为各种特殊文化之间交流的独特产物出现之时，就其基础而言即是"多元性的—文化的"。因此，每种文化的复杂性程度不应解释为某种天然的先定性的反映；毋宁说是由于特殊的历史经验而习得的制订符号结构和社会规则，并进而能够增多与其他文明交流和联系的能力的产物。举例来说，这种复杂性见诸伊斯兰文明、中国、日本、欧洲以及犹太文化。

事实上，接受跨文化和跨宗教挑战的一切社会都面临双重任务。首先是建立能够同其他文化共居的最起码的一般规则，这样的规则的性质是一般的，而不是普遍的，也就是说，它们的有效性属于就事论事和经验型的，不具备被援引为基础的任何正统性。其次是注重同其他文化的比照，以产生某些既是意识形态的又是实践的新形式的相容性。

这个多元文化模式直接来自文艺复兴时期形成的人类学理想，也就是诺伯特·埃利亚斯用"文明"（Civilisation）一词加以描述的理想，以同作为多样文化主义观念背景的"文化"（Kultur）理想相抗衡（埃利亚斯，1973、1975；迪蒙，1977、1983、1991）。"文明"模式或曰"公民"模式，颠覆了作为差异主义模式基础的自然—文化关系的观念。它拒绝赋予种种自然决定论以优先地位，而损害来自文明的自主规则。公民模式的创造和现代公民社会的创造是同时发生的，而现代公民社会显示出完全独特的意识形态的和制度特征。

因此，多元文化模式的公民进路，完全不同于多样文化主义模式所固有的、建立在自然基础上的进路。按照公民进路，文化不是解释人性所固有的问题并为之提供答案的不同方式。相反，文化被看作具体社会的符号结构，不同的社会无不以其自己的方式对种种宏大的自然决定论提出问题并进行管理。依据这样的观点，我们应该关注的不是按照决定论的自然模式来解释的社会关系观念，而是历史地和社会地思考人与自然关系的观念。

所以，从文明的观点来说，自然乃是自发的等级和差异——如果平等思想不进行干预而加以反对，在历史和社会的层面上可能形成歧视（社会的、身份的，等等）的等级和差异本身占据支配地位的场所。然而，从历史来看，这种平等的社会理念与其说是被视为人道主义思想媒介的基督教的发明，毋宁说是公民社会的发明，是构成奠定西方现代性的强大基石。

切勿将基督教与民主混为一谈

许多人由于往往不知不觉地产生的偏见而倾向于将宽容、平等和尊重多样性等民主价值看作基督教的直接遗产，仿佛基督教与民主是天然地孪生的。他们低估了这样一个事实，即就其结构本身而言，所有的一元神论都是强烈反民主的，上面我们已经说过，它们是建立在纵向权威原则基础上的一种具有普世追求的、排他的天启真理。此外，欧洲或者更普遍一点的现代西方的社会和政治理念是通过民主和平等主义来构建其模式的，与其说受到基督教的平等和个人主义模式——诸如马克斯·韦伯等另一些学者则追溯至自命为原始基督教社团的宗教改革派的新教模式——的启迪，倒不如说汲取了起源于基督教以前的——罗马或者希腊——公民模式的思想。正是古代整体论的（不是个人主义的）和平等的（不是等级制的）社会的典型模式，被贯彻于希腊民主和罗马共和政体，并在文艺复兴时期由确立了现代国家基础的法哲学家们重新加以运用。最后，也正是这个古代模式启迪了作为路德派改革核心的具有共同信仰的平等派团契的思想。

同样，确立社会成员的共同规则的理性观念本身，也是西方现代性内部的一个长期文明进程的结果。经历了16世纪和17世纪的宗教战争的经验之后，这个理性观念随同康德和启蒙运动哲学得到蓬勃发展，人们发明了公民理念作为各种不同的宗教诉求和多样的世界观平等地和平共处的领域。从建立在公民权利基础上的罗马共和制模式出发，经过马基雅维利对政治、伦理和宗教所做的分离，契约论的公民思想通过格劳秀斯和霍布斯以及后来的卢梭和康德的自然法学学说而形成，最终压倒了宗教、社会和政治领域的一切形式的自然决定论。如果说现代性并未促使各种符号的等级观和宗教的社会优势消失，那么反之，它给予了独特的主体以自由，解放了他们从公民和大众的平等出发选择各自的归属的能力，促使人们摒弃宗教在符号等级内占有最高地位的观念。

所以，人类学公民模式的基本特征既不是宽容，也不是道德人道主义，更不是理解为直接来自人民的权力的民主（这个理念可以追溯到古希腊，而不同于罗马的共和概念）。它体现了这样一种理念，即在集体生活和个人之间关系结构化进程中，人们从来不诉诸某些普遍的基础，不论是神权、公认的信仰，或者是历史和人类秩序的超验原则。相反，人们求助有益于某些特殊的矫正行动的一般规则，来组织日常历史实践活动中的集体生活。

那么，这些矫正行动究竟是什么，它们的特殊性何在？西方的现代性在汲取古代共和制法律模式的同时，实际上是自16世纪以来在民权和政治层面上已经停止诉诸的某些元社会基础——诸如种族、民族、性别的自然基础，以及全部超验和绝对性质的基础。为了界定个人和群体的身份，它援引社会现实中的契约或者法律模式，与这个模式相伴的是诸如契约、民法、法院的审判活动等特殊的符号设施的建立。这些被理解为集体意志执行场所的公民设施，旨在社会地吸纳、包容和整合个人和其他文化。这些公民设施本身确实是中立的，没有任何同自然基础观念有所瓜葛的内在含义。事实上，它们的唯一功能就是充当操作工具，其适用性完全取决于它们自身的社会功效（萨巴图奇，1976；加斯巴罗，2006）。

诚然，有人可以提出异议说，作为法律的这种矫正行动实际上不是中立的，存在法律为某些社会集团的意识形态服务的危险，因为这些集团手握统治霸权，而且有着利用法律来谋取私利的倾向。为了论证这样的异议也许站得住脚，还可以认为像诸如科学认识和技术等其他矫正行动一样，法律本质上具备一种强大的包容功效。比如像科学和技术一样，民法能够输出到我们的文化之外。它们之所以如此，恰恰是因为它们并非是通过原则的正统性，而是通过它们的具体矫正行动来界定自身的。正是这些整合和包容的公民设施，使我们能够同其他文化交往，尽管就世界观而言，存在分隔我们的深刻差异。

公民观念的筹码：一个模糊的三项式
（公民的、宗教的与意义的问题）

不同于自然论的自由主义，公民观念的基本假设在于确认——就社会层面而言——公民的平等先于一切差异属性并保证它们的自由行使。这种包容和契约实践不仅可以与一切自命为建立在具有普遍主义追求的价值观基础上的正统学说一刀两断，而且可以与各种生活形态的文化相对主义分道扬镳。

通过公民模式，差异主义鼓吹者捍卫的普遍性与特殊性之间的形而上学对立，被以普遍化（关于这个概念，参见下文）为一方与以各种不同文化在他们之间确立的关系——从来不是从抽象的孤立的认同，而是始终从具体的历史互动的视角来思考这些不同文化——为另一方的历史和次生的对立所替代。对于这种文明或者公民的关系思想来说，参照系的基本结构看来不是将个人的天然的特殊性与族群、民族、文化的特殊性联结在一起的类比性质的结构，而是作为社会角色的公民与国家的关系；而且，正是这种自主的契约关系被用于作为思考个人、社会群体、公民社会、法国家和民主（很少通过基础实体，而是大多通过建立确切的契约关系来界定的多重体制）的模式。

公民观念所蕴涵的关系模式，就其本质来说是人造的、可以随意延伸的、包容的和动态的。实际上，它的正当性直接来源自无论在具体的历史层面上或者在文化符号的层面上能够加以普遍化的能力。采用这样一个模式可以从此避免多样文化主义模式所固有的一系列风险。多样文化论的相对主义通过求助于确认文化多样性的自然基础来获得其正当性，这是大可怀疑的，它实际上被各种文化彼此间所确立的关系的相对化——历史的和比较的相对化所取代。从此，每一种文明被看作一个"过程"，一个始终与其他文明互动的流动实体，它的认同将与这类互动吻合。

多样文化与多元文化的立场各自以文化（Kultur）与文明（Civilisation）为依据，在宗教方面也有着不同倾向。众所周知，各派教会都赞同多样文化模式，同时又拒斥源自承认各种文明之间差异的伦理和文化相对主义。它们强调这个模式的个人主义一面，以维护意识自由的原则；但是，在社会层面上，它们坚持摒弃宗教私人化理念，也就是说反对将宗教归入私人领域层次。

但是，在多样文化主义的鼓吹者中间，并非只有教会公开宣扬关于各种宗教之间关系的明确立场。譬如说，为了分析文化之作为生活形态内部的世界新秩序，许多文化人类学家，主要是美国的学者们，赋予宗教以优先的符号价值，认为宗教是基本的认同标志（格尔茨，1972、2006）。这类著述完全赞同多样文化主义的各种假设，也就是说如我们所见到的那样，优先强调文化的符号向度（被认为是反映了"天赋"，文化的差异精神），而无视社会契约所包含的社会制度的向度。由此产生了这些独断的世界观——宗教之间互不相容的论断。一旦宽容无济于事，"文明的冲突"作为世界新秩序的产物将不可避免（亨廷顿，1998）。

实际上，多样文化主义模式旨在为宗教及其意义原则恢复名誉，将人的"精神表现"置于各种文明内的主导地位，而无视社会制度的能动性以及被认为是调节集体生活的各种设施（经济、法律、吸纳个人的社会规范，等等）。总之，研究主体意识所体验到的价值，研究语义域，研究意义的结构和符号的基础，压倒了具有社会和历史性质的对于客观的制度和符号逻辑的理解（韦伯，1964）。在文化主义者看来，宗教是符号生活的本源。宗教的存在价值为从属于自然决定论的存在问题提供了一个作为范例的答案，但几乎不能按照人们在必要时承认其人为和自主本质的社会生活的其他文化代码来解构。恰恰相反，它体现它所建构的社会所必需的一个前景。作为文化基础结构的宗教领域，应该既从文化体系的内部，又从其外部来开发其价值。因此，向各种跨宗教对话开放的教会，在美国被看重的宗教研究的许多部门，以及社会科学内部的"信众团契"与非信徒之间的许多争论，无不与多样文化主义的假设完全合拍。

由此可见，如果各种文化本质上是宗教文化，那么据说只有用以对它们内在地进行理解的解释学进路和跨宗教对话，才能避免各种文明的冲突。我们要顺便指出，如果说后现代主义解构了一切包罗万象的现代性理论（马克思主义、实证主义和科学主义、历史主义，等等，它们无不系统地服从于证实—证伪的准则），那么它毕竟拒绝把宗教纳入这个证实过程，而是倾向于将宗教看作可以理解生死和人类历史的一种学说。

多元文化的公民模式则赋予社会关系及由此衍生的诸如法律、政治、技术、社会组织和经济等制度，更普遍地说赋予社会生活的这一切代码以优先性，与试图摆脱社会生活的宗教代码相比，社会生活的代码同历史的偶然性、同人的行动的内在世界有着更直接的一致性。如人们所说，这些公民代码的特点在于它们本质上是操作性的，能够超越一切文化的差异而达到普遍化，尽管它们并没有被假设为普世的。这说明为什么多元文化公民模式主张者并不求助于信仰的激情，而是诉诸将人理解为多重历史角色的"理性之理性"，这些理性之理性分别属于社会的、经济的、政治的、制度的和符号的范畴，其中没有任何一个被认为是某一种特殊文化所固有的。这种注重人的理性的选择，促使不是教派的（在宗教上是中立的）和自由的（指政治上是中立的意义）国家得以出现。

公民革命的结果

这种深刻的公民革命思想必然结出累累硕果。我们要提到其中先后成为其他演进源头的三个结果。

第一个结果。具有同样权利和义务并通过某种集体意志联合起来的公民之间的共居，割断了建立在差异认同准则——自然的（种族、性别）或者超自然的（宗教认同）——基础上的一切归属和依附纽带。所有这一切公民身份之外的差异消解于被理解为具有历史和社会性因而是内在的和因时而变的公民平等之中。因此，公民平等没有任何客观的或者超自然的基础（这使人联想到霍布斯，他将宗教视为同任何超自然基础没有任何瓜葛的一种自然制度）。一切文化和宗教差异从此只能在法国家赖以为基础的公民平等内部来加以考虑。由此产生了人类学意义上的"公民社会"和"文明"的新范畴,"文明"自 16 世纪开始,独立于宗教及其神学基础。然而,重温这个历史过程,应该避免将这个运动看作某种法权的世俗化或者宗教价值和宗教模式的去宗教化。我们面对的不如说是一种崭新的、与神学思想和构成神学思想基本信条的逻辑彻底相悖的文化逻辑的确立。与马塞尔·戈谢似乎想要推进的看法(1985)相反,现代性的制度和知识并不是宗教理性世俗化的产物。它们是彻底取代建立在教条权威准则基础上的真理原则的一种选择。换言之,这些制度和知识用体现公民本质的事实确定性的经验的视域准则(法律、技术、历史编纂学),取代了源于某种启示真理的纵向的等级观正统学说。

实际上,确定性的经验准则在西方的宗教中并无先例。它是作为现代性的一个特殊发明出现的。按照法律和历史编纂学的范例产生经验确定性的科学和技术,不能以宗教的方式来加以思考,也就是说应该认为就其起源和历史发展的性质而言是独立于宗教的。可以和应该从科学和技术范式的内部,而不是从宗教权威范式出发,来探讨它们各自真理的局限(断言科学几乎不能经验地解释信仰的真理是毫无意义的,正如人们并不要求宗教科学地解释其教条一样)。

第二个结果。建立在包容的平等原则基础上的公民观念降生的第二个结果是谋求建立两个新的意义领域,或者如人们更喜欢说的那样,建立置于平等基础上的两个行动领域,即公民的领域和宗教的领域。随着现代性降生,前一个领域不仅彻底独立于后一个领域,而且最终包容了后一个领域。这说明为什么公民作为不仅具有政治和制度性质,而且具有符号性质的文化结构,能够通过文明概念作为独立的人类学向度而自立。这个概念具有更大的普遍化能力,因而比宗教更能包容包括宗教差异在内的各种文化差异。

第三个结果。它直接关系到宗教在公民社会中的地位。社会将宗教包容在公民领域里,这在今天是一个事实的法和法的事实,其地位本质上属于私人的范畴。这并非是削弱它的社会价值和符号价值,而是以平等的方式调节它对差异的合法表达,因为所有公民在被认为是以公正和中立的方式管理这些权利和差异的民事领域里,在宗教选择方面是平等的。所以,如果说在公众表达差异中,各种诉求(展示面纱、十字架、犹太人圆帽……)都是正当的,那么相反,不能伴随有符号上缺乏正当性、政治上破坏建立在公民平

文化多样性的假想与宗教的永恒性

等基础上的社会公约的行动。

因此，将宗教归入私人领域，不是反过来在符号上贬低其价值。这只是意味着承认宗教的或者非宗教的认同差异的极大多样性的存在，而承认这一点迫使国家在公民平等的内部调节差异的表达。两个原则启迪着这样一个逻辑：一方面，平等能够很好地包容差异；另一方面，越是平等，就越是能促使差异相互包容。

我们可能要问为什么诸如这里所介绍的反思实际上从来没有成为公众争论的话题。为什么在我们中间一直存在主导制度层面的公民导向与宗教的意义体系之间的这道鸿沟呢？如果赋予我们的文化以特色而具有公民性质的文化革命的历史是众所周知的和完整的（虽然常常被人们所忘记），那么反对像对待调节公民生活的其他任何符号代码一样来对待宗教这种抗拒态度究竟来自何方？事实是当人们今天追问价值的社会意义时，宗教的权威—真理论调重又泛起。我们所有人都在谈论科学知识的解释局限，却很少有人强调宗教真理的科学和历史的局限。在遵循科学法则时，我们的人类学意识迫使我们不能不把大多数历史的、科学的或者社会学的表象，大多数注定像昙花一现的意识形态所固有的历史—社会乌托邦视为独断的，而我们从这一原则出发，要求对非宗教的信仰进行验证。然而，我们常常忘记了源自公民社会体系的"信仰"与作为我们宗教观念基础的一元神论信仰风马牛不相及，也与一元神论所假设的不同世界秩序之间的结构等级毫不相关。我们不想坚持说，宗教类型的体系和制度应该服从我们认为历史的、人类学的、科学的、社会学的或者政治的观念必须服从的证实—证伪准则；恰恰相反，我们往往重视它们的社会文化影响力。总而言之，事态自身的发展表明，我们似乎正赋予宗教以某种意义的权威性，这种权威性在本质上不同于其他的权威性，这很好地证明了这个意义代码高等级的力量：我们一般以蕴含的方式，按照我们将它列入其中的基本原则的正统学说，将它置于公民生活的其他代码之上。

建立在包容的人人平等和执行集体意志原则之上的制度文化与属于宗教的意义向度之间的这种差距存在本身，在欧洲标志着世俗化方面的一个失败。前者被列入历史和公民生活的人道主义领域，而后者被抛入关于本源的元历史学之中。与教会的代表及某些后现代哲学家所坚持的言论相反，这样一种世俗化之所以失败，并非是因为它表明自身存在局限，或者是因为世俗化过程突然中断。而是因为我们，以公民思想的现代继承者自居的我们；因为我们，没有能将文明的使命推进到底的我们，尽管我们的文化投身于该使命，对历史和人的一切决定论观念——不论是自然决定论或者超自然决定论——提出质疑。

宗教学的挑战

构成我们世界观的意义原则的人道化未能推进到底，应该对这种无能负责的因素之一，毫无疑问是科学和学术层面上进行宗教研究的错误方式。就其历史起源而言，出自神学思想的宗教学本身常常竞相制造以公民生活的生产为一方与以宗教向度为另一方之间的鸿沟，一切宗教学往往借助与神学和哲学话语的论证相同的论据，执着地将这个向度说成具有某种固有的独立性和特殊性。然而，赋予一切宗教生产以某种附加的意义或者某种特殊的和不可还原的意义，等于在公众争论中重新引入某种形式的思维的原教旨主义。如果说"公民的现代性"由于不能生产一切宗教所固有的内在人文逻辑的历史重构，因而使得"宗教文明"的过程没有完成，那么这是由宗教学的许多代表的合谋造成的。由于不把宗教今天依然在西方行使的意义权力放进历史的框架加以质疑，我们正面临危险：无力将体现我们时代特征的各种现象的分析充分深入地进行下去。

这种历史批判的缺失，也成为现代社会科学的一些分支没有能力将宗教的这一意义权力整合进整个文明的根源。然而，宗教史和人类学通过经验证明，在许多社会中，符号和社会体系如何大多不是由宗教，而是由社会生活的其他代码（诸如亲属关系、政治结构、生产方式、符号逻辑等）主导的。自迪尔凯姆做出的奠基性贡献以来，这两个学科各自用自己的方式致力于证明，宗教只是诸多社会代码（政治、经济、法、与环境的关系等）中的一个代码，在构成文明的这个物质和符号价值交流和生产的总体系中，所有的代码都被动员起来。宗教在人们不赋予它以特殊的或者特权的地位条件下，是能够用破解其他代码的同样手段和视野来加以分析的。它能够提出的与其他代码不同的唯一特殊性则与它所确立的各种关系的性质相关。这就是人与非人的相异性之间的关系，而其他社会代码只涉及人类内部或者人与自然之间的关系（在科学的或者魔法的知识和实践形式下）。宗教所涵盖的关系的这种特殊性一旦得到承认，那么我们就应该同意说，它并非仅限于基督教世界观：神性的观念因它所属的社会参照系而异（古代的多元神论的诸神属于非常特殊的社会政治结构，完全不同于一元神论的唯一上帝；阿斯曼，2007；奥热，1982；韦尔南，1965）。宗教类型的社会代码丝毫也不是得到明证的；它像其他社会代码一样是文化自主的。在这样的意义上，不仅一切文化并非认同同一代码，而且一个代码一经产生，它并非必然以同样的方式在这个或那个文化中发生作用。况且，基督教的传教士们难道不正是首先发现没有宗教和神的其他文明存在的先驱吗（克拉斯特，1988）？

西方将现代性的宏大叙事（包括形而上学在内）付诸历史的批判和人类学的比较，这样做的后果是使它们的权威性的准则服从于确定性的经验准则，消解了它们的普遍主义的和总体的特征。为什么不以同样的方式对待宗教呢？首先，挑战是巨大的。西方世界今天面临极端复杂的文化和宗教差异这一尖锐问题。它第一次面对它们束手无策，其原因在于缺乏符号的中介，尽管现代性在不久之前曾经借助诸如形而上学、科学、目的论、历史哲学等普遍学说而握有这样的中介。其次，欧洲失去了其作为殖民帝国曾经使它获得保障的政治中心地位，由此产生了拥有一个可以加以普遍化的（丝毫也不是普世的）和比较的（丝毫也不是绝对的）文化模式，来构建新的公民知识的需要。在技术、体育、科学和通信的层面上，我们已经可以断言，这样的代码正在最多样的非西方文化中得到大规模采用。然而，如果说经济的、技术的、体育的、科学的、通信的代码之所以能输出并如此广泛地得到传播，并非是因为它们具有比其他代码更可取的某种正统基础或者意义价值，而是因为它们具有在实践上包容和整合文化差异并进而推进跨文化的相容性和普及化进程的能力。

这些包容性代码属于公民范畴，因为公民观念是孕育它们的现实存在和规范它们的使用的逻辑。我们看到，民法的好处正在于它并无自身内在的价值；它作为通过契约被公民采纳的自主规则体系而运作，其唯一目的乃是调节个人之间、个人与公共权力之间、个人与自然之间的关系。公民社会和民法拥有同样的起源、同样的结构和同样的操作逻辑。

在15世纪与16世纪之间，现代社会体系确立了与以往差异甚大的世界符号秩序。随着人们开始从被理解为建立在诸如法律、道德、政治、经济中所表达的那种自主契约和协议原则基础上的人与人之间的关系出发，来思考人与自然的关系（科学和技术）及人与神的关系（宗教），现代性同它的过去一刀两断（戈谢，2007）。今天绕开现代性的人类学意义及其为了达到公民社会而开启的历史过程，来谈论宗教与政治的关系问题，其结果只能是必然混淆两个不同的范畴。一方面是承认不同的文化代码（法律、政治、经济、宗教，等等）在我们文化内部的共存；另一方面是被假设为不可避免的它们的意义等级确立（西方的宗教代码在其中必然占据最高地位）的必要性。混淆这两个范畴的人们忘记了政治与宗教的和平共处乃是宗教战争以来现代公民社会的一个独特成果，正是这个成果结束了断言宗教高于政治的等级观话语。恰恰是公民社会始终在社会实践中促使这两个不同范畴共存相容。

因此，宗教学在政治与宗教关联的这种反思中应该发挥重要作用。宗教学肩负着一种记忆的责任：记住这种关联的历史。这样的反思和责任在当前的政治形势下具有举足轻重的重要意义。在今天面对宗教研究学术领域体制深刻重构过程的欧洲，尤其如此。对于宗教学来说，这种重构乃是一个机遇，借以证明宗教学并非在结构上没有能力从神学中解放出来，尽管由于历史的原因，它依然在体制上与神学联系在一起。所以，这也是宗教学重新确认自己的世俗和公民使命的机遇。

（陆象淦 译）

参考文献

阿斯曼，J.，Assmann, J. (2007) *Le Prix du monothéisme*, Paris：Aubier。
奥热，M.，Augé, M. (1982) *Génie du paganisme*, Paris：Gallimard。
克拉斯特，H.，Clastres, H. (1988)《La religion sans dieux：les chroniqueurs du XVIe siècle devant les sauvages d'Amérique du sud》，收入 F. 席姆特（主编），dans F. Schmidt (éd.), *L'Impensable polythéisme. Etudes d'historiographie religieuse*, pp. 95–122, Paris：Editions des Archives contemporaines。
德科拉，P.，Descola, P. (2005) *Par-delà nature et culture*, Paris：Gallimard。
迪蒙，L.，Dumont, L. (1977) *Homo Aequalis*, I：*Genèse et épanouissement de l'idéologie économique*, Paris：Gallimard。
迪蒙，L.，Dumont, L. (1983) *Essai sur l'individualisme*, Paris：Le Seuil。
迪蒙，L.，Dumont, L. (1991) *Homo Aequalis*, II：*L'idéologie allemande, France-Allemagne et retour*, Paris：Gallimard。
埃利亚斯，N.，Elias, N. (1973) *La Civilisation des mœurs*, Paris：Calmann-Lévy。
埃利亚斯，N.，Elias, N. (1975) *La dynamique de l'Occident*, Paris：Calmann-Lévy。
加斯巴罗，N.，Gasbarro, N. (1990)《La terza via tracciata da Raffaele Pettazzoni》，

Studi e Materiali di Storia delle Religioni, 56: 95 - 200。

加斯巴罗, N., Gasbarro, N. (2006)《Religione e politica. Potere di senso e prospettiva civile》, 收入 B. 博纳托 (主编), dans B. Bonato (éd.), *Religioni e politica. Verso una socieà post-secolare?*, pp. 23-65, Pordenone: Al Segno。

加斯巴罗, N., Gasbarro, N. (2007)《Storia delle religioni e società civile》, *Prometeo*, 97: 4 - 25。

戈谢, M., Gauchet, M. (1985) *Le Désenchantement du monde*, Paris: Gallimard。

戈谢, M., Gauchet, M. (2007) *Un monde désenchanté ?* Paris: Agora。

格尔茨, C., Geertz, C., (1972)《La religion comme système culturel》, 收入 J. 米德尔顿 (主编), dans J. Middleton (éd.), *Essais d'anthropologie religieuse*, pp. 19 - 66. Paris: Gallimard。

格尔茨, C., Geertz, C. (2006)《La religion, sujet d'avenir》, *Le Monde*, 4 mai。

戈德利耶, M., Godelier, M. (1984) *L'idéel et le matériel*, Paris: Fayard。

戈德利耶, M., Godelier, M. (1986) *L'énigme du don*, Paris: Fayard。

亨廷顿, S. P., Huntington, S. P. (1998) *Le Choc des civilisations*, Paris: Odile Jacob。

盖拉尼, M., Kilani, M. (2003)《Equivoques de la religion et politiques de la laïcité en Europe. Réflexions à partir de l'Islam》, *Archives de Sciences Sociales des Religions*, 121: 69 - 86。

盖拉尼, M., Kilani, M. (2005)《Il faut déconfessionnaliser la laïcité. Le religieux imprègne encore les imaginaires》, *Journal des Anthropologues*, 100 - 101: 37 - 48。

盖拉尼, M., Kilani, M. (2006)《La laïcité entre universalisme et hiérarchie》, *Journal des Anthropologues*, 106 - 107: 369 - 376。

勒努瓦, F., Lenoir, F. (2007) *Le Christ philosophe*, Paris: Plon。

《时代》, *Le Temps* (2007)《Samedi culturel》, Genève, 22 décembre。

列维-斯特劳斯, C., Lévi-Strauss, C. (1949) *Les structures élémentaires de la parenté*, Paris: PUF。

列维-斯特劳斯, C., Lévi-Strauss, C. (1958) *Anthropologie structurale*, Paris: Plon。

列维-斯特劳斯, C., Lévi-Strauss, C. (1962) *La pensée sauvage*, Paris: Plon。

列维-斯特劳斯, C., Lévi-Strauss, C. (1964 - 1971) *Mythologiques*, Paris: Plon。

曼奇尼, S., Mancini, S. (1999)《Les civilisations comme 'absolu esthétique'. L'approche morphologique de la Mittel-Europa》, *Diogène*, 186: 83 - 109。

曼奇尼, S., Mancini, S. (2000)《Historicisme allemand et anthropologie, ou de l'actualité d'un débat》, *Les Etudes Philosophiques*, 1: 17 - 35。

曼奇尼, S., Mancini, S. (2007) 'Comparatism in History of Religions: Some Models and Stakes', *Religion*, 37 (4): 282 - 293。

萨巴图奇, D., Sabbatucci, D. (1976) *Lo Stato come conquista culturale*, Rome: Bulzoni。

萨巴图奇, D., Sabbatucci, D. (2002) *La perspective historico-religieuse*, Paris: Arché。

斯托金, G., Stocking, G. (1968) *Race, Culture, and Evolution: Essays in the History of Anthropology*, New York: Free Press。

瓦拉迪耶, P., Valadier, P. (2007) *Détresse du politique, force du religieux*, Paris: Seuil。

韦尔南, J. P., Vernant, J. P. (1965) *Mythe et pensée chez les Grecs*, Paris: Maspero。

韦伯, M., Weber, M. (1964) *L'éthique protestante et l'esprit du capitalisme*, Paris: Plon。

Imaginaries of Cultural Diversity and the Permanence of the Religious

Silvia Mancini[*]

The contemporary national and international scene continues to present the general public with a stream of curiously uniform events, discourses and commentaries. They relate to the 'permanence of the religious', refer to public authorities' new sensitivity to the Christian heritage and that of the Churches, and produce intellectual but in fact secular discourses (from Luc Ferry to Clifford Geertz), whose field of meaning, based on faith and transcendence, is the essential protection that is supposed to save modern humanity from loss of cultural identity, existential crisis and the perils of relativism. In this context I also feel I need to comment on Nicolas Sarkozy's recent remarks, which have revived the debate on secularism in France; on the shocked reaction, widely publicized, of many intellectuals to the refusal of Rome's academics to welcome Benedict XVI for the beginning of the university's academic year; on the publication of many articles and books rediscovering the Christian message and its 'profound meaning' (Valadier 2007; *Le Temps* 2007; Lenoir 2007). We might wonder what these discourses

---

[*] Silvia Mancini is Professor of Comparative History of Religions at the University of Lausanne where she teaches Epistemology and Historiography of History of Religions, and Marginalized and Transversal Religious Traditions. Among her publications are 'Postface' to *Le Monde magique* by E. De Martino (Paris, 2004), 'Mimétisme et rite: de la lamentation funéraire à la phénoménologie de Padre Pio' (*Revue de l'Histoire des Religions*, 2004) and *La Fabrication du psychisme. Pratiques rituelles au carrefour des sciences humaines et des sciences de la vie* (Paris, 2006).

underlie, how we should interpret them and how far we can reconcile them with the trends on which our modernity is built.

The Current Position

What first strikes us about these discourses, which are intended to restore to the sacred the legitimating and founding role it is credited with today, is their convergence with the return of nationalist themes, given that religion is often presented as a significant national marker closely connected with the political sphere and values of identity. Indeed the issue of religion often recurs when it is a matter of the limits that should be imposed on integrating other cultures into Europe and the institutional measures that should be taken as strong religious identities emerge claiming a greater public visibility. At this point in history dominated by longstanding conflicts in the Middle East, the threat of terrorism, the proliferation of fundamentalist creeds, it seems in fact as though Europe was finding it hard to conceptualize in terms of *law* the ethical and cultural differences that the pluricultural system in which we are immersed makes particularly evident. In this situation it is clear that politicians, intellectuals and media have great difficulty in reminding us, or even themselves remembering, that a specific anthropological model defines and distinguishes western culture and characterizes it in relation to other civilizations. When it comes to identifying individuals and groups, that model is based chiefly on the egalitarian criterion of *inclusive citizenship*, which is expressed in the legally constituted state, rather than on *orthodox criteria of allegiances*, which are more ethnic, confessional, racial or gendered in nature.

However, if these difficulties arise it is because there has been marked out, not at the institutional but at the *symbolic* level, an area of meaning that truly matches the *civil model of inclusion and egalitarian generality* which exclusively defines our culture. And so it is because we have not been reminded, on the one hand, that only symbolic meanings matching our 'civil' -and not religious-model are able to eliminate the cultural prejudices that crop up here and there in current debates on the 'return of the sacred' and 'religious identities' understood as strong social carriers; and on the other hand that these prejudices are the direct legacy of monotheism seen as a religion of *foundations* -so that all the monotheisms, by their exclusivist nature, claim to be founded on principles thought of as absolute and universal, whose authority lies in a metahistorical and metasocial transcendence (Assmann 2010; Augé 1982). Indeed it is precisely this which contrasts with the contractual and civil conception underlying all our modern institutions and cultural practices. We have here on one hand an egalitarian, inclusive socio-political model based on contract and the arbitrary (in the positive sense of the word); and on the other a range of values, experienced in the west as transcendent, universal and necessary foundations, on which many discourses are nowadays being superimposed about the return in force of religious dentities and their mutual compatibility-discourses that again and again use phrases such as 'the end of the grand narratives of modernity' (Marxism, scientism, philosophies of history, secularism…), 'the advent of a post-secular, post-modern phase', 'God's revenge', 'the return to a fundamental questioning about the meaning of life and values' and so forth.

However it is really and truly a matter of asking whether the thinking evolved by anthropology and comparative history of religions is not capable of arriving at a different diagnosis, in contrast to these clichés which often come from the most conservative sections of civil and political society-and it is true that the keenest spokespeople for the idea of the 'comeback of religion' are in fact the supporters of the neo-liberal model and the new world order. But what then are the real implications of their discourse? This question prompts a prior one, which is: what is the origin of the contradiction mentioned earlier, which runs through a Europe divided between an institutional model, on the one hand, that is based on inclusion and egalitarian generalization of rights and, on the other hand, the difficulty with seeing in terms of rights differences in values and world views revealed by pluri-ethnic society?

It is a fact that obvious secularization has clearly occurred on some levels of civil society. It is also a fact that the symbolic secularization of the meaning universe structuring the western world view appears to have failed. The proof of this failure is manifested especially in the attribution to religion of a 'meaning power', an instituting function and an extra semantic charge which are still extremely strong. The proof also lies in the fact that the west persists in seeing other civilizations-as well as their symbolic and social hierarchies-in religious terms (Gasbarro 2006, 2007; Sabbatucci 2000; Kilani 2003, 2005, 2006). Now we need to bring to mind the historical causes of this contradiction and identify its significant elements.

Multiculturalism, a Way of Viewing Relations between the Political and the Religious

In Switzerland and other European countries the Churches' representatives have a strong tendency to think of relations between civilizations in terms of relations between religions. From this arise many initiatives designed to set up a dialogue between religions which is supposed to defuse conflicts. It is completely understandable that, since they come from the monotheistic tradition, the Churches are encouraged to see relations between different civilizations in terms of theological differences (and more generally in terms of different world views). And so there is an impulse towards reciprocal toleration which finds its institutional expression in the federative model of multiculturalism and cohabitation between communities. This federalist notion of religious communities is based on the idea that relations between human beings are governed by a system of shared cultural, especially ethical, values situated beyond both politics and law.

However, the Churches are not the only ones to ask the question about differences between civilizations in terms of religious differences. A number of spokespeople for civil society also perform this shift. And so we see many politicians, intellectuals, media ⋯, faced with the multiplicity of symbolic perspectives thrown up by globalization, asking the question, like the Churches, about the diversity and compatibility of cultures in terms of differences between 'world views', 'value systems', 'concepts of life', which we need to ensure cohabit without too much conflict. As for the Churches themselves, they all refer, whether implicitly or explicitly, to a differentialist anthropological model known as 'multiculturalist'. This model emphasizes differences between peoples, the 'differential value' of cultures, seen as primary as regards the historical processes set in train by exchanges between civilizations and the socio-cultural complexity related to these processes. According to this perspective differences between cultures would be in part reduced by virtue of a kind of moral and symbolic equality attributed to them as 'forms of life' -that is, different ways of facing and solving the basic problems of the human condition.

After going into a decline in the 1960s and 70s, which were strongly affected in anthropology by the attempt to develop *intercultural*-type approaches (Lévi-Strauss 1970, 1993, 1996, 1964 − 71; Godelier 1986, 1999; Descola 2005), the *multicultural* or 'differentialist' model is nowadays attracting renewed interest in the social sciences. According to its adherents, cultures-seen in and for themselves-live side by side, each one expressing its own symbolic inclination, its original 'genius', its specific social potential. What is the origin of this anthropological model? It has its roots in pre-romantic historical particularism-in particular that of Johann Gottfried Herder and his followers. Franz Boas, founder of American cultural anthropology, imported it from Germany into the USA where it was revised by the science of culture (Stocking 1968; Mancini 1999, 2000, 2007). This differentialist model rests on the idea of a kind of organic solidarity linking together a people's setting, language, institutions, customs, arts and religion. It is this solidarity that is thought to give the people's spirit its original imprint. Now, setting aside the risks of conservative or even racist distortions of this notion, two of its elements should be stressed.

The first is that the idea that a 'cultural spirit' might be inherent in civilizations goes together with a liberal perspective. Indeed symbolic structures would simply be the most appropriate responses to mankind's natural needs. This is how, in a multicultural society, the management and regulation of relations between the respective symbolic structures of each social group would fall on the market in values and 'perspectives on life'. Since a spirit directed and legitimized by nature could not bear the constraints of social rules, it would in fact only be necessary to let that spirit express itself freely and to attempt to illuminate its specific content. In a multicultural society several 'forms of life' exist cheek by jowl without meeting; in order to avoid conflicts between them a policy of recognition-the modern version of toleration-becomes the institutional remedy and political correctness its formal guarantee (Gasbarro 2006, 2007). If we envisage confrontation between individuals and groups in terms of individualism (which is the case with multiculturalism, which classifies cultures as individualities), toleration and political correctness seldom turn out to be effective in guaranteeing institutional and social equity among existing cultural groups, because their *differential status* wins out over the *civil principle of equality* (Dumont 1983: 296 -8; 1991: 269).

The second element that needs to be stressed is that any general theory aiming to understand modernity in a systemic globalizing way is accused, from a differentialist perspective, of rationalist illusion harking back to the Enlightenment-an illusion to be deconstructed in this case in favour of a return to the basic relationship between the universalism of nature and the particularism of cultures. Cultural neo-relativism, which is so fashionable nowadays, has its origin there, legitimized on the ethical level by implacable arguments drawn from nature and its laws. In the interplay of relations between cultures nature is for all and each culture is for itself. The best one will win and its victory will be the sign of a predestination, a spiritual superiority that will now be proved by the success achieved economically, politically and militarily. Thus it is no accident that the multicultural model was born and spread mainly in the countries with an American protestant, liberal culture, then into Europe from the 1980s.

Pluriculturalism, Another Way of Seeing Relations between the Political and the Religious

The second model, which could be called 'pluriculturalist', does not take its inspiration from the historical particularism of pre-romantic or romantic origin which established a fundamental continuity between the spirit of cultures and nature. It is the most representative product of the civil or contractual tradition emerging from European modernity as it began to be formed in the late 16th century. This model is pluricultural in the sense that it does not see cultures as concrete incarnations of a particular spirit and with an essential identity, but rather as historically determined artefacts thrown up by the permanent interaction between different societies. That is why each culture is, in its basis, 'pluricultural' since it appears as the original result of exchanges between specific cultures. Each culture's degree of complexity can therefore not be interpreted as a reflection of a natural predestination; instead it will be the consequence of its ability, gained as the result of specific historical experiences, to develop symbolic structures and social rules that in their turn are likely to increase exchanges and relations with other civilizations. (This complexity appears in Islamic civilization, for instance, in China, Japan, Europe and in Jewish culture.)

Indeed every society that has met the intercultural and inter-religious challenge has found itself facing a twofold task. First the task of establishing minimal general rules for possible cohabitation with other cultures-rules whose nature is less *universal* than *general* in that their effectiveness is *factual* and *empirical* and is not based on any sort of *orthodoxy* invoked as its foundation. Then the task of fostering a symbolic encounter with the other cultures with a view to producing new forms of compatibility, both ideological and practical.

This pluricultural model comes directly from the anthropological ideal that was formed in the Renaissance, to which Norbert Elias applies the term 'civilization', in contrast to the ideal of 'Kultur', which serves as a backdrop to the multiculturalist vision (Elias 1994; Dumont 1977, 1983, 1991). The model of 'civilization', or civil model, reverses the notion of the nature/culture relationship that underlies the differentialist model. It refuses to give priority to natural determinisms to the detriment of the arbitrary rules emerging from civilization. The invention of the civil model and the social invention of modern civil society are concomitant, with the latter being characterized by utterly original ideological and institutional features.

The pluricultural model's civil approach thus differs radically from the one based on natural foundations that is peculiar to the multiculturalist model. According to the former, cultures do not embody different modalities of interpreting and providing answers to problems inherent in human nature. By contrast they are seen as *symbolic structures* of concrete societies which problematize and manage, each in its own way, nature's great determinisms. From this perspective we are dealing less with a conception of social relations interpreted in a natural and determinist style than with a conception of relations with nature seen in historical and social terms.

So, from the viewpoint of *civilization*, nature is the place where hierarchies and spontaneous differences dominate-the same hierarchies and differences that, historically and socially, are likely to cause discrimination (social, of status, etc.), unless thinking about equality intervenes to contradict them. But historically this social idea of equality was hardly invented by Christianity seen as a vehicle for humanist thought. Rather it was invented by civil society, the supreme foundation-stone upon which western modernity rests.

On the Importance of not Confusing Christianity and Democracy

There are many who, in a sometimes imperceptible sideways shift, tend to see a direct legacy from Christianity in the democratic values of toleration, equality and respect for diversity-as if Christianity and democracy ran naturally side by side. They underestimate the fact that, by their very structure, the monotheisms are supremely anti-democratic since-as was mentioned earlier-they are based on a principle of vertical authority from which comes a revealed, exclusive truth with universal claims. In addition, the social and political conception of Europe and more generally the western world, the model for which is formed by democracy and egalitarianism, is inspired less by the Christian egalitarian, individualist model (which some authors, such as Max Weber, see as going back to the reformed communities modeling themselves on the first Christian communities) than by the pre-Christian civic model (of Rome or Greece). It is this model, typical of the holistic (not individualistic), egalitarian societies of antiquity, which was applied in both Greek democracy and the Roman *res publica* and was taken up at the Renaissance by those philosophers of law who stand at the origin of modern states. Finally it was this same ancient model again which inspired the idea at the heart of the Lutheran Reformation of a community of equals sharing the same faith.

And so the notion of a reason establishing rules common to a society's members is the consequence of a long process of civilization in western modernity. After the experience of the wars of religion in the 16th and 17th centuries, it took off with Kant and Enlightenment philosophy when the *civil* was invented as a place of egalitarian, peaceful cohabitation for the different manifestations of the religious and for a plurality of world views. From the model of the Roman *res publica* based on civil rights, and through the separation made by Machiavelli between politics, ethics and religion, contractual, civil thought was formalized by Grotius and Hobbes's, then Rousseau and Kant's jusnaturalism, and finally won out over all forms of natural determinism in the religious, social and political spheres. Though modernity has not eliminated religion's symbolic hierarchies and social priorities, it has nevertheless left private individuals free to choose their respective allegiances based on civil and public equality-we are very far from a conception where religion occupies the highest place in a symbolic hierarchy.

Thus the basic characteristic of the civil anthropological model is neither toleration nor moral humanism, nor democracy understood as the power emerging directly from the people (an idea that goes back to ancient Greece and is not the same as the Roman concept of *res publica*). Instead it lies in the fact that, in the structuring of collective life and relations between individuals, appeal is never made to universal foundations-whether this means a divine right, a shared faith, principles transcending human history and order. By contrast appeal is made to general rules applied in certain specific orthopractices in order to organize communal life in day-to-day historical practice.

What might these *orthopractices* consist of and what is their specificity? Taking as its inspiration the legal model of the ancient *res publica*, western modernity has in fact refrained since the 16th century from appealing, in civil and political matters, to metasocial foundations (such as the natural foundations of race, ethnicity, gender, but also any transcendent, absolute basis). To define the identities of individuals and groups it appeals instead to a contractual or legal model of social reality, a model that goes together with setting up specific symbolic machinery such as contract, civil rights, the legal activity of courts, etc. This civil machinery, understood as the place where the collective will is exercised, is designed to include, integrate socially and gain the adherence of individuals and other cultures. This civil machinery is in fact neutral in itself, without an intrinsic meaning that refers to any idea of natural basis. Indeed its only status is to function as operational tools whose validity depends exclusively on their inclusive social effectiveness (Sabbatucci 1976; Gasbarro 2006).

Of course it could be objected that this orthopractice of the law cannot in fact be neutral, protected from the risk of being recruited to serve ideologies emerging from hegemonic social groups, who are inclined to use them for their sole profit. However well-founded that objection, it is nevertheless the case that, like other orthopractices such as scientific knowledge or technology, the law has by nature a considerable inclusive performative reach and that, like science or technology, civil rights are likely to be exported outside our culture. This is so precisely because they are defined less by their orthodoxy of principle than by their concrete orthopraxis. And it is just this civil machinery for integration and inclusion that allows us to communicate with other cultures, despite the profound differences that separate us as regards world view.

Issues around the Civil Idea: an Unclear Trio (the Civic, the Religious and the Question of Meaning)

Unlike naturalist liberalism, the fundamental premise of the civil idea is to state that civil equality takes precedence in the social sphere over all differential allegiances and guarantees the free exercise of them. This practice of inclusion and contract makes it possible to break, not only with any view appealing to an orthodoxy based on values claiming to be universalist, but also with the cultural relativism of forms of life.

With this civil model the metaphysical opposition between universal and particular defended by advocates of differentialism is replaced by the historical, contingent opposition between generalization on the one hand (for this idea see below) and on the other the relationship which different cultures establish among themselves-and they are never seen in their abstract isolated identity but always in their concrete historical interactions. For the relational thinking of civilization or the civil, the basic structure is not the analogical one which links the individual's natural specificity to that of the ethnic group, the nation, the culture; it is rather the relationship of the citizen as social actor to the state; and it is that relationship, a contractual, arbitrary one, that here functions as a model to think the human person, the social group, civil society, the legally constituted state, democracy (all of them institutions defined less by an essential substance than by establishment of precise contractual relations).

The relational model underlying the civil idea is by its very nature artificial, extendable at will, inclusive and dynamic. Indeed its legitimacy flows directly from its ability to be generalized at the concrete historical, as well as the cultural-symbolic level. Adopting such a model then makes it possible to avoid a whole raft of risks inherent in the multiculturalist model. Legitimized by the appeal to natural founda-tions that justify the diversity of cultures, multiculturalist relativism is in fact likely to be replaced by historical and comparative relativization of relations that cultures have set up among themselves. Each civilization will then be apprehended as a 'process', a mobile entity in constant interaction with others, and its identity will be composed of those interactions.

Multicultural and pluricultural stances, which relate to *Kultur* and *civilization* respectively, are also expressed differently in the sphere of religion. We know the Churches adopt the multicultural model at the same time as rejecting the ethical and cultural relativism that flows from recognizing differences between civilizations. They emphasize the model's individualist side in order to safeguard the principle of freedom of conscience; however, at the social level they tend to reject the idea of the privatization of religion which involves relegating it to the private sphere.

But the Churches are not the only ones among the advocates of multiculturalism to take a precise stance on relations between religions. In order to describe the new world order within those forms of life called cultures, a number of cultural anthropologists, mainly American ones, give religion a privileged symbolic value, considering it as a basic marker of identity (Geertz 1966, 2006). This understanding is in complete accord with the assumptions of multiculturalism, which, as we have seen, privileges the symbolic aspect of culture (thought to reflect its 'genius', its differential spirit) to the detriment of the socio-institutional dimensions brought out by the social contract. Thus we see the incompatibility between those totalizing world views, religions. When toleration fails then the 'clash of civilizations', the consequence of a new world order, becomes inevitable (Huntington 1996).

In fact the multiculturalist model tends to rehabilitate religion and its 'principles of meaning' insofar as it privileges in civilizations 'spiritual' expressions of mankind to the detriment of socio-institutional dynamics and machinery designed to regulate communal life (economics, law, social norms for gaining individuals' adherence, etc.). In essence the study of values experienced by subjective consciousness, of semantic ranges, of meaning structures and symbolic foundations is given precedence over an understanding of objective institutional and symbolic logic which is social and historical in nature (Weber 2002). For culturalists religion is the seat of symbolic life. Its existential value, which provides a pragmatic answer to the problems of an existence subject to natural determinisms, cannot be deconstructed in the same way as the other cultural codes of social life, whose artificiality and arbitrariness may be accepted. On the contrary, religion embodies a perspective necessary to society, which it institutes. The religious domain, as a fundamental structure of culture, must be promoted both within and outside the cultural system. Thus the Churches, which are open to dialogue between religions; a large number of religious studies departments, whose importance in the USA is well known; as well as many debates between the 'community of believers' and non-believers, even within the social sciences, all fit perfectly within the assumptions of multiculturalism.

So we are told that, if cultures are essentially religious cultures, only a hermeneutic strategy aimed at understanding them from within and inter-religious dialogue will allow us to avoid the clash of civilizations. We should note in passing that though post-modernism deconstructs all modernity's globalizing theories (Marxism, positivism and scientism, historicism, etc., which have been systematically subjected to the criterion of verification/falsification), it nonetheless refuses to subject religion to this verification process, preferring to see it as a comprehensive doctrine of life, death and human history.

The pluricultural, civil model on the other hand gives priority to social relations (and thus to institutions such as the law, politics, technology, social organization, the economy, etc.) and more generally to all those codes of social life that, compared with the religious code-which claims to be exempt from social life-fit more immediately with historical contingency, the immanent world of human action. The characteristic of these civil codes, as we have said, lies in the fact that they are by their very nature operational, capable of being generalized to all cultures, over and above the differences between them, because they cannot be laid down as universals. That is why the advocates of the pluricultural civil model appeal less to the impulses of faith than to 'reason's reasons', which see human beings as historical actors-those reasons being now social, now economic, political, institutional and symbolic, without any of them being thought peculiar to one culture in particular. This option in favour of human reason made it possible for states to arise which are non-confessional (neutral in religious matters) and liberal (in the sense of neutral in politics).

The Consequences of the Civil Revolution

This civil thinking, which was profoundly revolutionary, was to turn out to have important consequences. I shall mention three of them, which in their turn led to other developments.

First consequence. Cohabitation among citizens with the same rights and duties, and united by a *common will*, breaks any link of allegiance and dependence based on differential criteria of identity, be they natural (race, sex) or supernatural (religious identity). All those extra-civil differences are absorbed within a civil equality whose nature is understood as historical and social and so *immanent* and *contingent*. Civil equality therefore lacks any objective or supernatural basis (we think of Hobbes, who makes religion a natural institution which in no way depends on a supernatural basis). And so cultural and religious differences are thinkable only within *civil equality*, on which the legally constituted state now rests. Thence come the new categories of 'civil society' and 'civilization' in the word's anthropological sense-since in the 16th century 'civilization' became autonomous in relation to religion and its theological foundations. However, in rereading this historical process, we should avoid seeing that dynamic as a kind of secularization of the law, or a laicization of religious values and models. Instead we are dealing here with the establishment of a totally unprecedented cultural logic, radically foreign to theological thought and the logic of the foundations that structure it. Modernity's institutions and knowledge are not the result of a secularization of religious reason-contrary to what Marcel Gauchet (1997) seems to suggest. They are rather a radical alternative to a truth principle based on the criterion of dogmatic authority. In other words, those institutions and that knowledge replace vertical, hierarchical *orthodoxy* emanating from a *revealed truth* with the empirical horizontal criterion of *factual certainty*, civil nature (law, technology, historiography).

In fact the *empirical criterion of certainty* has no precedent in western religion. It seems to be a specific invention of modernity. Science and technology, which have, like law and historiography, produced empirical certainties, cannot be thought of in religious terms, that is, as independent of religion by the very nature of their origin and historical development. It is within their paradigm, rather than from the paradigm of religion's authority, that we can and must ask ourselves about the limits of their respective truths (it is banal to say that science is not capable of explaining empirically the truths of faith-just as we do not ask religion to explain dogmas scientifically).

Second consequence. The second consequence of the advent of a civil conception based on the principle of inclusive equality should be sought in the establishment of two new meaning fields or, if you will, two spheres of action on an equal footing: the *civil* and the *religious*. With modernity not only did the first term become radically autonomous with respect to the second, it ended up including it. That is why the civil, as a cultural structure whose nature is not only political and institutional but also symbolic, managed to gain the upper hand as an autonomous anthropological dimension through the concept of civilization. This notion has a greater capacity for generalization, so it is more capable than the religious of including cultural differences-including religious ones.

Third consequence. This has to do directly with the status of religion in civil society. The social inclusion of religion in the sphere of the civil is today a de facto right and a legal fact whose status relates essentially to what is *private*. It is not a matter of lowering its social and symbolic value but of regulating in terms of equality its legitimate exercise of difference, since in the area of religious choice citizens are equal with regard to the civil sphere, which is supposed to manage those rights and differences in an equitable and neutral manner. Therefore, if in the public exercise of difference demands (displaying the veil, the crucifix, the kippa⋯) are legitimate, on the other hand they cannot be accompanied by actions that symbolically delegitimize and politically destructure the social pact based on civil equality.

So placing religion in the private sphere does not mean symbolically subordinating its value. It simply means recognizing the existence of a wide variety of differences of identity, whether religious or not, a recognition that obliges the state to regulate their exercise within civil equality. Two principles inspire this logic: on one hand equality may very well include differences; on the other there is more equality the more we manage to make them mutually compatible.

We may wonder why thoughts such as the ones presented here are almost never publicly debated. Why is there this persistent gulf between the civil orientation that dominates the institutional area and the meaning system of the religious? If the history of the cultural revolution, which was civil and distinguishes our culture, is well known and integrated (though too often forgotten), where does this resistance come from to treating religion like any other symbolic code regulating civil life? It is a fact that, when today we ask questions around the social significance of values, the argument as to the authority-truth of religion comes up again. We are all ready to discuss the interpretive limits of scientific knowledge, but too few of us will lay down the scientific and historical limits of religious truths. Following the rules of science we demand proof of non-religious beliefs, basing ourselves on the principle that ouranthropological consciousness forces us to see as arbitrary most historical, scientific or sociological representations, from historico-social utopias to ideologies criticized as being ephemeral. However, we are too forgetful that 'beliefs' emerging from civil social systems have nothing to do with the monotheistic faith that underlies our conception of religion, nor the structural hierarchy it postulates between the different orders of the world. We are not inclined to claim that religious systems and institutions should be subject to the criteria of verification-falsification to which we submit historical, anthropological, scientific, sociological or political ideas; on the contrary we tend to talk up the strength of their socio-cultural impact. In the end we seem to attribute to the religious, as if it went without saying, a meaning authority different in nature from other authorities-which definitely proves the hierarchical strength of that meaning code which we are inclined to place, generally implicitly, above other codes of civil life by virtue of a foundation *orthodoxy* we credit it with.

The very existence of this gap between institutional culture, based on the principle of inclusive equality and exercise of the collective will, and the dimension of meaning attributed to the religious-the former situated in the humanist sphere of history and civil life, the later promoted into a metahistory of foundations-indicates a failure of secularization in Europe. Contrary to what the Churches' representatives and certain post-modern philosophers claim, if that secularization has failed, it is not because it may reveal its existential limits or because a process of laicization may have been sharply interrupted. It is we, the modern heirs to a civil thinking, who should be criticized; we who have not managed to carry through to the end the civilizing task our culture had embarked upon by problematizing any deterministic vision of history and humanity-be it a natural or supernatural determinism.

The Challenge of the Science of Religions

One of the factors responsible for this inability to carry through to the end the humanization of the principles of meaning that structure our world view probably lies in a wrong way of proceeding with the study of religions on the scientific and academic level. Emerging from theological thought because of its historical origin, the science of religions has itself too often contributed to widening the gap between what civil life produces on the one hand and the religious dimension on the other-a dimension that it persisted in presenting as having its own autonomy and specificity, often using the same arguments as theological and philosophical discourse. But crediting every religious production with extra meaning, or a specific and irreducible meaning, is the same as reintroducing into public debate a form of fundamentalism of thinking. If, because it was unable to produce a historical reconstruction of immanent human logic, which is every religion's peculiar feature, 'civil modernity' left unfinished the process of 'civilizing religion', that happened with the complicity of many representatives of the science of religion. If we do not problematize by historicizing it the meaning power that religion still exercises in the west, we are unlikely to push far enough analysis of the phenomena characterizing our era.

That failure of historical critique is also the reason for the inability, shown by some sectors of present-day social science, to integrate into the whole of civilization that same meaning power of the religious. However, the history of religions and anthropology have shown empirically how in many societies the most important symbolic and social systems are not governed by religions but rather by other codes of social life (such as kinship, political structures, forms of production, symbolic logic …). Since Durkheim's founding contribution the two disciplines have worked, each in its own way, to show that religion is only *one* social code among others (politics, economics, law, relations with the environment, etc.), all of them being mobilized in this global system for communicating and producing material and symbolic values that is a civilization. Provided religion is not given a special or privileged status, it is amenable to being analysed with the same tools and perspectives as the other codes mentioned. The only specificity it can claim compared with them concerns the nature of the relations it deals with, that is, relations between human beings and non-human alterity, whereas the other social codes involve solely relations between humans or between humans and nature (in the form of scientific as well as magical knowledge and practices). Once we have accepted the specificity of the relations dealt with by religion we have to agree that it should not be restricted to the Christian world view: the idea of divinity varies with the particular social system in which exists (the divinities of the old polytheisms, which are part of very particular socio-political structures, are quite different from the monotheisms' one god; Assmann 2010; Augé 1982; Vernant 1983). The religious social code is not at all obvious; it is *culturally arbitrary* like the others, in the sense that not only do all cultures not share the same code but also that, when this happens, the code does not necessarily operate in the same way from one culture to another. And were Christian missionaries not the first to uncover the existence of other civilizations without religion or gods (Clastres 1988)?

The west has subjected modernity's grand narratives (including metaphysics) to historical criticism and anthropological comparison, which has had the result of subjecting their authority criteria to the *empirical criterion of certainty* and doing away with their universalist, totalizing character. Why should we not do the same thing with religion? It is an important matter. The western world is today faced with the radical nature of extremely complex cultural and religious differences. For the first time it is dealing with them without having any symbolic mediations, whereas once modernity had some, with its universals such as metaphysics, science, finalist philosophies of history, etc. Furthermore Europe finds itself lacking the political centrality which its colonial empire had guaranteed. Thus we need to have a cultural model that is *generalizable* (but not *universal*) and *comparative* (not *absolute*), on which we can build a new civil body of knowledge. In the area of technology, sport, science and communication we can already recognize that such codes are being adopted on a massive scale in the most diverse non-western cultures. But if economic, technological, sporting, scientific, communication codes are exported and spread to this extent it is not because they are based on any orthodox foundation or meaning value that presents itself as preferable to others-but rather because of their ability *in a practical way to include and integrate* cultural differences and so to *start up the process of* compatibility and intercultural generalization.

These inclusive codes belong to the civil sphere because the reality that has given rise to them, as well as the logic that regulates their use, is civil. In the same way civil law, as we have seen, does not have any intrinsic value; it functions as a system of arbitrary rules adopted in contract by citizens with the sole aim of regulating relations between individuals themselves, between individuals and the authorities, and between the individual and nature. Civil society and civil law share the same origin, the same structure and the same operational logic.

Between the 15th and 16th centuries the modern social system set up a symbolic order of the world very different from the one that had preceded it. Modernity broke with its past when people started to see relations between humans and nature (science and technology) and with divinity (the religions) on the same basis as relations between humans themselves, which were understood as resting on arbitrary, contractual and conventional principles such as are expressed in the law, morality, politics, economics (Gauchet 2007). Today, approaching the issue of relations between religion and politics, while ignoring the anthropological significance of modernity and the historical process it set in train to end up with civil society, is resulting in a fatal confusion between two different registers. On the one hand *recognition of the coexistence* within our culture *of different cultural codes* (law, politics, economics, religion, etc.); on the other *the need*, assumed to be inevitable, *to establish their hierarchy of meaning* (a hierarchy in which the religious code would infallibly occupy the apex). Those who confuse these two registers forget that since the wars of religion the peaceful cohabitation of politics and religion has been the original result of the moderns' civil society, which put an end to the hierarchical discourse affirming the supremacy of religion over politics. It was also that civil society which made those two distinct registers compatible in the practice of social life.

The science of religions therefore has an important part to play in this thinking about the articulation between the political and the religious. It has a duty to remember the history of that articulation. The thinking and the duty are crucially important in the current political context. And that is so particularly in Europe where we are at present witnessing a process of profound institutional restructuring in the academic field of religious studies. That restructuring is the opportunity for the science of religions not to display a structural inability to free itself from theology when, for historical reasons, it may still be institutionally connected to it- it is the opportunity for that science to reaffirm its secular, civil vocation.

References

Assmann, J. (2010), *The Price of Monotheism*, translated by Robert Savage. Stanford, CA: Stanford University Press.

Augé, M. (1982), *Génie du paganisme*. Paris: Gallimard.

Clastres, H. (1988), 'La religion sans dieux: les chroniqueurs du xvie siècle devant les sauvages d'Amérique du sud', in F. Schmidt (ed.), *L'Impensable polythéisme. études d'historiographie religieuse*, p. 95 -122. Paris: éditions des Archives contemporaines.

Descola, P. (2005), *Par-delà nature et culture*. Paris: Gallimard.

Dumont, L. (1977), *Homo Aequalis, i: Genèse et épanouissement de l'idéologie économique*. Paris: Gallimard.

Dumont, L. (1983), *Essai sur l'individualisme*. Paris: Seuil.

Dumont, L. (1991), *Homo Aequalis, ii: L'idéologie allemande, France-Allemagne et retour*. Paris: Gallimard.

Elias, N. (1994), *The Civilizing Process*, translated by Edmund Jephcott. Oxford: Blackwell.

Gasbarro, N. (1990), 'La terza via tracciata da Raffaele Pettazzoni', *Studi e Materiali di Storia delle Religioni*, 56: 95 -200.

Gasbarro, N. (2006), 'Religione e politica. Potere di senso e prospettiva civile', in B. Bonato (ed.), *Religioni e politica. Verso una società post-secolare?* p. 23 -65. Pordenone: Al Segno.

Gasbarro, N. (2007), 'Storia delle religioni e società civile', *Prometeo*, 97: 4 -25.

Gauchet, M. (1997), *The Disenchantment of the World: A Political History of Religion*, translated by Oscar Burge with a foreword by Charles Taylor. Princeton, N. J.: Princeton University Press.

Gauchet, M. (2007), *Un monde désenchanté?* Paris: Agora.

Geertz, C. (1966), 'Religion as a Cultural System', in *Anthropological Approaches to the Study of Religion*, ed. by Michael Banton, p. 1 -45. New York: Praeger.

Geertz, C. (2006), 'La religion, sujet d'avenir', *Le Monde*, May 4.

Godelier, M. (1986), *The Mental and the Material: Thought, Economy, and Society*, translated by Martin Thom. London/New York: Verso.

Godelier, M. (1999), *The Enigma of the Gift*, translated by Nora Scott. Chicago: University of Chicago Press.

Huntington, S. P. (1996), *The Clash of Civilisations*. New York: Simon & Schuster.

Kilani, M. (2003), 'équivoques de la religion et politiques de la laïcité en Europe. Réflexions à partir de l'Islam', *Archives de Sciences Sociales des Religions*, 121: 69 -86.

Kilani, M. (2005), 'Il faut déconfessionnaliser la laïcité. Le religieux imprègne encore les imaginaires', *Journal des Anthropologues*, 100 -101: 37 -48.

Kilani, M. (2006), 'La laïcité entre universalisme et hiérarchie', *Journal des Anthropologues*, 106 -107: 369 -76.

Lenoir, F. (2007), *Le Christ philosophe*. Paris: Plon.

Le Temps (2007), 'Samedi culturel', Geneva, December 22.

Lévi-Strauss, C. (1964 -1971), *Mythologiques*. Paris: Plon.

Lévi-Strauss, C. (1970), *The Elementary Structures of Kinship*. London: Social Science Paperbacks.

Lévi-Strauss, C. (1993), *Structural Anthropology*. Harmondsworth: Penguin Books.

Lévi-Strauss, C. (1996), *The Savage Mind*. Oxford: OUP.

Mancini, S. (1999), 'Les civilisations comme "absolu esthétique". L'approche morphologique de la Mittel-Europa', *Diogène*, 186: 83 −109.

Mancini, S. (2000), 'Historicisme allemand et anthropologie, ou de l'actualité d'un débat', *Les Etudes Philosophiques*, 1: 17 −35.

Mancini, S. (2007), 'Comparatism in History of Religions: Some Models and Stakes', *Religion*, 37 (4): 282 −93.

Sabbatucci, D. (1976), *Lo Stato come conquista culturale*. Rome: Bulzoni.

Sabbatucci, D. (2000), *Prospettiva storico-religiosa*. Rome: seam.

Stocking, G. (1968), *Race, Culture, and Evolution: Essays in the History of Anthropology*. New York: Free Press.

Valadier, P. (2007), *Détresse du politique, force du religieux*. Paris: Seuil.

Vernant, J. -P. (1983), *Myth and Thought among the Greeks*. London: Routledge & Kegan.

Weber, M. (2002), *The Protestant Ethic and the Spirit of Capitalism*. New York & London: Penguin Books.

编后记

2010年中国社会科学院推出了中国社会科学论坛，全年举办了18场国际学术研讨会，"现代社会生活方式的文化根源"是其中之一。

本次研讨会的成功举办得益于多方面的支持。国际哲学与人文科学理事会副秘书长、《第欧根尼》英法文版主编L. M. 斯卡兰蒂诺先生推荐并帮助联系了国外知名学者，国际合作局吴波龙处长和文献中心张树华副主任对会议的筹备工作给予了指导和积极关注，文献中心刘振喜处长带领科研处及研究部的一批青年人出色地完成了从筹备到召开等一系列繁杂的工作，在此一并致以由衷的谢意！

武寅副院长专程到会做了精彩的致辞，黄长著学部委员和朝戈金学部委员用流畅的英语主持了会议并做了点睛评论，提升了会议的学术品位，在此致以特别的谢意！

当然，我们更要感谢到会发言的中外学者和论文集的撰稿者，感谢他们的支持与合作！

最后要感谢的是参加会议论文的翻译、校对及编辑等项工作的诸位同人，他们是王文娥、杜鹃、陈源、贺慧玲、高媛、萧俊明。

编　者
2011年4月

图书在版编目(CIP)数据

现代社会生活方式的文化根源/萧俊明主编. —北京：社会科学文献出版社，2013.12
 （中国社会科学论坛文集）
 ISBN 978-7-5097-4598-4

Ⅰ.①现… Ⅱ.①萧… Ⅲ.①生活方式-关系-传统文化-研究 Ⅳ.①C913.3 ②G04

中国版本图书馆 CIP 数据核字（2013）第 097745 号

·中国社会科学论坛文集·
现代社会生活方式的文化根源

主　　编 / 萧俊明

出 版 人 / 谢寿光
出 版 者 / 社会科学文献出版社
地　　址 / 北京市西城区北三环中路甲 29 号院 3 号楼华龙大厦
邮政编码 / 100029

责任部门 / 皮书出版分社 （010）59367127　　责任编辑 / 柳　杨　周映希
电子信箱 / pishubu@ssap.cn　　　　　　　　　责任校对 / 岳爱华
项目统筹 / 郭　峰　　　　　　　　　　　　　　责任印制 / 岳　阳
经　　销 / 社会科学文献出版社市场营销中心　（010）59367081　59367089
读者服务 / 读者服务中心（010）59367028

印　　装 / 北京季蜂印刷有限公司
开　　本 / 787mm×1092mm　1/16　　　印　张 / 15.75
版　　次 / 2013 年 12 月第 1 版　　　　字　数 / 275 千字
印　　次 / 2013 年 12 月第 1 次印刷
书　　号 / ISBN 978-7-5097-4598-4
定　　价 / 59.00 元

本书如有破损、缺页、装订错误，请与本社读者服务中心联系更换
▲ 版权所有 翻印必究